THE PALSGRAF CASE:
COURTS, LAW, AND SOCIETY IN 1920s NEW YORK

WILLIAM H. MANZ*

LexisNexis™

* A.B., College of the Holy Cross; M.A., Northwestern University; M.L.S., Long Island University; J.D., St. John's University School of Law; Senior Research Librarian, St. John's University School of Law. The author is a resident of Rockville Centre, N.Y., and regularly uses the Long Island Rail Road.

Library of Congress Cataloging-in-Publication Data

Manz, William H.

The Palsgraf case: courts, law, and society in 1920s New York / William H. Manz.

    p. cm.

ISBN 0-8205-6372-2 (softbound)

1. Palsgraf, Helen, b. 1884 — Trials, litigation, etc. 2. Long Island Railroad —
    Trials, litigation, etc. 3. Torts — New York (State). I. Title.

KF228.P346M36 2005

346.74703'2 — dc22   2005025593

ISBN 1-8205-6372-2

Editorial Offices
744 Broad Street, Newark, NJ 07102 (973) 820-2000
201 Mission St., San Francisco, CA 94105-1831 (415) 908-3200
701 East Water Street, Charlottesville, VA 22902-7587 (434) 972-7600
www.lexis.com

(Pub.03210)

ACKNOWLEDGMENTS

Thanks are owed to persons at the following libraries, archives, and offices for their assistance:

Albany Medical College Alumni Office
Association of the Bar of the City of New York Library
Brooklyn Historical Society
Brooklyn History Division, Brooklyn Public Library
Cold Spring Harbor Laboratory Library
Feinberg Library, Plattsburgh State University
Humanities and Social Science Library, New York Public Library
Kings County Supreme Court Library
Lockport Public Library
Long Island Division, Queensborough Public Library
Long Island Studies Institute, Hofstra University
Newburgh Public Library
New Rochelle Public Library
New York City Municipal Archives
New York County Lawyers' Association Library
New York State Archives
New York State Library
Onondaga County Historical Society
Onondaga County Public Library
St. John's University Archives
Schoharie County Historical Society
Science, Industry, and Business Library, New York Public Library
University of Pennsylvania Alumni Office
Watertown Public Library
Yale University Archives

Special thanks are owed to the following for their assistance: Long Island Rail Road historian Ron Ziel; Dr. Dale Preece of the Sandia National Laboratories for insights into the effects of explosions; fireworks consultant Charles Weeth; Edward J. Murphy, the retired general attorney of the Long Island Rail Road; Mrs. Elizabeth W. Smith, the niece of Matthew W. Wood; attorney Alan W. Borst, Jr., for arranging the telephone interview with Mrs. Smith; Mrs. Palsgraf's grandson, William Palsgraf; Grace White Lohr; Dr. Rachel Yehuda of Mt. Sinai Hospital for comments regarding post-traumatic stress syndrome and Mrs. Palsgraf's symptoms; retired roofer Philip DeSantis for information on the roofing industry in the 1920s and 1930s; Richard Tuske of the Association of the Bar of the City of New York Library, and Paul Henrich and Jacqueline Cantwell of the Kings County Supreme Court Library for providing numerous records and briefs of LIRR cases; Nuchine Nobari of the New York County Lawyers' Association Library for providing microfilm of vintage *New York Law Journals*; Bill Mills of the New York Law School Library for checking on what information might be available in school records regarding Matthew W. Wood and William McNamara. Thanks are also owed to Professor Lawrence Joseph of St. John's University School of Law for his helpful suggestions during the preparation of the law review article that became the basis for this book.

TABLE OF CONTENTS

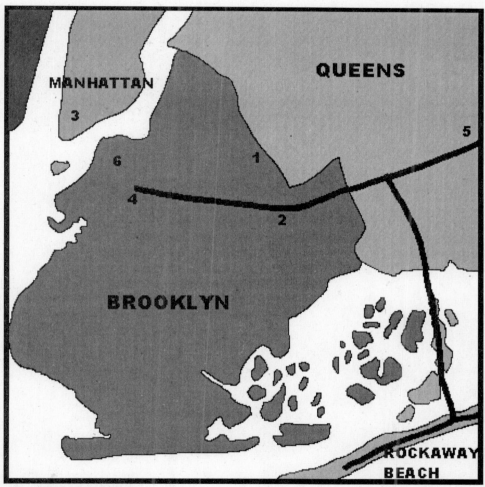

1 – Palsgraf Apt.
1 – Palsgraf Apt.
2 – East N.Y. Sta.
3 – Woolworth Bldg./Wood Office
4 – Flatbush Ave. Sta.
5 – Jamaica
6 – Kings County Courthouse & Borough Hall

INTRODUCTION

Palsgraf v. Long Island Railroad Co.[1] enjoys unique fame in the history of American law. Declared a "legal institution" as long ago as 1938,[2] its hold on the legal community's popular imagination goes far beyond what might be expected even for a well-known torts opinion written by a famous judge. It is the one case remembered by attorneys long after law school graduation. Everyone who has sat in an American law school torts class can recall the basic facts — the crowded railroad platform, the running men, the dropped package, the explosion, the falling scale, and the poor woman who lost a $6,000 judgment. Interest in the case has produced a short film, at least four published cartoons, and the annual "Palsgraf Days" celebration at the University of Georgia Law School, begun by Professor R. Perry Sentell in 1963.[3]

Although it was decided in 1928, *Palsgraf* survives as an enduring favorite among legal academics and has been the subject of countless articles on tort doctrine. As an outstanding example of the intersection of legal scholarship and ordinary human life — a personal injuries lawsuit against a common carrier that became a vehicle for resolving a difficult question of negligence law — it has been a basis for discussions of Benjamin Cardozo's judicial technique, the influence of his personal background on his opinions, and his attitudes toward women and the poor. Largely lacking from the copious *Palsgraf* literature, however, has been consideration of the case as an historical event. A notable exception is Judge John Noonan's "The Passengers of Palsgraf," a chapter in his 1976 work, *Persons and Masks of the Law*, which utilized the trial record and offered new facts about the attorneys, judges, and the Long Island Railroad. Additional information also emerged in a 1978 *Harvard Law Record* article based on an interview with Mrs. Palsgraf's daughter, Lillian,[4] and a 1991 *Georgia Bar Journal* article by Professor Sentell where new details were provided by other family members.[5] However, most discussions of the case take their facts from Cardozo's opinion, with some adding minor embellishments or new factual errors, such as stating that the package exploded on impact,[6] claiming that the wheels ran over the package,[7] describing the contents of the package as firecrackers,[8] or referring to Mrs. Palsgraf as an elderly widow.[9]

The most immediate question that arises when considering the case from an historical perspective is its apparently bizarre fact pattern, one that has been described as "the supreme illustration of a freak accident,"[10] a "law professor's dream,"[11] and "as improbable as a Rube Goldberg cartoon."[12] As told, *Palsgraf* is a sort of legal "urban legend"[13] — an allegedly true, but improbable tale related to each new class of law students. As with any unlikely story, however, *Palsgraf* invites skeptical analysis. Questions about the facts usually focus on the accuracy of Cardozo's version of the events. He may effectively portray Mrs. Palsgraf as an unforeseeable victim, but critics maintain that "the facts as stated seem to violate the laws of physics,"[14] and that the opinion describes an event that "could not possibly have happened."[15] Less reverently, *Palsgraf* has been described as a "sham," "a crock," and "a preposterous case."[16] However characterized, the facts raise the question of how a package of fireworks described as "small," exploding at track level, and that apparently injured only Mrs. Palsgraf, could possibly have toppled a heavy scale located "many feet away."[17]

The *Palsgraf* facts have been retold countless times in books and law review articles and, like more conventional urban legends, Cardozo's impossible version of the event has proved remarkably resistant to criticism or correction.[18] This is not because the legal community is disinterested in the truth and prefers a good story to a more mundane reality. Instead, it results from a greater concern with studying the opinion rather than the event that generated it. The legal community's failure to explore the history of *Palsgraf*, or to question or re-analyze its facts is unfortunate because the case was narrowly decided at every court level, and knowledge of the actual event is a vital component in the debate that it has inspired. As one commentator has noted, "even details which are purely extrinsic to any participant in the process have an effect on the understanding of the case."[19]

Beyond the immediate facts are misleading impressions regarding the contending parties. It might seem that *Palsgraf* was an unequal struggle between a large and wealthy corporation and a poor working class woman. However, the Long Island Railroad was hardly an invincible corporate empire. In reality, it was beleaguered on many fronts and highly vulnerable to lawsuits by sympathetic plaintiffs with able legal assistance. Such was the case with Mrs. Palsgraf, who had an experienced attorney with a more impressive legal education than most of the railroad's legal department or outside counsel, and who had the means and ability to effectively contest the case all the way to the state's highest court. In contrast, the railroad's lawyers were usually at a disadvantage in negligence actions; their employer usually received little sympathy from juries and was accorded no favorable treatment from the appellate courts.

An understanding of the case is also enhanced by more knowledge about the lives and careers of the members of the bench and bar involved with the case. Although *Palsgraf* has now assumed legendary status, for the attorneys involved it was just one more case, seemingly far less important than others they had encountered. However, the way they handled the litigation was crucial in determining whether it would reach the Court of Appeals. As for the judges, during their collective careers they had already been called upon to decide high-profile civil actions or trials arising from notorious crimes. For them *Palsgraf* would have had no special significance. The case may have arisen from an unusual accident, and did pose an interesting legal problem, but the financial stakes were small, and public interest in the outcome was entirely lacking. However, as with the attorneys, the judges' backgrounds and attitudes were critical to the outcome. A different trial judge might have dismissed the case, probably consigning it to legal oblivion. If the Appellate Division had reversed the trial court, or had there been no dissent, the case could have ended there. Without Judge William S. Andrews' famous Court of Appeals dissent, and the narrow 4–3 vote, critical elements in the story would be missing.

Finally, it is useful to view *Palsgraf* and its participants within the context of their times. The lives of the participants were shaped by the socio-economic forces of the day, and the careers of the judges were often determined by partisan politics and the results of presidential, gubernatorial, and mayoral elections over which they had no control. As for the case itself, its progress through the courts demonstrates how the civil court system operated in the 1920s, and reveals how exponential urban population growth, new technologies, and a burgeoning economy created ongoing problems for the legal system that persist to this day.

Chapter 1
THE ACCIDENT

There is nothing about the Long Island's Rail Road's East New York Station in Brooklyn that suggests anything of significance ever happened there. Trains arriving today emerge from a tunnel into a gloomy concrete-and-steel station located beneath a viaduct carrying Atlantic Avenue. The pale blue paint used to cover steel beams and other metal surfaces does nothing to brighten its dreary appearance. The surrounding area, viewed through openings between the support columns, is a drab urban landscape, the result of East New York's transformation into an urban ghetto that started in the 1960s.[1] On a typical mid-day trip, no riders get on or off when the train arrives, and some rush-hour commuter trains pass right through without halting.

The station and its environs presented an entirely different picture in the mid-1920s. Spurred by the construction of several elevated transit lines, East New York was a rapidly growing commercial and industrial area. Newly-built tenements and other low-cost housing were built, becoming the homes of Jewish, Polish, and Lithuanian immigrants. Immediately around the LIRR station at Atlantic and Van Sinderen Avenues were such enterprises as the Western Electric Company, the National Marble and Tile Works, the Supreme Lumber and Wrecking Corporation, several garages, and the East New York Continuation School.

During the 1920s, the station itself looked far different from today's covered concrete-and-steel structure. Located at ground level and open to the sky, it consisted of two raised platforms, over 600 feet long.[2] Passengers purchased tickets at a one-story office/waiting room on the south side of Atlantic Avenue. Westbound passengers could then reach their platform by using a raised walkway over the tracks. Eastbound passengers, like Mrs. Palsgraf, could get to the platform simply by crossing the street and climbing a few steps. Both eastbound and westbound platforms were high enough to permit passengers to step directly into the open doors of the waiting cars. Wooden walls separated the platforms from Atlantic Avenue; in several places the platform was covered with a roof to shelter passengers from the elements. In one contemporary photo, the main part of the platform appears to be concrete. A second photo, that has appeared for years in the Prosser torts casebook, taken from the far west end of the station, shows that the platform, at least at that end, was constructed of wood planks.[3]

The station at East New York served the LIRR's electrified double-tracked line running between busy downtown Brooklyn and Jamaica, the largest commercial center in the Borough of Queens. It also handled trains headed for the railroad's then highly-profitable branch line to Rockaway Beach. Located on a long sandy peninsula separated from the rest of Queens by Jamaica Bay, Rockaway was a popular destination for city residents seeking a day at the shore. It was the home of such long-gone establishments as Thompson's Amusement Park, offering ocean bathing, swimming pools, various amusements and inexpensive places to eat. Even for those who had a private car, reaching these attractions by road then required a long circuitous drive around the bay, making the LIRR the quickest, most convenient means getting to the Rockaway beaches.[4]

The LIRR facility was easily accessible to the traveling public. Just to the east, high above the railroad's right of way, were platforms of the Brooklyn-Manhattan Transportation Corporation's Atlantic Avenue station, serving six elevated train tracks. Established in 1896 as the Brooklyn Rapid Transit Company, by the mid-1920s the BMT operated an extensive network of elevated and subway lines throughout Brooklyn and parts of Queens. Three of its elevated lines, the Broadway, Fulton, and Canarsie, were served by the Atlantic Avenue station, making the LIRR station a busy transfer point for passengers also using BMT trains.

On Sunday morning, August 24, 1924, the East New York station was crowded with passengers. The forecast for the day was for good weather, and although in the *Palsgraf* legend the day is always described as hot, temperatures that morning were only in the mid-seventies, not particularly high by the standards of a New York City August.[5] As the throng of passengers on the platform waited, a train arrived from the Flatbush Avenue station in downtown Brooklyn. Since the Atlantic Avenue line had been completely electrified since 1905, this train would have consisted of all-steel electrically-powered coaches.[6] Painted in the Tuscan red color of the LIRR's parent corporation, the Pennsylvania Railroad, they proudly bore the name "Long Island" in block gold letters above the windows. As this train began to slowly pull out, bound for Jamaica, two or three men carrying bundles rushed onto the platform, darted through the waiting passengers, and ran for an open car door. The first man boarded safely, but the second dropped his bundle as he was being assisted by two railroad conductors.[7] Moments later, the station was rocked with a large explosion.

The result of this now infamous last-minute attempt to board a LIRR train rated attention from almost all the local newspapers and was even reported outside New York.[8] Because other detailed sources of information regarding the explosion, including a police report, internal railroad accident or damage reports,[9] and the LIRR's legal department case files, are unfortunately no longer available, these newspaper stories are the earliest surviving accounts of the event.[10] The *New York Times*, the *New York Herald Tribune* and *Long Island Daily Press* gave the story front-page treatment. The *New York World* and *New York Evening Journal* placed their articles on the first page of an interior section, while the other dailies located their versions on various inside pages. These articles appeared along with others on events of passing interest from August 24, 1924, including far more serious accidents, a double murder involving a lawyer, stolen chicks, potential zeppelin stowaways, and even speculations about civilization on Mars. Events of more ongoing interest meriting attention that day were the anti-Ku Klux Klan Texas gubernatorial campaign of "Ma" Ferguson, and Clarence Darrow's defense of the Chicago "Thrill Killers," Nathan Leopold and Richard Loeb.

The newspaper accounts all contain the same basic facts — three men carrying bundles appeared on the crowded platform of the East New York station, one of which exploded when dropped. In all but two of the stories, the men were identified as "Italians,"[11] who were presumed to be taking fireworks to a celebration in Queens or on Long Island. In most articles, all three were said to have been carrying bundles. The dropped package was variously described as an "unwieldy package,"[12] "a large bundle,"[13] and "a large package."[14] The contents were uniformly described as fireworks and/or bombs. Two reports, assuming that the exploded package had similar contents to one later found at the scene, stated that it contained six such bombs, each eighteen inches in length and four inches in diameter.[15] No articles named railroad employees as the cause of the fallen package. Most stated merely that the man dropped it, while three, including the *New York Times*, claimed that the accident resulted when the crowd jostled one of the men. They also said that the package fell between the station platform and the train. Only the *Times* and *Evening Journal* claimed that the package had dropped all the way to the tracks.

All the articles described the explosion as severe. Five headlines called it a "blast."[16] The *New York Herald-Tribune* described it as a "terrific detonation,"[17] and the *Brooklyn Daily Eagle* called it "terrific explosion."[18] The *New York Times* reported that it was heard "for several blocks."[19] Both the *Times* and the *Long Island Daily Press* stated that "there was a terrific roar, followed by several milder explosions, and a short lived pyrotechnic display."[20] The *Times* report stated that "pieces of the big salute bomb shot up to the platform."[21] Five articles claimed that the explosion consisted of a rapid sequence of detonations.[22]

Several papers, including the *New York Times*, characterized the scene on the platform after the explosion as one of "panic." The *Brooklyn Daily Times*, *New York Daily News*, and *New York Herald-Tribune* added the force of the explosion knocked down thirty or forty people. The *New York Sun* described a "wild scramble for safety [with] [w]omen and children . . . swirled along the platform."[23] The story in the *New York World* referred to a "stampede" and indicated that "the crowd . . . surged backward to a medley of shrieks."[24] The *Brooklyn Daily Eagle* wrote that "the crowd was bowled over in its tracks, part through shock and part through fear," adding that "[t]he usual number of women fainted."[25] The dramatic nature of the events is also attested to by the descriptions of the scene after the explosion. Crowds of the curious were reported to have flocked to the station, and ambulances from several hospitals arrived. Firemen appeared, led by Battalion Chief Elmer Mustard. The police presence included Acting Captain James G. Gegan of the Bomb Squad and detectives from the Rockaway Avenue police station.

Descriptions of the amount of damage done by the fireworks explosion varied. The *Brooklyn Daily Eagle* mentioned only broken windows in the passenger coach, while the *New York Herald-Tribune* and *Brooklyn Daily Times* indicated only that the roadbed had been damaged. The *New York Times* stated that the explosion broke the windows in the railroad car, ripped away part of the platform, and overthrew a penny scale, smashing its glass and wrecking its mechanism. Similar descriptions, including the damage to the scale, appeared in the *New York Sun* and *Long Island Daily Press*. Only the *Times* and the *Daily Press* provided information about the distance of the scale from the explosions, stating that it was "more than ten feet away." The newspaper stories were consistent in their reports of injuries. Most gave the number of injured as thirteen.[26] Physical injuries to others on the platform were reported as burned hair, burns on the wrist, shoulder abrasions, and lacerations. Only three men were said to have required hospital treatment. Two, Joseph Coyle and Richard Seeman, were identified as Long Island Railroad policemen.

The appearance of Gegan and the Bomb Squad indicated that the police initially believed that there was at least the possibility that the explosion had been caused by anarchists, communists, or Italian gangsters known as the Black Hand.[27] Founded in 1914, the squad had spent the World War I years investigating suspected Black Hand bombings and attempting to foil the sabotage plots of anarchists and German agents. Immediately after the war, it had participated in raids against radicals during the so-called "Red Scare." Gegan's tactics sometimes proved controversial. He had been briefly arrested in 1920 for allegedly using the "third degree" on a suspect, and in 1921 had been attacked by the American Civil Liberties Union for "unlawfully raid[ing] private houses and apartments, seiz[ing] papers without warrants . . . and treat[ing] private property of law-abiding citizens with complete disregard of ordinary courtesy and propriety."[28]

Whatever their tactics, the Bomb Squad was combating a real danger as was demonstrated in September 1920, when a bomb hidden in a horse-drawn wagon exploded at the corner of Wall and Broad Streets in the heart of the financial district. The blast had killed thirty persons instantly and injured over 300 more. Those responsible were not apprehended and rumors of other potential bombings followed, including alleged plots against the Customs House and the Sea Beach line of the Brooklyn Rapid Transit Company. The city briefly had a nasty scare in January 1922 when a major explosion occurred only a few blocks from the Wall Street bombing site. However, it was quickly determined that the blast had been caused by sewer gas. Similarly, despite initial suspicions that actual bombs might have caused the LIRR station explosion, the police quickly determined that it was a fireworks-related accident.

Chapter 2
THE PARTIES

When three papers, the *New York Times*, *Brooklyn Daily Eagle*, and *Brooklyn Daily Times*, printed complete lists of the injured, they included a woman whose last name was variously spelled "Polsgraf," "Polsgraff," and "Golsgraf," and who was described as suffering from shock. Helen Palsgraf, the woman whose name the newspapers failed to spell correctly,[1] was a forty-year-old lifelong resident of New York City. She was one of twin daughters born in 1884 to German immigrants, Herman Spilger, a blacksmith/spikemaker, and his wife Catherine.[2] Her place of birth was a tenement located at 608 East 17th Street on Manhattan's Lower East Side.[3] Although she is known to generations of law students as Helen, her given name at birth was Jacobine.[4] According to the Palsgraf family, she disliked the name, and would instead use Lena or Helen, and Helen was the name she blurted out when questioned at the scene of the explosion.[5] At least for official purposes, Lena appears to have been the name she used most often. It appears on her marriage certificate, the birth certificates of two of her children, her death certificate, and in the 1900, 1920, and 1930 census reports.[6]

The 1900 census reports sixteen-year-old Lena Spilger working as a tobacco stripper (involving sorting, smoothing, and deveining tobacco leaves), presumably in one of Manhattan's many cigar factories. Three years later, she married twenty-four-year-old Michael Palsgraf, a tinsmith employed in the roofing trade. The Palsgrafs initially lived on Keap Street in the Williamsburg section of Brooklyn, not far from the Navy Yard. By the time their two older children, William and Elizabeth, were born,[7] they had relocated a few miles east to an address on Maujer Street, near the heart of Williamsburg's old German neighborhood. By 1920, the family had moved to a basement apartment at 238 Irving Avenue in the Ridgewood area of Brooklyn, a heavily German working/lower middle class neighborhood that straddles the border between Brooklyn and Queens, where their fellow tenants included a trucking foreman, a waiter, a driver, a grocery store manager, a machinist and a baker.

Michael Palsgraf's roofing job as a tinsmith was a skilled occupation involving the construction of the then-common tin roofs, as well as the installation of flashing around stacks, gutters, downspouts, and skylights. With Brooklyn growing rapidly, such an occupation would have provided steady work six days a week, and a living wage.[8] However, sometime between 1920, and 1927, Mrs. Palsgraf had separated from her husband, and unless he continued to provide some kind of financial assistance, her income was limited to the $8 per week she

earned doing housework, and the $10 per month she was allowed for perform-
ing janitorial duties in her building. This meant that her income totaled only
about 45% of the weekly income needed for a fair standard of living for an
industrial worker living in Brooklyn.[9]

Mrs. Palsgraf's encounter with legal history began with plans for a Sunday
outing to Rockaway Beach with her daughters, Elizabeth, fifteen years old,
and Lillian, twelve. The trip would most likely have begun with a short walk to
the BMT's Myrtle Avenue elevated station, located only a block-and-a-half south
from the family's Irving Avenue apartment. The BMT train would have taken
them to the line's Atlantic Avenue elevated station in East New York. From
there, the Palsgrafs would have descended to street level, purchased tickets at
the LIRR office, and then crossed the street to the station platform. After climbing the steps, Mrs. Palsgraf and Elizabeth turned right and took up a position
next to a penny scale, while Lillian turned left, heading for a newsstand to
purchase a paper. As she reached the newstand, she looked back and saw two
men running for the train, one of whom dropped his bundle as he was helped
aboard. After the explosion, she was unable to reach her mother because the of
thick smoke and the crowd rushing for the stairs; she was reunited with her
when a policeman led Mrs. Palsgraf to the benches by the newsstand.

When the scale fell, Mrs. Palsgraf was struck on the arm, hip, and thigh. After
the accident she said she "could just about walk alone . . . [and] shook and
trembled from head to foot."[10] She was given drinks at the scene by a police officer and an ambulance doctor, before eventually taking a taxi home. Her physical injuries consisted of some small bruises on her shoulder. A few days later,
she began stuttering and stammering. She was treated for her injuries by a
neighborhood physician, Dr. Karl A. Parshall, an 1899 graduate of Albany Medical College, whose home and office were at 317 Bleeker Street in Ridgewood,
just a short distance from the Palsgraf apartment. Over the next two months,
the doctor saw Mrs. Palsgraf at his office two or three times a week. For her
nervous condition, he prescribed bromides and nerve tonics, stopping treatment at various intervals to see if her condition would be better or worse without them.

The day after the accident, Mrs. Palsgraf was visited by a man she later
described as a railroad doctor. However, the visitor was almost certainly a
claims agent since the railroad would have been too parsimonious to actually
employ a physician.[11] That the man was merely a claims agent is also suggested by the fact that he did not examine her, asking only about the accident.
Since Mrs. Palsgraf's physical injuries were relatively minor, it is likely that this
visit produced either no offer of a financial settlement, or one that was
extremely modest. In any event, sometime during the next month, still suffering from the effects of the accident, and forced to give up her outside cleaning
work, Mrs. Palsgraf decided to see a lawyer about suing the Long Island Railroad.

The Long Island Railroad was one of Greater New York's major common carriers. In 1924, the railroad operated 366.27 miles of track and leased another 27.01 miles;[12] its assets totaled $114 million.[13] It was chartered in 1834 as a route for passenger traffic from Brooklyn to Greenport on eastern Long Island's North Fork, where ferry connections to a rail line in Connecticut would permit travel all the way to Boston. Unfortunately for the LIRR, the completion of a direct rail link through Connecticut to Boston rendered this service obsolete. Since its main line to Greenport ran through the relatively unpopulated center of Long Island, the railroad eventually began constructing or acquiring other lines that served the Island's main villages. In 1871, this included obtaining a lease on the New York and Rockaway Railroad (purchased in 1901), that provided the route Mrs. Palsgraf intended to take to Rockaway Beach.

Continually mired in financial problems, the LIRR finally achieved prosperity after 1880 when it was reorganized and expanded under the leadership of wealthy banker Austin Corbin. Corbin was killed in a carriage accident at his New Hampshire estate in 1896, and in 1900, the Pennsylvania Railroad acquired controlling interest in the LIRR for $6,982,000.[14] The acquisition was part of a major expansion plan. The Pennsylvania wished to extend its tracks from New Jersey into New York City by either a Hudson River bridge or tunnel, build what would be Pennsylvania Station in the heart of Manhattan, and acquire the LIRR's East River tunnel and its freight facilities in Brooklyn and Queens.

By the mid-1920s, the public face of the LIRR was its vice-president, George "Boots" LeBoutillier, a six-foot tall, 200-pound, native of Ohio who professed to be fond of golf and big game hunting. He had worked his way up through the Pennsylvania system, and had been named head of the LIRR division in 1923. LeBoutillier's difficulties included the perception that the LIRR was a stepchild of the Pennsylvania Railroad, but his most basic public relations problem was that he was running the least popular of common carriers, a commuter railroad. Worse, it was a line that simply could not keep up with the exponential growth in the number of passengers and the population of the area it served. In 1900, the total population of Long Island was 1,452,611, but by 1930, it would almost treble to 4,147,413.[15] LIRR passenger traffic rose at an even faster rate, going from 12,300,000 in 1900 to 43,000,000 in 1915, to 73,000,000 in 1920,[16] and then to 92,991,010 in 1924, the year of the Palsgraf accident.[17]

This huge increase in passenger traffic brought with it an endless stream of complaints about service. LeBoutillier may have boasted that the LIRR provided "fast, clean, adequate electric passenger train service,"[18] but articles and letters in the New York press complained of poorly-maintained equipment, a lack of cleanliness, meaningless schedules, and overcrowded trains. One commuter once complained to the *New York Times* that "[t]he New York subway is not, at its worst, more uncomfortable than Long Island Railroad trains, nor more dangerous."[19] Serious shortcomings were also noted in a 1924 New York Public Service Commission report that said only 68% of trains leaving New York were on time, and that the line suffered from poor equipment and dirty cars. The LIRR also suffered from bad publicity caused by proposed service cuts, smoke pollution from freight yard steam engines, and even the death of a polo pony.[20] Naturally, such complaints made the railroad a popular target for politicians and leaders of civic groups. Charles S. Colden, the attorney for a Flushing taxpayers organization, characterized the railroad's attitude as one of "the public be damned."[21] Schedule cuts led a spokesman for the Rockaways Chamber of Commerce to complain that "the municipalities are 'lambs being led to the slaughter.'"[22] A complaint of a different type was voiced by Maurice Hotchner, the lawyer for the Association of Long Island Commuters, who accused the LIRR of caring only about service between New York and Jamaica, thus retarding the Long Island real estate boom.

The critics overlooked or failed to mention the expensive improvement projects made necessary by the constant expansion of the LIRR's passenger load. During July 1923, LeBoutillier claimed that the LIRR had spent $7,000,000 on various upgrades and announced a ten-year $84,000,000 improvement plan.[23] The following April, the railroad announced the largest improvement budget in its history, with plans to spend $4,000,000 on such items as sixty new steel passenger cars, four new passenger locomotives, and two new passenger stations.[24] Accordingly, the LIRR management maintained that the public "enjoyed modern equipment and good service . . . and the stockholders get nothing."[25] This remark highlighted another problem for the railroad, its chronic financial problems. The Pennsylvania's operation of the LIRR got off to a promising start with the company announcing improved operations and increased earnings for fiscal 1901 — $4,862,347, with a net income of $195,609.[26] Unfortunately, this favorable financial picture would not last. Although the railroad earned $22,143,571.83[27] in 1924 and had an overall net income of $4 million,[28] its finances remained in a questionable state. It had not paid its stockholders a dividend since 1896, and would not until 1928.[29] In fact, in 1927, LeBoutillier claimed that the railroad was "one jump ahead of the sheriff."[30]

At the heart of the LIRR's financial problems was its heavy dependence on passenger fares. Approximately 70% of its income came from this source, with only 30% from freight, the reverse of most other rail lines.[31] This meant that to increase revenue, the LIRR management had to ask for increased fares, bringing more controversy and bad publicity. When the railroad insisted it needed higher fares, the public and politicians naturally took an exactly opposite view. In 1924, New York City Mayor John F. Hylan appeared at a hearing considering the issue, pointed an accusing finger at LeBoutillier, and announced, "if it's war you want, we are ready to start whenever you are."[32]

In addition to the cost of equipment and service upgrades, the railroad also faced large expenses for grade-crossing eliminations aimed at preventing the all-too-frequent collisions between trains and motor vehicles.[33] In 1911, it reported expenditures of $15,000,000 in the past decade to eliminate dangerous crossings.[34] In 1923, the railroad maintained that it had done as much if not more than any other line in the country to eliminate the crossings, noting that it had eliminated over 300 at an expense of approximately $20,000,000.[35] Four years later, LeBoutillier estimated that grade-crossing elimination would cost the LIRR $18,250,000 over the next five years. In addition to elimination costs, the railroad also expended large sums of money to employ watchmen at crossings, and to install crossing gates, alarm bells, lights, signs and signposts.

Grade-crossing accidents had always been a problem for the LIRR; for example, five persons had been killed when a train struck a large tally-ho coach on Memorial Day in 1897. However, these accidents assumed a whole new dimension in the age of the automobile. An early indication of the bad publicity car-train collisions could generate came with the 1907 death of Dr. Edward J. Gallagher and his fiancé at a crossing in St. Albans, Queens; the *New York Times* headline announced "Victims Wrapped in Gasoline Flames."[36] Two years later, the article on the death of another doctor, William G. Terwilliger, at the Wreck Lead (now Island Park) crossing, reported that the bodies of the victims had hung briefly from the overhead telegraph wires. More unwelcome press coverage resulted from another accident at the same crossing on August 3, 1913, that killed two prominent socialites, William Laimbeer and S. Osgood Pell, and their chauffeur, and severely injured Mrs. Nathalie Laimbeer.[37]

The railroad, complaining bitterly about reckless "automobilists," responded to the problem with a public education campaign consisting of posters and newspaper ads. Unfortunately, this sort of effort did little to reduce the large number of reckless drivers who risked death at the crossings. A *New York Times* article published in September 1915 reported that so far that year eighty-five motorists had driven through lowered gates with fifty-nine of these crashing through the barrier; one of the four reported crossing deaths was a railroad watchman run down by the automobile he was attempting to warn.[38] Ten years later, little had changed; in August 1925, the railroad reported 365 incidents of vehicles crashing through gates thus far that year.[39] Although many accidents were clearly the result of careless or reckless driving, collisions between LIRR trains and motor vehicles during the 1920s produced many lurid headlines that hurt the railroad's image. These included: *Killed With Babes Going to Baptism, Mother and Two Children Die as Train Hurls Them to Third Rail from Automobile*;[40] *Fifty-Mile Express Wrecks Fire Truck; 2 Dead, 2 Dying*;[41] *Ex-Detective Dies as Train Hits Auto; Henry Bischoff's Car Is Cut in Two on Long Island Crossing in Ronkonkama*;[42] *3 Killed, 2 May Die as Train Hits Auto*;[43] *Two Are Crushed and Burned Under Train When Auto Skids Through Gates at Crossing*;[44] *Long Island Train Hits Crowded Bus*;[45] and *Three Men Killed as Train Hits Auto.*[46]

Equally damaging to the railroad's prospects with local juries were highly-publicized accidents involving passengers. Although fatal accidents were relatively infrequent, the fear of violent and random death on the rails had existed in the imagination of the traveling public since the mid-nineteenth century. The awful consequences of railroads' negligence had twice been dramatically demonstrated to New York City residents during the early years of the twentieth century. In 1902, one New York Central train ran into the rear of another in Manhattan's Park Avenue tunnel, killing fifteen passengers. A far worse disaster struck the Brooklyn Rapid Transit Company fifteen years later, when a train traveling at excessive speed derailed as it entered a tunnel near the Malbone Street station in Brooklyn. Two passenger cars smashed against the wall of the tunnel and were demolished, killing ninety-seven persons.

In contrast, the LIRR managed to avoid any passenger fatalities during this period. The last series of fatal accidents involving the LIRR all occurred in the short span of nine months in 1892–93. In December 1892, the railroad suffered a major construction accident at Long Island City during work on its East River tunnel. A worker using a steam box to thaw out 100 pounds of dynamite caused a major explosion that killed him and four other people, injured twenty, and reportedly broke every pane of glass within a three-block radius. The following June, a train on the railroad's Manhattan Beach line derailed, throwing three cars against an embankment, killing seven passengers. In August, at the Laurel Hill station in Long Island City, a train from Rockaway Beach crashed into the rear of a Manhattan Beach train, killing a railroad brakeman and fifteen passengers, and injuring an estimated forty others. Thereafter, the LIRR managed to avoid accidents resulting in passenger deaths. In 1908, an electric motor exploded on a train bound for Rockaway Beach, setting the coach afire, but all the passengers escaped without injury. Fifty passengers were injured in a head-on collision near the College Point station in 1913, but the three fatalities were all railroad employees. Thus by 1916, when the railroad had gone almost twenty-three years without a passenger fatality, its general solicitor, Joseph F. Keany, optimistically proclaimed, "we don't kill anyone nowadays but reckless automobilists at grade crossings."[47]

Unfortunately, as operations grew and the number of passengers carried increased, the railroad's luck eventually ran out. In April 1918, the 30th Infantry Regiment suffered its first violent fatalities, not in combat against the Germans on the Western Front, but while riding the LIRR from a training facility at Camp Upton in Suffolk County to College Point, Queens. Three soldiers among the 700 troops aboard were killed, and thirty-six were injured, when a split rail caused eight cars of their ten-car train to leave the tracks near Central Islip. Another serious accident took place in February 1921 when a motorman ran past a red signal causing a five-car express to crash broadside a seven-car local on the Atlantic Avenue line, injuring fifty passengers, but causing no fatalities. In July 1924, less than a month before the *Palsgraf* accident, fifty passengers were injured, and a thirty-year-old Flushing stenographer, Walburta Buck, was killed at the Sunnyside Yards when a prematurely thrown crossover switch derailed a commuter train and caused it to crash against an electric locomotive on an adjoining track. Railroad-hating Mayor Hylan proclaimed that the accident was caused by "gross negligence,"[48] and a Long Island congressman remarked: "It is about time the [LIRR] officials began to realize they are carrying human beings and not cattle."[49] The report to the ICC stated that the speed of the derailed train was in excess of the maximum limits and that railroad employees were not properly informed about rules on operating crossover switches.[50]

Three more major mishaps followed during 1926, accidents that would have been fresh in the memory of those who sat on the *Palsgraf* jury. In April, fifty passengers were injured, two seriously, when a work train backed into an east-bound six-car train at the Nostrand Avenue station in Brooklyn. One of the injured, forty-year-old father-of-four Anthony Baul, pried from the wreckage by firemen using hooks, axes, and acetylene torches, lost both legs and died the next day. A far worse accident took place in August, when a train derailed near Calverton in Suffolk County and crashed into a pickle factory, killing seven, including five passengers and the engineer and fireman, and injuring twenty-eight (twenty-one passengers and seven LIRR employees). One of the dead, affluent Manhattan stockbroker Harold L. Fish, suffocated when part of a par-lor car was buried in salt from the pickle works. In September, there was yet another accident, when a baggage train struck the rear of a rush-hour passen-ger train. Four passengers were injured, and 55,000 commuters were affected by delays caused by the accident.[51]

There was more bad publicity in October 1926 when a Suffolk County grand jury investigating the Calverton wreck stated: "We condemn the Long Island Railroad in emphatic terms for the apparent lack of proper inspectors and inspection and the use of obsolete switches which fail to measure up to the standard of approved and modern specifications."[52] No railroad officials were indicted because of the Calverton crash, but this had happened on other occa-sions. In 1907, after the grade-crossing accident that killed Dr. Gallagher and his fiancé, Ralph Peters, then president of the railroad, was arrested and had to post a $60,000 bond. In 1923, the railroad's general superintendent, chief of police, and several LIRR employees were indicted for manslaughter in connec-tion with fatal grade-crossing accidents.[53] Nothing came of these indictments, but in 1924, after a special grand jury investigation of the Sunnyside Yards derailment, three LIRR employees were indicted; the employee who caused the accident by negligently throwing a switch was later convicted of manslaughter and sentenced to sixty days in the workhouse.

Chapter 3
THE ATTORNEYS

When Mrs. Palsgraf decided to seek legal redress from the Long Island Railroad she was about to encounter a legal profession that had been utterly transformed by the vast industrial and commercial growth of the late nineteenth and early twentieth centuries. In 1870, the population of the area that would become Greater New York was 1,478,103.[1] By 1920, four years before the *Palsgraf* accident, it would be 4,776,883.[2] In 1870, New York City had a lawyer population of only 1,283,[3] but by 1927, an estimated 20,000 were practicing within its boundaries.[4] The increase was reflected in law school enrollments. In 1910, Fordham Law School had 215 students and Brooklyn Law School 289.[5] By 1924 these numbers had risen to 1,480 and 2,283 respectively.[6] By 1926, the total enrollment for all the city's law schools was 10,280, including 2,790 at the newly-opened St. John's Law School.[7]

A loss of a sense of collegiality developed as the number of lawyers grew along with the city's population. The influx of persons with immigrant backgrounds also resulted in a stratification of the bar. A major report issued in 1921 stated that it was divided into two groups, graduates of full-time day law schools who handled business and commercial affairs for the affluent, and those who had attended part-time night schools who represented persons of limited or moderate means, often in ethnic neighborhoods.[8] Many of the latter were what has been termed "personal plight practitioners,"[9] attorneys who were compelled to constantly seek one-time clients to represent in negligence, divorce, and criminal cases.

Inevitably, those in the upper levels of society began to express concern about both the numbers of lawyers and the perceived decline in their quality. In 1914, Columbia University President Nicholas Murray Butler complained that "under present conditions graduates of the best university schools of law find themselves side by side with practicing lawyers whose keenness and apprehension do not conceal their intellectual poverty, and whose insinuating address is too often a cloak of unworthy character."[10] The next year, legal scholar John Henry Wigmore maintained that "[t]he bar is overcrowded with incompetent, shiftless, ill-fitted lawyers, who degrade the methods of the law and cheapen the quality of services by unlimited competition."[11] Much the same sentiments were expressed in 1922 by Harlan F. Stone, Dean of the Columbia Law School, who claimed that the profession included "increasing numbers of men of mediocre ability and inadequate preliminary education," adding that it was the duty of law schools to "dissuade the man of ordinary ability and meager education from beginning law study."[12] There were also concerns about women applicants. Speaking in 1927, Allan Fox, a member of the Committee on Character and Fitness, worried about the applications of "girl typists" who "clearly can never become competent lawyers."[13]

A target of those bemoaning the alleged oversupply of ill-educated lawyers was the evening law school. They questioned whether faculty and students could function properly in class after a day's work. Defenders of the evening schools responded by praising the character and dedication of evening students. They also questioned the supposed overall superiority of day students. As one commentator noted, "[l]oafing in fraternity houses, chalking billiard cues, or testing out proficiency in auction pinochle, and the like are accomplishments not unknown to the day law student. . . ."[14]

Those who wanted some college preparation as a prerequisite for law study focused on bar candidates' lack of knowledge of literature, history, and American traditions. Tales were told of candidates who thought that Andrew Jackson was a Civil War general and that the Battle of Marathon was fought between the *Monitor* and the *Merrimac*, or those whose idea of a biography was John Erskine's recent best-selling novel, *The Private Life of Helen of Troy*. Others were concerned with the purported ignorance of lawyers and law students coming from immigrant groups or the working and lower middle classes. John G. Agar of the Committee on Character and Fitness, warned that the threat presented by a lack of knowledge of the "basic principles on which American traditions are based."[15] He cautioned: "Unless we are to be Russianized, [bar] candidates must be made to familiarize themselves with these basic principles on which American principles are based."[16] Similarly, George Wickersham, president of the exclusive Association of the Bar of the City of New York, and former attorney general during the Taft administration, complained about foreign-born lawyers who lacked "the faintest comprehension of the nature of our institutions, or their history and development."[17]

Critics accused members of the Character Committee of class prejudice. New York City Assistant Corporation Counsel Benjamin Greenspoon reacted to their complaints by stating that they knew nothing about the human side of "boys south of Fourteenth Street."[18] However, proponents of a more exclusive bar waved aside suggestions that they were motivated by anything more than concern for the profession. Former Democratic presidential candidate John W. Davis denied that proposals for raising qualifications stemmed from selfish motives, stating: "Nothing is more fantastic and absurd."[19] Others disputed the argument that a more exclusive bar was somehow unfair to young men from the poorer classes. One commentator, a supporter of some college education for law students stated: "Once we realize that the lawyer's preliminary education is a matter of as great importance to the public as the doctor's, we shall forget this 'poor boy' nonsense and think of giving more scholarships to young men of ability ready to make sacrifices in order to enter a noble profession."[20]

Not all the complaints about lack of attorney quality came from elite members of the bar. As one commentator has observed, "[h]ow could the profession serve as a means of upward mobility and status definition for the middle and lower-middle classes . . . if there was nothing distinctive about them and they were open to every person, qualified or not?"[21] In 1916, while running for the supreme court, Philip A. "Doc" Brennan, a leading Brooklyn attorney who had not attended law school, complained of "low ethical standards and slovenliness," adding that "[s]ome lawyers mistake crust for craft and skill and some mistake gabbiness for courage."[22] Even flamboyant Brooklyn criminal defense lawyer Edward J. Reilly, a graduate of St. Lawrence University's Brooklyn Law School, found fault with the modern 1920s attorney, stating: "The old school lawyer has disappeared. In his place we find a product of a machine law school in a colored shirt, a loud tie, vulgarity stamped all over his face, no conception of ethics, decorum, or that he happens to be of an honorable profession and not a soap box. . . . A lawyer should have a background of breeding, culture and associations."[23]

According to critics, the chronic problem of ambulance chasing — involving personal injury lawyers who employed runners or solicitors to obtain cases, or who paid doctors and policemen to alert them to possible clients — was closely related to the alleged oversupply of new lawyers "dumped by our law factories upon a helpless public."[24] They also saw a close connection between the practice and those with recent immigrant backgrounds, Catholics, and Jews. Complaints about ambulance chasing were hardly new. In 1905, a group of insurance, railroad, and street railway companies announced the foundation of "The Alliance Against Accident Frauds" to detect and deter shyster lawyers, ambulance chasers, and dishonest physicians. A year later, Assistant Corporation Counsel George L. Sterling inveighed against "detestable little accident suits [against New York City], which are actually cooked up by unscrupulous lawyers who have early information on accidents."[25] An apparent blow was struck against ambulance chasing by the Court of Appeals in 1904 when it ruled that employing laymen to procure cases was a violation of § 74 of the Code of Civil Procedure.[26] In 1917, the New York State Legislature made a gesture toward reform by amending § 270 of the Penal Law to make it unlawful "to make it a business to solicit payment for a lawyer, or to furnish attorneys or counsel or an attorney and counsel to render legal services" in the City of New York.[27] However, the court ruling and the new law did nothing to curb the problem since, as Brooklyn supreme court Justice Mitchell May noted, the courts simply "closed their eyes to it."[28]

By late 1927, renewed complaints about ambulance chasing caused the president of the Association of the Bar to announce the appointment of a special committee to study the problem.[29] This was followed by hearings conducted for the Appellate Division by Justice Isidor Wasservogel, held from February to August 1928. Over 1,100 witnesses appeared, generating over 10,000 pages of testimony. Among the many abuses attributed to accident lawyers were the concocting of fraudulent claims and the filing thousands of meritless suits. Common tactics allegedly included oral retainers, and showing accident victims newspaper clippings reporting big awards and photos of large checks. A major concern was that poor persons, such as Mrs. Palsgraf, were being victimized by unscrupulous lawyers who settled cases on terms beneficial to themselves, while utterly ignoring the welfare of their unfortunate clients.

Although Mrs. Palsgraf's name and address were available in the *Brooklyn Daily Eagle* of August, 25, 1924, her case did not end up in the hands of one of the Borough's many negligence lawyers. If she was insisting on obtaining a substantial amount from the railroad, her case would not have been attractive to an attorney whose practice relied on obtaining rapid small settlements of personal injury cases. Any amount that the railroad might offer would have been very small. Worse, the case was factually difficult — boarding slowly moving trains and streetcars was not uncommon, and the railroad had no notice of the explosive nature of the package, which belonged to an unknown passenger — meaning there was a real possibility it that could be dismissed. Furthermore, even if a monetary judgment was obtained, the case would require additional time and expense since the railroad would almost certainly appeal to the Appellate Division, and even to the Court of Appeals.

Critics of the bar would have found nothing to object to about the attorney who took Mrs. Palsgraf's case, Matthew Wills Wood,[30] one of many persons from upstate New York who arrived in the city during the late nineteenth century. Wood, a Methodist, was born in 1875, and grew up in Middleburgh, a village of approximately 2,000 people, located in Schoharie County, about thirty-five miles southeast of Albany. The village was part of a hop-growing region that supplied breweries in Albany, Utica, and elsewhere. In 1895, it enjoyed a brief moment of fame when the Middleburg National Bank was the target of "Count" Maximilian Shinburn, a well-known professional bank burglar credited with stealing millions of dollars during his career, and whose previous exploits included successful burglaries in Europe, New York City, Boston, New Hampshire, and Ohio.

Wood was a graduate of Middleburgh High School who entered the University of Pennsylvania's Wharton School in 1897. He did not start college until he was twenty-one, an event that coincided with the entry by his father, Boyd Hudson Wood, into the booming real estate market in the Bay Ridge section of Brooklyn.[31] Born in 1844, the elder Wood was one of thirteen children of a Montgomery County, N.Y., farmer, Abram Wood. As a young man, he had been a canal boatman, but took up growing hops after his wife, Elizabeth, inherited a Middleburgh hop yard. During the mid-1890s, he began acquiring and developing properties in Brooklyn. Finally abandoning hop growing, he established a building/contracting firm, the Boyd H. Wood Corporation, and moved his entire family to Bay Ridge. The success of his business is evidenced by its construction of up to 150 buildings and business blocks,[32] and the $101,888 estate he left when he died in 1922.[33]

After receiving his B.S. degree, Matthew W. Wood enrolled in New York Law School where he served as president of the senior class. He graduated with honors and was one of four students from the 132-member class to receive awards, winning the $100 second prize, given for an essay, "Liability of a Private Corporation for its Torts of it Agents Committed in Ultra Vires Transactions," and for correctly answering a large number of legal questions. Instead of entering law practice, Wood then enrolled as a one-year student at Yale Law School. This was not a post-graduate course, but involved becoming part of Yale's third-year class and earning another L.L.B. Such dual degrees were made possible by a split in legal education methods. New York Law School followed the text-based method of its founder, Theodore Dwight, and like most law schools of the period required only two years of study. Yale, which had adopted the Langdell case method of instruction, had instituted a three-year program in 1896.

At Yale, Wood fared as well academically as he had at New York Law School. He successfully competed in a writing competition to become an associate editor of the *Yale Law Journal*,[34] won the Addison Porter essay prize for "Application of the Sherman Anti-Trust Act to Organized Labor," and when he received his second L.L.B. in 1904, he was one of only three graduating seniors in class of sixty-three to receive his degree *magna cum laude*.[35] The speaker at his graduation was former Secretary of War Elihu Root, who told the class: "To preserve and foster such a living faith of the people in the supreme value of the great impersonal rules of right which underlie our system of law is the highest and ever-present duty of the American lawyer."[36] Deciding not to do post-graduate work because he didn't want to add on more degrees,[37] Wood passed the bar exams of New York, Connecticut, and Massachusetts, and took a position with the lower Manhattan firm of Wing, Putnam & Burlingham. The next year, he moved to the Title Guarantee and Trust Company, located at 146 Broadway, and by 1908, he had opened his own law office at 80-82 William Street. When the Woolworth Building opened in 1913 at 233 Broadway, Wood relocated there immediately.

Wood described himself as a man with no hobbies, although he was a fan of University of Pennsylvania football, writing on more than one occasion to the *Brooklyn Daily Eagle* complaining about the paper's coverage of the team.[38] Until 1922, the bachelor attorney, who would not marry until 1929, lived in a stone-fronted row house in Bay Ridge with his widowed father, his sister, Hazel, her husband, and their children. Unfortunately, Wood did not get along well with his brother-in-law, Victor D. Borst, a patent attorney from Middleburgh. Since Borst was a Democrat and Wood a Republican, they argued about politics and issues like United States entry into World War I (Wood was opposed). As a result, when Boyd H. Wood died in 1922, the Bay Ridge home was sold and Wood was forced to make new living arrangements; thereafter his contact with his sister was limited to weekly phone calls.

By the time Mrs. Palsgraf became his client, Wood had over twenty years experience in both trial and appellate courts. A member of the New York County Lawyers' Association, he was one of a minority of attorneys to have a rating in *Martindale's American Law Directory* for ability and ethics. His was the highest level possible for both legal ability ("very high to preeminent") and general ethical standards ("very high").[39] Within the limits imposed at the time, he did his best to promote his law practice. He was one of a small minority of solo practitioners to place a professional card in the *Martindale's* and *Hubbell's* legal directories. He paid an extra fee every year to be among the attorneys whose names were listed in bold type in *Bender's Lawyer's Directory*. He was also listed annually in *Who's Who in New York*, *Who's Who in the East*, and *Who's Who in Law*.

Wood's office in the Woolworth Building also served to promote his practice. As a 1912 advertisement for the building stated: "Every tenant will acquire for his business some the building's enormous advertising value."[40] Then the tallest building in the world at 792 feet, and popularly known as the "Cathedral of Commerce," it was a prestige address. Clients coming to Wood's office entered through an arched entrance facing Broadway and passed through an ornate three-story cruciform-shaped lobby with a vaulted ceiling decorated with Byzantine-style colored glass mosaic tiles. Marble and gleaming bronze in a Gothic design framed the doors of the then-state-of-the-art elevators that took them to the attorney's office on the thirty-fourth floor at speeds of up to 700 feet per minute; once at that level, they would have enjoyed a fine view of lower Manhattan.

In addition to practicing law, Wood was involved in several business enterprises. Early in his legal career, he was the director and secretary of the Concentrated Milk Company, the director and secretary of the Yale Equity Company, and the vice-president of the Boyd H. Wood Corporation. In 1914, he also started his own real estate/construction company, the Penn-Yale Corporation, in whose name he put properties he'd purchased with his own funds. While the company held the properties, rents were collected, and bank loans secured to pay for repairs and/or improvements to prepare the properties for resale.[41] His non-legal social activities included memberships in the University Club of Brooklyn and the Bay Ridge Masonic Lodge.

Wood was not primarily a negligence lawyer. A fellow attorney once described his practice as being "on the commercial side of the law, in real estate and Surrogate's practice, and things of that description."[42] His card in the 1920 edition of *Martindale's American Law Directory* indicated that he practiced in all civil and criminal courts, and paid special attention to "probate and commercial matters."[43] His listing in the 1924 *Hubbell's Legal Directory* stated that he had a "general practice in all state and federal courts," accorded "special attention to the interests of non-resident heirs," had a "commercial department," and handled "bankruptcy matters."[44] The 1928 *Martindale's* entry was "General Practice in all Courts, Specializing in Trial Work and Real Estate Law."[45] It also listed references in New York, London, Edinburgh, and Hamilton, Ontario.

The diversity of Wood's practice is reflected in cases where there are published pre-*Palsgraf* appellate decisions. These include an estate action,[46] the foreclosure of a mechanic's lien,[47] a divorce,[48] attorney misconduct,[49] an action against the employee of a brokerage house for failing to sell stock when it reached a certain price,[50] and a demurrage case.[51] His reported negligence actions are, like *Palsgraf*, factually difficult cases involving injuries to working class Brooklynites. In the first of these, he represented Mrs. Edith M. Wensley who badly injured her knee in a fall caused by a large cut left in the street by the Edison Electric Illuminating Company's installation of light poles. Suits were filed against both Edison Electric and the City of New York, which had issued the permits for the work. At the trial, held during December 1915, both defendants denied any negligence and produced eighteen witnesses to testify on their behalf. However, the jury returned a verdict of $3,500 for the injured woman and $500 for her husband for loss of consortium. Both defendants appealed, but only the loss of consortium judgment against the City was reversed.[52]

Wood was less successful in 1921, when he represented Elizabeth Day, a forty-four-year-old Brooklyn housewife, who, like Mrs. Palsgraf, had been injured while using public transportation during an outing with her two daughters. She had been aboard a street car operated by the Brooklyn City Railroad Company when it was struck by a large horse-drawn milk truck belonging to the Sheffield Milk Company. The street car and truck were traveling in opposite directions down a snow-covered street. As they drew alongside one another, the wheels of the truck slued on an icy rut, causing it to smash against the side of the street car, breaking two windows and splashing milk over a passenger. The collision allegedly threw Mrs. Day across the car, injuring her back and side.

Wood filed suit against both the milk company and the street car line. The case was factually difficult since the milk company could claim that its truck could not have avoided the streetcar, while the railway's position was that its car was traveling on fixed rails and could do nothing to miss the truck. Wood contended both defendants were negligent — the milk company because its driver attempted to navigate the narrow passage between the curbside snow banks and the tracks, and the railway because the operator failed to slow down while passing the milk truck. When the jury agreed with defense contentions that the accident was unavoidable, Wood appealed to the Appellate Division. The verdict for the defendants was affirmed, although one justice dissented on the grounds that the verdict was against the weight of the evidence.[53] In his opinion, he made the same point about Mrs. Day that many have made about Mrs. Palsgraf — that she had been sent out of court despite being a passenger injured through no fault of her own.[54] Because of the dissent, Wood was able to take the case to the Court of Appeals, but it affirmed the Appellate Division decision in a per curium opinion.[55]

In another factually difficult case, tried in 1925, Wood represented Joseph Hild, a worker injured at the Brooklyn Navy Yard. Hild had accepted $576.30 in worker's compensation, but then sued for $25,000, claiming he'd only agreed to the smaller amount because of misrepresentations made by his former employer. Unimpressed with Hild's claims, the court dismissed his case. Wood's ultimately unsuccessful efforts to get the case reheard took him all the way to the Court of Appeals.[56] In another negligence action, first tried approximately one year before *Palsgraf*, Wood won a verdict for Gladalyn Richter, a nine-year-old who had been on her way to Sunday school when she was struck by a car and suffered a broken leg. The defendant driver, James Hallaren, was represented by Philip A. "Doc" Brennan, the former general counsel for the Brooklyn Rapid Transit Company, who frequently represented the LIRR. Wood's witnesses testified that the vehicle had defective brakes, that the car was being driven in an erratic manner, and that Hallaren had crammed three passengers into a two-seater car, including a young woman who had been sitting on his lap. Brennan twice moved that the case be dismissed on the grounds of contributory negligence, but veteran jurist Norman S. Dike allowed the case to go the jury, which awarded the injured girl damages of $6,500. However, when the case went to the Appellate Division in December 1926, it ordered a new trial, holding that finding the girl free from contributory negligence was against the weight of the evidence.[57]

It was not negligence cases, however, that brought Wood some visibility and newspaper headlines. During 1908 and 1909, he served on a legal committee advising civic groups that wanted top priority for construction of the Fourth Avenue subway in Brooklyn. The proposed line was of vital interest in the borough because it would spur development and raise land values — a definite benefit for Wood's father's business, the Boyd H. Wood Corporation. Fearful that the City would incur so many financial obligations that its constitutional debt limit would be exceeded, thus delaying subway construction, Bay Ridge realtor David Meyer filed suit in July 1908, with Wood as one of his attorneys. Although the suit sought an injunction against all subway construction, the intent of the action was not to stop the building of the Fourth Avenue line, but to get a court ruling that determined the true limits of the municipal debt.[58] A referee's determination of the City's debt limit was appealed to the Appellate Division, and then to the Court of Appeals, where it was determined that the City could incur the debt necessary for the subway construction.[59]

Wood was only one of several attorneys assisting pro-subway civic groups, but in January 1914, he made headlines in his own right when he involved himself in the latest controversy over the activities of a radical clergyman, Reverend Charles Bouck White.[60] White grew up in Middleburgh at the same time as Wood, graduated from Middleburgh High School, and earned an A.B. from Harvard, *magna cum laude*. In 1901, after attending divinity school and being ordained a minister, he gained notice with *The Book of Daniel Drew*, a well-received fictionalized "autobiography" of the nineteenth century railroad speculator who aided the takeover of the Erie Railroad by financiers Jay Gould and Jim Fisk. His next literary effort, *The Call of the Carpenter*, sparked controversy because it described Jesus as a social activist. Socialist leader Eugene V. Debs called it the best book he'd read since *Les Miserables*,[61] but its publication eventually led to the White's dismissal from his post as head rector of Trinity Neighborhood House in New York City.

The radical clergyman's next novel, *The Mixing: What the Hillport Neighbors Did*, incensed not theological conservatives, but Matthew W. Wood and his former neighbors in Middleburgh. Published in late 1913, it was intended, according to White, to show the "decadence of the rural communities in this country."[62] It related how dedicated young people, following White's social activist ideals, transformed a backward small town inhabited by ignorant bigots. The fictional Hillport was easily recognizable as Middleburgh, and worse, White used the names of actual town residents. There was even a character named "Mat Wood," a young man who hung around on street corners with other youths until he was sent off to YMCA training school so he could become the head of the town's new recreation department.[63]

After reading the book, Wood wrote to both White and the publisher, Doubleday & Page, complaining about its portrayal of Middleburgh and its inhabitants. He received no satisfaction from the radical clergyman, who repeated his allegations about the town's residents, calling them "peasants" and "bleaters typical of a country community."[64] Believing that the novel constituted criminal libel, a misdemeanor, Wood sent a copy of the book to Manhattan District Attorney Charles S. Whitman along with a letter asking that charges be brought against the author. When this news reached the press, Wood told a reporter from the *Brooklyn Daily Eagle* that in his opinion White "ought to be put in jail."[65] He also wrote to the editor of the *Middleburgh News*, stating that he was "incensed at the portrayal of the leading citizens of the village" and asking for assistance in having *The Mixing* suppressed.[66]

However, the decision on whether to prosecute White rested with Whitman. In June 1914, he wrote back to Wood, reporting that an assistant had reviewed the novel and it had been determined that "the public interests do not require the institution of criminal proceedings by me because of anything published in the book. . . ."[67] However, by then Wood already had the satisfaction of seeing White behind bars. In May 1914, the clergyman staged a protest during Sunday services at Manhattan's elite Calvary Baptist Church, dubbed the Church of Standard Oil by socialist novelist Upton Sinclair, because it was attended by millionaire John D. Rockefeller, Jr. White was arrested and sentenced to a six-month term in the New York City workhouse on Blackwell's Island.[68]

The case that brought Wood the most visibility occurred in 1918 when he was assigned as co-counsel for the teenage "choirboy murderer," Paul Chapman. The sixteen-year-old Chapman, who had once sung in the choir of the fashionable St. Bartholomew's Church, had participated in a bungled burglary of a Brooklyn cigar store that left the proprietor, Henry R. Regensberg, and his brother-in-law, Samuel Regensberg, dead, and his wife, Jennie Regensburg, in critical condition with four gunshot wounds. When the police arrived, seventeen-year-old Hughes Davis, the perpetrator who appears to have done all the shooting, attempted to hide in the building's dumbwaiter. When discovered, he fired at the police and was shot five times and killed. Meanwhile, Chapman was able to walk away from the scene unnoticed, but was apprehended later.

At his trial, Chapman claimed he hadn't carried a gun, had fired no shots, and had urged Davis not to use his gun. Wood and his co-counsel, Brooklyn attorney William R. Murphy, argued that Chapman had abandoned the burglarious enterprise. They also unsuccessfully tried to have the indictment dismissed on the grounds that it stated that the crime had been committed with a revolver, but that testimony showed that a pistol was used. They produced as character witnesses a choirmaster and eight public school teachers who recalled that Chapman had been a "bright obedient boy."[69] Despite the efforts of his attorneys, Chapman did not make a good impression on the jury, reportedly seeming far shrewder than his years, and appearing indifferent to the proceedings. Although the jury took less than an hour to convict their client, one observer, an experienced court reporter, praised the efforts of Wood and Murphy, stating that the defendant "was assigned two lawyers as counsel who probably got their first experience as murder counsel in this trial. . . . Nevertheless, they defended Chapman well and ably . . . [and] no lawyer, however experienced and clever, could have affected the verdict of 'Guilty.'"[70]

After their client was convicted, Wood and Murphy shifted their efforts to avoiding the death penalty, arguing that the court should have considered Chapman's abandonment of the crime before it was consummated by Hughes Davis. Wood also wrote to the *Brooklyn Daily Eagle*, protesting that: "The State of New York . . . is about to forfeit . . . the life of a boy whose mind is scarcely mature enough to weigh the serious consequences of his acts. . . . Is it just in this advanced stage of our civilization?"[71] After Chapman was sentenced to death on February 19, similar protests arrived from all over the country; the *Brooklyn Daily Eagle* published letters not only from local correspondents, but from upstate Oneonta and Grand Rapids, Michigan.[72] Eventually, Governor Charles S. Whitman would receive petitions signed by over 30,000 people asking clemency for Chapman.[73]

Chapman's case was argued before the Court of Appeals on Oct. 10, 1918. Assistant District Attorney Henry C. Anderson characterized Chapman as "a dangerous and vicious criminal" who needed money for an assignation with a married woman.[74] In contrast, Wood stressed his client's youth, stating: "It seems there is an unbearable inconsistency in the criminal law. . . . Which holds a boy of the age of 16 years and ten days, of good parentage and good record, to the same rigid and absolute degree of accountability as a hardened criminal of adult age."[75] Writing for a unanimous court, Judge Frederick Collin declined to consider Chapman's age, stating: "Our duty and our power in capital cases are clearly defined and established. They are not changed, they are neither less nor more rigid or compelling because of the age, character, or standing of the convicted defendant."[76] In concluding, Collin did note that Chapman might yet be granted clemency.[77] This is exactly what happened, when ten days later, Chapman's youth prompted Governor Whitman to grant executive clemency.[78]

Three months before the *Palsgraf* trial, Wood was back in Kings County Supreme Court for the retrial of the *Richter* case. On February 18, 1927, it was heard before the recently-elected Justice Charles J. Druhan, who had spent his legal career as an assistant corporation counsel. Doc Brennan again represented the driver, Hallaren, and seeking to establish contributory negligence, closely questioned the Richter girl about many steps she'd taken into the street before being struck by the car. After hearing all of Wood's witnesses, Druhan, satisfied that there was contributory negligence as a matter of law, dismissed the case; Wood then appealed to the Appellate Division.

About this time, Wood was also involved in legal proceedings of a personal matter. In January 1927, he was sued over the possession of a Brooklyn house by thirty-year-old Italian-born Mrs. Elizabeth Ingrao, allegedly a widow whose husband had died on a business trip to Italy. Although the deed was in the name of the Boyd H. Wood Corporation, Mrs. Ingrao claimed, "[i]t's really mine, because I picked it out and spent all my money in the expectation that Mr. Wood and I would marry."[79] In November 1926, she obtained an injunction to prevent her eviction, and installed double locks on the doors and windows. However, she indicated to the press that she did not fear a forcible ejection because "Mr. Wood is too much of gentleman for that."[80] Claiming that she and Wood had had an affair for five or six years, and had been engaged to marry until recently, she also filed a breach of promise suit against the attorney.[81]

Wood had an entirely different version of the story. He said that he had known Ingrao only as an interpreter in law cases. He claimed she had told him that she wanted to buy a home, but had only $1,000; he refused to finance a deal for her, but instead purchased the Brooklyn residence, put it in the name of the Boyd H. Wood Corporation, and leased it to her for $100 a month. As evidence, he filed with the court a copy of the lease signed by Mrs. Ingrao. He stated that she had paid no rent since June 1926, and requested the court to order either that the rent be paid to him or that it be held on deposit until the lawsuit was decided. Wood also denied stories of a romantic involvement, stating that Mrs. Ingrao was not a widow as she claimed, but was really married and the mother of a child. The case was scheduled for trial in mid-April 1927 before Justice William B. Carswell, who as a member of the Appellate Division, would be one of the justices to hear the first *Palsgraf* appeal the following October. Despite earlier claims that her affair with Wood had been "notorious" in the neighborhood and promises of "scandalous revelations," Mrs. Ingrao dropped her suit over the house as soon as it was called for trial. The *Brooklyn Daily Eagle* reported she had "quit cold" and that Wood had agreed to a discontinuance if she vacated the premises within three weeks.[82]

As for how Mrs. Palsgraf came to engage Matthew W. Wood nothing is known; perhaps she or someone of her acquaintance had once seen Wood's name in the papers. Her choice could have been influenced by the location of his office high in the prestigious Woolworth Building, which literally and figuratively set him far above local negligence attorneys whose offices clustered around Court Street in Brooklyn. Another possibility may be Wood's involvement in the building and real estate businesses. The Palsgrafs might have known about Wood either because roofer Michael Palsgraf was familiar with the Boyd H. Wood Corporation and/or the Penn-Yale Corporation, or had actually worked on one of their construction or renovation projects. As for Wood, an attorney from a prosperous family with an apparently successful law practice and outside business income, it was a case on which he could afford to take a chance.

Like Matthew W. Wood, the Long Island Railroad attorneys had offices in a New York City landmark; for them it was Manhattan's Pennsylvania Station. Completed in 1911, the station was massive granite structure that covered two city blocks. Its exterior featured large columns along its eastern side and twenty-two 5,700-pound stone eagles positioned over the entrances. Large carriageways took passengers inside the station to a marble waiting room with a 150-foot-high vaulted ceiling; a glass vaulted ceiling supported by wrought-iron beams covered the concourse. When it opened, the Pennsylvania Railroad proudly proclaimed that it "epitomizes and embodies the highest development of the art of transportation." [83]

Located in the huge station's Room 341, the LIRR legal department was headed by its general solicitor, Joseph F. Keany, the son of Irish immigrants, Patrick Francis Keany and his wife Anne. Keany's father had arrived in Brooklyn from Boston in the 1860s, working first as a brewer and then as a wholesale liquor dealer. The younger Keany attended local parochial schools, and then earned B.A. and M.A. degrees at St. John's College. While working as a tea auctioneer, he attended New York Law School and then clerked for two law firms before being admitted to the bar in 1896. He then joined the railroad's legal department, serving as chief clerk and junior attorney under William J. Kelly who later became the presiding justice of the Appellate Division, Second Department. Keany became the LIRR's head attorney in 1904, and was named general solicitor in 1916. The numerous cases he handled for the railroad illustrate the full range of legal problems handled by his department. In addition to many employee accident cases and major negligence actions were a Montauk Indian land claim[84] and charges of violating the federal Locomotive Boiler Inspection Law.[85] Other cases included disputes over tax assessments[86] and grade-crossing elimination costs,[87] and a brokerage house challenge the LIRR's management as a Pennsylvania Railroad subsidiary.[88] Keany's stated philosophy on representing the railroad was that the less an attorney said in court the better it was for him and his client.[89]

A life-long bachelor, the general solicitor lived his entire life at 470 Washington Ave. in Brooklyn. Politically, Keany was a strong supporter of Governor Alfred E. Smith, and regularly contributed to his political campaigns. Like his father, the railroad attorney was very active in Roman Catholic affairs. A vigorous defender of the Church, he was in demand as a graduation and after-dinner speaker, and made appearances at Sunday communion breakfasts. He served as trustee of St. John's College, which awarded him an honorary doctor of laws in 1913, and belonged to the St. Patrick's Society, the Emerald Society, the Holy Name Society, and the Catholic Benevolent Society of Brooklyn. Keany's most significant service was as a member of the board of directors and vice-president of the Roman Catholic Orphan Asylum Society. A large organization that ran several orphanages, the Society was regarded as especially important in Catholic circles since its purpose was to ensure that orphans would be brought up in their parents' faith. Keany staunchly defended the orphanages against critics who claimed they caused dependence and a lack of self-reliance in children. He acknowledged the superiority of a real home environment and maintained that the Society actively sought homes for its charges, but claimed that they were hard to find because modern 1920s women had other more remunerative ways to supplement their incomes. All his service to Roman Catholic causes was rewarded in 1920, when he was named a Knight of St. Gregory by Pope Benedict XV.

Keany's staff included two attorneys who had studied at Columbia Law School, Louis Carruthers and Alfred Augustus Gardner. Carruthers graduated from Columbia in 1899, and joined the LIRR's legal department in 1901. He was active in lawn tennis circles, served as president of the prestigious West Side Tennis Club in Forest Hills, Queens, and took an active part in the financing and construction of the Club's tennis stadium.[90] Carruthers does not appear to have been directly involved with handling negligence actions. Instead, reported cases where he appeared for the LIRR include such issues as liability for the cost of a new bridge over a right-of-way,[91] whether a change in a grade crossing was required,[92] and whether the LIRR was liable for damages to businesses while a street was closed during grade-crossing construction.[93]

Like Carruthers, Alfred A. Gardner was a tennis enthusiast. He was an 1887 graduate of Harvard College, who attended Columbia, and was admitted to the bar in 1899.[94] After briefly working for the LIRR, he served as the general solicitor for the Interborough Rapid Transit Company and the Interborough Metropolitan System. Gardner returned to the LIRR in 1913 as assistant general counsel. For several years, his cases included negligence actions, including the *Terwilliger* grade-crossing accident,[95] but by the 1920s, the reported cases where he represented the railroad concerned tax and business matters.[96] He also had the unenviable task of representing the railroad at the contentious fare-hike hearings held during the 1920s.

The other members of Keany's staff during this period were fellow Irish-Catholics who had attended local law schools. The most senior of this group was his younger brother, Matthew J. Keany. The younger Keany was an 1897 graduate of New York Law School who had served in the LIRR's real estate department until 1904, when he moved to the legal department and became a trial lawyer. Other experienced attorneys at the Pennsylvania Station office during the 1920s were Michael V. Ahern, Dominic B. Griffin, who specialized in trying negligence cases, and Edward Newburn.[97] William McNamara, who would try the *Palsgraf* case, fits the image of the hard-working, dedicated evening law student extolled by defenders of the night schools. McNamara was from Brooklyn. He first worked for the LIRR as a teenage clerk, attending evening classes at New York Law School at the same time that he married and started a family. He received his law degree in 1923, receiving second prize honors at graduation, and then moved up to the LIRR legal department; he was admitted to the bar in 1924. At the time of the *Palsgraf* trial, he was thirty-three years old and had two young children. Another recent addition to the department was William J. O'Brien a graduate of St. John's College and Fordham Law School, who joined the railroad as a clerk in 1924, and became an attorney in 1926.

For cases it regarded as particularly important, the LIRR employed prominent outside counsel. One high-profile attorney who represented the LIRR was Morgan J. O'Brien, a former Appellate Division justice, who was once suggested for the United States Supreme Court. O'Brien appeared as counsel for the railroad in a 1912 real estate case,[98] and more importantly in 1921 as co-counsel with Alfred A. Gardner in a successful effort to lift an injunction against a fare hike.[99] O'Brien was even more prominent in New York City Catholic affairs than Joseph F. Keany; he was a Knight of St. Gregory, a friend of both Cardinal Farley and Cardinal Hayes, once had an audience with Pope Pius XI, and received a papal blessing on his fiftieth wedding anniversary. Equally prominent was sometime-LIRR outside counsel Henry A. Uterhart, who had A.B., M.A., and L.L.B. degrees from Columbia, and whose list of clients included financier J.P. Morgan, and "almost every millionaire on Long Island."[100]

Keany also employed outside counsel well known in the locality where a case was being heard. In 1910, when the LIRR was sued for $156,000 by the Forest Fish and Game Commission for allegedly not cutting weeds, brush and grass along its rights of way in Suffolk County, retired Suffolk County Judge Timothy M. Griffing returned to his old courthouse to represent the railroad.[101] In 1924, when the railroad faced federal forfeiture proceedings against Vice President George Le Boutellier's private railway car, which had been seized at Penn Station by Prohibition agents after it was found to contain twenty-two cases of wine, whiskey, and gin, Manhattan Congressman Royal H. Weller was hired to handle the case.

For a highly-publicized 1926 trial in Queens County Court involving charges that locomotive smoke coming from a rail yard violated penal and sanitary codes, the LIRR's special counsel was William J. Morris. Morris, an assistant district attorney, who later served as Queens County Bar Association president and become a judge, may have had the most difficult experience of any of the LIRR's outside attorneys. After obtaining a delay in the start of the case, he was surrounded by an angry crowd and was unable to leave the courthouse until court attendants intervened. At the trial, held during a major heat wave that caused six deaths in the City, angry housewives presented packets of soot as evidence. However, the railroad escaped liability when the jury failed to agree.

Similarly, for negligence cases, Keany primarily relied not on his own staff, but on outside attorneys. When Mrs. S. Osgood Pell engaged former New York City Mayor Robert A. Van Wyck to represent her in the $250,000 suit arising from the 1913 Wreck Lead grade-crossing accident, Keany countered with prominent attorney Martin W. Littleton.[102] Littleton had served in Congress and had been the Borough President of Brooklyn from 1904-05. He was the lawyer who in 1908 had successfully represented eccentric Pittsburgh millionaire Harry K. Thaw at his second trial for the killing of noted architect Stanford White.[103] During this period, Keany also utilized the services of Henry A. Uterhart's partner, John J. Graham, a horse racing fan known for his successful defense of a man charged with bookmaking for taking private bets at Belmont Park.[104] Also representing the LIRR on many occasions was Colonel William C. Beecher, a negligence expert, and the second son of famous clergyman Henry Ward Beecher, who also represented the New York Society for the Suppression of Vice and the New York Society for the Prevention of Crime. For three Suffolk County cases — two grade-crossing accidents and an injured trespasser — Keany used the services of Judge Griffing.[105] In three other Suffolk negligence actions, he engaged Rowland C. Miles, an important local Democrat and the President of the Northport National Bank.[106]

By the 1920s, the attorneys who most often represented the LIRR in personal injuries cases were Philip A. "Doc" Brennan, the former general counsel of the Brooklyn Rapid Transit Company, and his brother, Thomas J. Brennan, an experienced trial specialist, whose other clients included the Nassau Electric Railroad Company, the Brooklyn Heights Railroad Company, and the New York, New Haven & Hartford Railroad. Doc Brennan was the more high-profile of the two brothers. After obtaining a medical degree from Long Island College Hospital in 1892, he had studied law and was admitted to the bar. He then developed a highly successful law practice, which included some sensational criminal cases, including the successful defense of a city magistrate accused of hugging and kissing a girl in his chambers. After giving up his association with the BRT because the financially hard-pressed common carrier could no longer afford his services, he won several well-publicized civil suits, including $13,000 for Dr. Alma Webster Powell, a singer injured in a New York Central Railroad crash, and a $100,000 judgment for wealthy oilman Harry F. Sinclair in a suit over a racehorse.[107] Brennan was also active with Keany's favorite charity, the Roman Catholic Orphan Asylum Society, belonged to various leading Brooklyn social organizations, and played a major role in the founding of St. John's Law School.

When defending the LIRR in cases where there was the possibility of contributory negligence or inconsistencies in the evidence, Brennan could subject witnesses to aggressive cross-examination. Such was the case with John C. Whiting, a clergyman who fell from a train in January 1921. At the trial a year later, the forty-five-year-old plaintiff limped to the witness stand and testified about the fall in which he suffered a broken arm, a broken leg, broken ribs, and two broken collarbones, his long and painful recovery, and his continuing disabilities. In his testimony, he appeared to claim that he had fallen from a type of car that the railroad maintained was not part of the train in question. Thus, on cross-examination, Brennan questioned him in detail and at length about every aspect of his testimony. When the best Whiting could do in recalling how he had fallen was: "I felt myself going out," Brennan concluded with: "Pardon me, Mister. That is all you can tell us about it?"[108] The hospital physician who treated Whiting was also questioned closely, with Brennan utilizing his medical knowledge to challenge virtually all the doctor's statements about the plaintiff's condition.

Doc Brennan lost the *Whiting* case, but during the 1920s he and his brother had their share of trial court successes on behalf of the LIRR. Thomas J. Brennan was able to have set aside a $15,000 verdict for Frank D'Aurio, a LIRR trackwalker hit by a train.[109] He also won a verdict in favor of the railroad in the case of Leon Goodrich, a tired and ill boater who was struck and killed by a train while resting on a Jamaica Bay trestle,[110] and a dismissal of the case of Thomas V. Brick, a LIRR tugboat crewman who fell overboard and drowned.[111] He prevailed again in a suit over the death of nineteen-year-old Mary M. Kelly who had fallen through an open car doorway, when a favorable jury charge resulted in a verdict for the LIRR[112] Trial court successes for Doc Brennan included obtaining dismissals in the case of Frank Maiorano, a motorist killed at a Suffolk County grade-crossing, by convincing the judge that the plaintiff, who had ignored a warning bell, could not have known the device was malfunctioning and had been ringing constantly for hours,[113] and of the suit of passenger Myra Paige Wiren who slipped and fell while getting off a LIRR train on a dark and rainy night.[114]

Chapter 4

THE LAWSUIT

Because of Mrs. Palsgraf's extremely limited means, it is almost certain that Matthew W. Wood took her case on a contingent basis. Before the fireworks explosion she was making only $8 a week, and her accident-related injuries had caused her to quit work, reducing her earned income to zero. Her son, William, was of working age at the time of the accident, and thereafter both of her daughters found employment, but it is still extremely unlikely that after covering her living costs that she could have gathered the extra funds required to finance her lawsuit. She would have had to pay Wood's fee, cover filing costs, and pay any required medical witnesses, an impossible task for someone who, at the time of the trial, had still not paid her personal physician's $70 bill.

Attorneys could not provide clients with living expenses, but they could advance the funds necessary to litigate the case and then obtain reimbursement from the recovery. However, they were barred from making such advances as an inducement.[1] As Cardozo wrote in 1929: "The law does not say that an attorney is guilty of misconduct by the voluntary advance of expenses of a lawsuit to a client too poor to pay the cost of justice. It does say that there is misconduct if he makes or promises the payment to discharge an obligation assumed in return for his retainer."[2] As for contingent fees, under the system as practiced in New York during the 1920s, they could be 33 1/3% for a pre-trial settlement, and as high as 50% for a judgment.

There is no evidence that Wood's dealings with Mrs. Palsgraf were in any way improper, but the strictures of the Penal Law were no deterrent to widespread attorney wrong-doing, and by the late 1920s the contingent fee system was under constant attack by critics. In May 1927, the American Bar Association averred that "the fee . . . is at the bottom of the bulk of lawyer-abuses."[3] In August, in a speech to the Commercial Law League of America, United States Attorney Charles H. Tuttle denounced contingent fees, stating that they "breed more evil than any other practice in the American bar today."[4] The noted millionaire lawyer and businessman Samuel Untermyer reacted to Tuttle's speech by acknowledging that the contingent fee system spawned gross abuses, but maintained that greater regulation, not abolition, was the solution to the problem, observing, "[t]o say to a poor litigant that he cannot get into the courts because he has not the money with which to pay counsel would be the height of folly, injustice and brutality."[5] Future New York Court of Appeals judge Albert Conway expressed similar sentiments, arguing that eliminating the contingent fee would force poor plaintiffs to use inexperienced attorneys who would be no match for "the well trained, experienced and well-paid lawyers and claim departments of insurance companies."[6] When Tuttle renewed his attack on the existing contingent fee system, he called it "not only the chief cause of congested court calendars, but also . . . a menace to the legal profession."[7] However, he did allow that abolition was not the solution and suggested that all contingent fee agreements be filed as open public documents. Increased regulation was also the approach suggested by Justice Wasservogel's 1928 study of ambulance chasing, which recommended cutting the contingent fee to 33 1/3%, and putting retainer agreements under the control of the court.[8]

However, like attempts to end ambulance chasing, efforts to curb contingent fees failed. In 1929, the Assembly Judiciary Committee unanimously killed bills to reduce the contingent fee to 33 1/3%, bar oral retainers, delay for fifteen days the retaining of a lawyer after an accident, and subject settlements and releases to court approval. The Committee's actions reflected the hostility of critics who regarded court supervision of fee agreements as "insulting,"[9] and the opinion of upstate attorneys that the bills were "ill-considered," "dangerous," and the result of hysteria in New York City.[10]

The *Palsgraf* litigation began with a summons dated September 27, 1924, and served on October 2, 1924.[11] Wood's complaint followed on November 14, 1924, describing the railroad's alleged negligence as "failing to make and enforce proper rules and regulations . . . so that . . . persons on the platform . . . might be reasonably free from injury."[12] It claimed that the railroad had a duty to prevent bringing onto its platforms "fireworks and other flammable and combustible materials. . . ."[13] The complaint noted that Mrs. Palsgraf was lawfully on the platform and that she was or was about to become "a passenger for hire."[14] It provided the time and location of the accident, and stressed that the platform was crowded. The explosion is characterized as sudden and violent. The complaint described Mrs. Palsgraf's injuries as "grievous, serious, and painful . . . [including] shock to the nervous system [and] . . . loss of control of the organs of speech."[15] The alleged cause of Mrs. Palsgraf's injuries differed from subsequent trial testimony. The complaint stated that she was "violently jostled, shoved, crowded or pushed by the force of said explosion or by the crowd of other passengers . . . or by both said . . . explosion and jostling, so that the plaintiff was knocked down or against certain of the platform stairs."[16] No mention was made of the infamous scale. The complaint concluded with the statement that Mrs. Palsgraf's injuries could well be long-lasting or even permanent, and that she faced the possibility of large future medical expenses.

The amount of damages demanded was $50,000,[17] although Wood most certainly did not believe that he could obtain anything close to that. $50,000 was a figure then frequently used in complaints in negligence actions against common carriers, so that sum may simply have struck him as appropriate for a personal injury complaint against the LIRR. It could also have been meant to impress on his client that her case was being taken seriously. However, it certainly was not going to intimidate Joseph F. Keany, whose career with the LIRR had included handling far more serious lawsuits than one over minor physical injuries and an alleged speech impediment. The answer, served on December 3, contained the LIRR's standard response in negligence actions. It admitted only that the LIRR was a domestic railroad corporation organized under the laws of the State of New York, that it operated trains in Brooklyn, and that it maintained a station in East New York. It denied each and every other allegation in the complaint.

Regardless of the amount demanded, it is likely that Keany viewed any potential LIRR liability as quite small. He would have been aware from the newspaper accounts, internal railroad accident reports, and the LIRR claims agent's visit to Mrs. Palsgraf, that she had suffered no serious physical injuries because of the August fireworks accident. Presumably, he also would have known that the railroad was being sued by a low-income plaintiff. Since potential liability was heavily influenced by earning capacity, only judgments and settlements for affluent victims were likely to be expensive. When the Park Avenue tunnel disaster killed and injured many high-income professionals, the New York Central had been forced to pay awards as high as $100,000[18] and out-of-court settlements of up to $45,000.[19] Causing the deaths of high-income persons had also proved expensive for the LIRR. William G. Terwilliger, the doctor killed in the 1909 Wreck Lead grade-crossing accident was thirty-five-years old and earned $5,000 a year; the jury awarded his widow $45,110.11,[20] a judgment upheld by the Appellate Division and the Court of Appeals.[21] In 1914, a jury awarded $29,364.68 for the death of socialite S. Osgood Pell, killed at the Wreck Lead crossing, which then led to a reported $50,000 settlement for the death of William Laimbeer and the injuries to his wife.

In the Malbone Street crash, where victims were less affluent, the average reported wrongful death settlement was still $34,332 for men, but only $7,462 for women.[22] For non-fatal injuries, however, the median settlement was just $500.[23] That disaster also demonstrated the hard-nosed attitude of public carriers when litigating and negotiating damage amounts, even in egregious accidents where they were forced to admit liability. When injured plaintiffs made claims against the BRT, its general counsel, Doc Brennan, used his knowledge of medicine, as he later did in the *Whiting* case, to challenge the extent of plaintiffs' injuries in an often successful effort to hold down the amounts of awards.

Mrs. Palsgraf probably had lower income than any of the Malbone Street victims; she had only been earning $8 a week as a cleaning woman, and at the time of the suit, had been forced to stop working for only a short time. Furthermore, unlike the BRT, the LIRR was not in a position of having to admit liability. As it did later in court, it would have insisted that it could hardly be responsible for what passengers brought onto its platforms in wrapped packages. Thus, any set-

tlement offer that the railroad's attorneys might have made after receiving
Wood's complaint would have been extremely small, at best only a few month's
wages, and the then-amount of her doctor's bill. Although, at the time, many
personal injury cases were settled for $25 to $100, this type of offer was hardly
one that Mrs. Palsgraf or Wood appeared prepared to accept.

Since the railroad did not make an acceptable offer, Mrs. Palsgraf had a considerable wait before she had her day in court. Congested court calendars were
a long-standing problem in the New York City area, affecting municipal, county,
supreme, and federal courts. The Kings County Supreme Court had been two
and one half years behind schedule in 1904; by 1928, despite a large increase
in the numbers of justices, the court was still two years, two months behind.[24]
For Mrs. Palsgraf, court congestion meant that it took about two and one-half
years after the complaint was served for her case to reach the top of the calendar.

Factors cited as contributing to calendar congestion included insufficiently
prepared cases, poorly drafted complaints and answers, and inadequately
trained trial counsel. Some critics also charged that that the courts were being
tied up because of large numbers of unworthy actions. In fact, a large number
of suits did produce only modest results; 25% of Kings County trials resulted in
verdicts of under $1,000.[25] However, the underlying cause of continual court
congestion was not inept attorneys or an overly litigious society, but rapid population growth and the development of the automobile. Negligence suits constituted 88% of New York City cases, and of those 75% arose from automobile
accidents.[26] Proposed solutions included adding more justices, compulsory automobile insurance with damages determined by an administrative board, mod-
ernizing court administration, encouraging attorneys to waive jury trials, and
raising court fees, which in Brooklyn were only $3 for a note of issue, with an
additional $6 for a trial.[27]

Others argued that what was really needed was for judges to work harder.
Kings County Republican leader Jacob Livingston blamed Democratic justices
for congestion, complaining that three of them together tried fewer cases than
Republican Justice James C. Cropsey. Cropsey himself objected to the usual six-
hour court day and the up-to-thirteen-week vacations enjoyed by some judges.
He urged that there be a nine-to-five court day, stating: "Any judge who is physically well should be able to hold court for seven hours a day."[28] He also suggested that judges take shorter vacations and that trials be held during a
summer session.

The large backlog of pending cases occasionally produced special efforts to
reduce the size of the calendar. In May 1925, it was reported that Justice
Edward Lazansky of the Second Judicial District had had disposed of 118 cases

(including forty-six settlements) in the recently ended term.[29] He managed this feat by taking no recesses and sometimes remaining in session until 10 p.m. and then resuming at 9 a.m. Later that year, five Brooklyn justices agreed to dispose of 600 cases in one week.[30] In January 1927, the First Department Committee on Court Congestion announced that all cases on the calendar would be called in an effort to facilitate settlements and to eliminate "dead" cases.[31] The next month, ten justices in Manhattan and the Bronx were reported as having disposed of 7,632 cases in a single week.[32] Such efforts, however, were hardly the solution to the problem. By the end of 1927, the courts of the Second Judicial District would be 23,762 cases in arrears.[33] Conditions were no better in the Supreme Court, First Department, where a report issued in May 1927 by attorney Joseph F. Crater,[34] the secretary to the Calendar Committee, indicated that the courts were now 30,000 cases behind, and falling further behind at a rate of 5,000 cases a year.[35]

Palsgraf was part of this flood of litigation. Less than a month before the trial, the case was one of 22,024 on the calendar for the Second Judicial District,[36] and it would be one of 1,859 tried in the first six months of 1927.[37] Mrs. Palsgraf's wait for a court date ended finally ended on May 24, 1927. *Palsgraf v. Long Island Railroad Co.*, case number 8,798, had risen to the top of the Kings County Supreme Court calendar and was listed in the pages of the *New York Law Journal* as one of those about to go to trial.[38]

Chapter 5

THE TRIAL

The *Palsgraf* case was assigned to Justice Burt Jay Humphrey, one of the most experienced trial judges in the state. Since the evidence of negligence against the railroad was less than compelling, and Wood's case was vulnerable to a motion to dismiss, the identity of the trial judge could be crucial. This had been recently demonstrated by Wood's two *Richter* trials. Charles L. Druhan, whose attitudes toward contributory negligence may well have been influenced by his long career as an assistant corporation counsel, dismissed the case after hearing Wood's witnesses. In contrast, Norman S. Dike, who allowed the case to reach the jury, had been a judge since 1908. Humphrey had been on the bench even longer than Dike and had experienced virtually every possible courtroom situation. He presumably had confidence in his ability to decide difficult questions, and his kindly nature boded well for a sympathetic defendant in a close case. In addition, Humphrey professed to be a supporter in the jury system, believing that although they were not perfect, juries were the best method for determining questions of fact.

Although he had only been on the supreme court bench since January 1926, Humphrey had served as county judge in Queens from 1904 to 1925. He took a practical view of the human condition — that it was "prone to error," but that if it were otherwise, "there would be no judges, and perhaps no newspapers."[1] As for the law, he conceded that it was not an exact science because "the human element and personal interest keep it from attaining the perfection that it has in theory."[2] The sixty-one-year-old justice was married, but childless; he and his wife, Frances, lived in a large home in Jamaica, where for a time the judge kept cows, chickens and pigs. Active in local affairs, he belonged to the Queensborough Chamber of Commerce, the Jamaica Chamber of Commerce, the Crescent Athletic Club, and the Jamaica Club.

Humphrey was popular with the practicing bar. Lawyers reportedly admired him because of his courtesy, honesty, and the respect he accorded them. His personal manner was described as cordial, friendly, tolerant, and never too busy to listen. When told of Republican leader Jacob Livingston's complaint that Democratic justices didn't hear enough cases, he quipped: "If Jake would follow me around he would see that I work."[3] Humphrey's lack of pretense was demonstrated early in his judicial career when an attorney, unable to find the judge in his chambers, decided to look for him at his home. Upon arriving, he found Humphrey milking a cow. He explained to the lawyer that the hired man was away, but "I can milk as well as he. This is a part of the close to the soil programme that keeps people human."[4] The attorney then made his presentation while Humphrey continued with his milking.

Humphrey had followed a circuitous route to Queens County. He was born on April 23, 1866, in the Tompkins County village of Speedsville, the son of farmer Edward L. Humphrey and Manette Smith Humphrey.[5] His early education took place in a school described as a "primitive red structure with one teacher and a dozen classes."[6] He graduated from high school in Owego, in Tioga County, and since his family's finances ruled out law school, he instead read law in the Binghamton offices of supreme court Justice Charles E. Parker and County Judge George F. Andrews. Admitted to the bar in 1890, Humphrey moved west to Seattle to establish a law practice. There, he was elected a justice of the peace, and appeared several times before the Washington Supreme Court.[7]

Humphrey's fortunes changed radically for the worse with the Panic of 1893. Across the nation, businesses failed, factories closed, and the unemployed walked the streets. In Seattle, with potential clients unable to afford legal services, Humphrey's law practice suffered badly. Finally, in 1897, after struggling financially for several years, Humphrey and his wife decided to return to Binghamton. With barely enough money to pay for the train fare home, they made the long trans-continental trip to New York. After reaching New York City's Grand Central Station, they made a spur-of-the-moment decision to take a train to Jamaica, Queens. Finding that the then-small community reminded him of his hometown, Humphrey decided to stay and open a law office.

In Jamaica, Humphrey engaged in the general practice of law, gaining visibility through several well-publicized cases. In 1902, he won acquittals in two murder cases, one involving a man accused of fatally shooting a policeman, and the other, a nineteen-year-old jockey who killed a boarder who had insulted his mother. His most notable civil case was on behalf of a black woman who wanted to enroll her granddaughter in one of Jamaica's all-white primary schools. Like every other attorney who challenged the village's segregated schools in court, Humphrey was unsuccessful; the court rejected his arguments and upheld Jamaica's segregated school system, citing the recently-decided *Plessy v. Ferguson*.[8] Other Humphrey clients included local farmers, irate over having to pay assessments for an electrification project that had little likelihood of immediately benfitting their area, and saloonkeepers angry that brewers were passing on to them the cost of a special Spanish-American War tax.

Humphrey was provided with the opportunity to run for county judge by the local political boss, Joseph "Curly Joe" Cassidy. The son of an immigrant Irish florist, the curly-haired, mustachioed Cassidy was a tough politician from Long Island City. A former city councilman, he rose to prominence through his battles with Long Island City's mayor, Jerome Patrick "Battle Axe" Gleason, himself a formidable political boss known for physically assaulting his opponents. The flamboyant Cassidy, who was also known as "Hungry Joe," "Genial Joe," and "the King of Queens," served two terms as borough president. He lived an opulent lifestyle, reportedly owning a steam yacht, trotting horses, a farm in California, and a vacation home in Rockaway. A frequent target of corruption charges, Cassidy's political career ended in 1914, when he was convicted of selling a supreme court justice nomination to ex-Congressman William Willett. He later served one year in Great Meadows and Sing Sing prisons; Cassidy died in 1920 at the age of fifty-four.[9]

Burt Jay Humphrey's judicial ambitions were in the hands of a man like Cassidy because the New York Constitution of 1846 had made all state judicial offices elective.[10] Intended as a reform, the Constitution ended a system of appointive judges that dated from colonial times. The change was made with little discussion, and has been attributed to "the most sanguine optimism . . . regarding the value of popular elections," and the belief that all officers ought to be elected by the people.[11] In practice, the judges may now have been elected by the people, but nominations for judicial office rather quickly came under the control of political bosses. This situation was regularly denounced with little effect; a state-wide referendum on appointive judges was defeated by a wide margin in 1873, and subsequent efforts at change went nowhere.

In 1899, political influence over the judiciary was considered by the Mazet Committee, a group formed by the legislature to investigate corruption in New York City. A highlight of the investigation was an appearance by Tammany Hall chief, Boss Richard Croker. Testifying candidly, Croker stated that judicial nominees were "assessed" for campaign costs.[12] He also expressed the view that judges should remember the organization when dispensing patronage, just as any good party member would. The penalty for ignoring such requests was detailed for the Committee by ex-Justice Joseph F. Daly who told of being denied renomination after twenty-eight years on the bench in part because he refused to appoint a Tammany man as chief clerk of the court of common pleas.

The issue of appointive judges arose again during the Constitutional Convention of 1915; Presiding Justice George Ingraham told the Judiciary Committee that the elective system for judges had failed, at least in New York City, "where men were compelled to mortgage the future if not seldom their immortal souls to get on the bench."[13] He added that the notion that the people elect judges was just a "popular fiction": "The men who wear the ermine are picked by political leaders."[14] Despite Ingraham's scathing remarks, again no change was made in the method of selecting judges.

The futility of challenges to the selections of a strong party organization was demonstrated by the 1917 First Judicial District Democratic primary between Tammany Hall's candidate for the supreme court, party regular City Court Justice John V. McAvoy, and Thomas E. Rush, the surveyor of the Port of New York. Rush, a bitter rival of Boss Charles F. Murphy, was so angered by McAvoy's nomination that he quit the Tammany Hall organization and entered the primary. After McAvoy won by a large margin, Rush charged election fraud and demanded a recount. Mistakes and irregularities were discovered, but the final official count left Tammany Hall's candidate comfortably in the lead.

Once nominations for judicial office were settled, the general elections were largely coat-tail events, heavily influenced by the results of races at the top of the ticket. Press coverage was generally limited to the inclusion of judicial candidates' names when reporting nominations and election results. There were occasional exceptions, such as the 1916 supreme court justice race between Republican Justice James C. Cropsey, the former Kings County district attorney who had sent "Curly Joe" Cassidy to jail, and the Democratic candidate, attorney Philip A. "Doc" Brennan. Brennan and Cropsey had clashed several years earlier when the lawyer was defending a police officer charged with assault and the judge was the police commissioner. Reacting to an announcement that his opponent would make political speeches, Brennan launched a vigorous attack on his rival's record as a judge and district attorney, calling him "cold-hearted and cruel,"[15] a "Jekyll and Hyde,"[16] an "ingrate,"[17] and a "hammer-thrower."[18] However, Brennan's verbal creativity in attacking Cropsey's record was to no avail. He lost by over 22,000 votes, when Republican gubernatorial candidate Charles S. Whitman easily defeated Democrat Samuel Seabury in the counties of the Second Judicial District.[19]

Burt Jay Humphrey has been portrayed as an accidental judge because he was given little chance to win when first nominated. However, it was no accident that he was chosen when a nomination became available. "Curly Joe" Cassidy was an ally of former Queens County Clerk John H. Sutphin, the leader of the Jamaica-based Fourth Ward Democratic Club. Humphrey was a founding member of and treasurer of that 800-member organization and had taken an active part in Cassidy's successful 1901 campaign for borough president, appearing as a speaker at several rallies. His name had been mentioned in the press as a possible candidate for public office on several previous occasions — for municipal judge in 1899 and 1901, and for Congress in 1902. In 1903, Cassidy, now the absolute political boss of the county, was running for re-election, and his slate needed a candidate for county judge. However, the nomination was regarded as worthless because the incumbent Republican-Fusion candidate was Harrison S. Moore, a thirty-year Queens resident and the popular president of the county bar association. Moore was regarded as unbeatable, and no Democratic lawyer was interested in running against him. Humphrey, who had always wanted to become a judge, accepted the opportunity to run and made regular appearances at campaign rallies. The pro-Democratic press praised him as "a young man of splendid ability, exalted reputation, and high moral courage,"[20] but privately he was given little chance to win.

Unexpectedly, the Democratic judicial nomination proved to be not nearly as worthless as predicted. Incumbent Fusion mayor, reformer Seth Low, was running for re-election in 1903, and the Tammany Hall leadership was determined to oust him. Their candidate was the popular President of the Board of Alderman, George B. McClellan, son of the Civil War general. In addition to a popular candidate at the top of the ticket, Democrat Humphrey benefited from the recent split of Queens County. When Greater New York City was formed in 1898, the heavily-Republican towns of Hempstead, North Hempstead, and Oyster Bay split off from Queens County and became the new Nassau County, depriving Moore of badly-needed votes. On Election Day, McClellan defeated Low by almost 60,000 votes citywide, and by over 6,000 votes in Queens. Aided by the McClellan sweep, the entire Cassidy slate prevailed at the polls, with Humphrey defeating Moore by over 4,300 votes.[21]

The most noteworthy event of Humphrey's first term as county judge was his role as the hero in a classic "lost boy" story, reported by newspapers as far away as Washington, D.C.[22] While out for a walk in woods near his home on a chilly April evening in 1909, Humphrey was alerted to the boy's presence by the child's dog. By following the agitated pet, he discovered the boy, and personally returned him to his parents. During his second term, Humphrey drew praise from the local Suffragette Party leader, Florence Eno, for his role in obtaining justice for sixteen-year-old Clara Ellert. In 1914, Mrs. Ellert had visited the Queens County Courthouse to inquire about the case of her recently-arrested husband. There, she encountered two Cassidy followers, who, instead of finding her a lawyer, took her across the street to the Democratic Party clubhouse and assaulted her.[23] When District Attorney Matthew J. Smith, a Cassidy organization man, did not press the case, Humphrey saw that charges were brought against the two men, one of whom was later convicted. In a letter to the *New York Times*, Mrs. Eno praised Humphrey's "absolutely fearless attitude and splendid help," and stated that it would have been impossible to get any indictments without his assistance.[24]

After his re-election as county judge in 1915, Humphrey's ambitions turned toward the state supreme court, but his efforts to secure a nomination were repeatedly frustrated. He ran in the Democratic primary in 1917, but fared poorly, finishing fourth in a five-candidate race. The next year, when he failed to get the endorsement of party boss Maurice Connolly, he considered running in the primary as an insurgent candidate, but reconsidered when Governor Alfred E. Smith appealed for party unity in wartime. Humphrey finally received a nomination in 1920, but like every other Democrat running in the Second Judicial District, was defeated as part of Republican presidential candidate Warren G. Harding's landslide victory.

In 1925, Humphrey unexpectedly received another chance to run when the expected supreme court nominee, Queens District Attorney Richard S. Newcombe unexpectedly withdrew. Humphrey was nominated instead because Connolly decided he did not want to create a district attorney vacancy that would then be filled by an appointee of Governor Smith. Humphrey's opponent in the general election was a well-respected incumbent, Republican James C. Van Siclen, who was seeking re-election after completing a fourteen-year term. Van Siclen was endorsed by a long list of prominent persons including former Republican governor, Supreme Court justice, secretary of state, and 1916 presidential candidate Charles Evans Hughes, and 1904 Democratic presidential nominee Judge Alton B. Parker. However, no endorsements mattered when Tammany Hall mayoral candidate, the colorful James J. "Jimmy" Walker, crushed his hapless Republican opponent, Frank D. Waterman, by over 400,000 votes, and carried the entire Democratic city slate to victory. In the judicial contest, Humphrey outpolled Van Siclen by over 70,000 votes, running up big margins in Brooklyn and Queens.[25] Unfortunately for Connolly, retaining Newcombe as district attorney did not save his political career. When a sewer contracts scandal developed two years later, the district attorney's investigation was taken over by Smith appointees. The following year, Connolly was indicted for conspiracy to defraud the City. After resigning as borough president, he was convicted and served ten months in the Welfare Island Penitentiary.

While serving as Queens County judge, Humphrey presided over both the criminal and civil terms. His civil cases included a tomato-throwing incident, displaced chickens, a dispute over the use of a tent between two evangelists, and a personal injury suit that involved a hands-on demonstration of the proper use of a pressure cooker that filled the courtroom with the aroma of corned beef and cabbage. In the criminal term, he passed sentence on over 1,200 persons, including horse thieves, swindlers, burglars, and murderers.[26] Two murderers whom he sentenced to death were executed. The first was Peter Nunziato, who went to the electric chair in 1921, after his conviction for the mugging-related murder of Wilfred P. Kotkov, a professor at the Manhattan Jewish Theological Seminary.[27] A death sentence was also imposed on Albito Mastrota who had been so anxious to inherit his uncle's $50,000 estate that he strangled the man in his bed and then faked an intruder-related murder scene; Mastrota was executed on June 12, 1924.[28]

Humphrey's trials were a popular subject for the local papers, and his quotable comments at sentencing were frequently reported. He reserved his harshest remarks for hardened or particularly vicious criminals. In imposing a thirty-nine-year sentence on an arsonist who admitted to setting fires to three tenement houses because life had been dull since he'd left the army after World War I, Humphrey said: "You are a most dangerous man. I am going to give you the longest sentence I can."[29] On another occasion, he said, "I am going to do all I can to stop holdups in Queens if I have to send every young loafer in this county to prison for life."[30] Not all of Humphrey's remarks made at sentencing were so serious. To one would-be producer of homemade liquor, Humphrey stated: "When a necktie manufacturer starts to make bootleg whiskey two things are likely to happen — either there will be an explosion because he does not understand the operation of a still or the whiskey is apt to be poison. I would impose a jail sentence if it wasn't for the fact that you have gone back to the necktie business."[31]

Of all the judges who heard *Palsgraf*, Humphrey would have been most familiar with the LIRR. Like other residents of Queens County, he would have read about the railroad's various difficulties in the local press. He was also probably a frequent passenger. Since he resided in Jamaica, the railroad would have provided him with the easiest route to Manhattan, and would have been a convenient means of travel to the county courthouses in the Second Judicial District — downtown Brooklyn, Long Island City in Queens County, Mineola in Nassau County, and Riverhead in Suffolk County. Humphrey's experiences with the LIRR also included several courtroom encounters. In 1910, he fined the railroad $500 for maintaining a nuisance by closing a public highway, ruling that the rights to lay out streets accorded the citizens of Jamaica by a 1734 royal grant prevailed over rights claimed by the LIRR under its 1834 charter. In 1923, he presided when the LIRR's general superintendent, chief of police, and several others were indicted for manslaughter in connection with fatal grade crossing accidents. A year later, he was the judge who granted the district attorney's request for a special grand jury to investigate the Sunnyside Yards derailment. He also presided at several trials where the LIRR was the defendant in negligence actions. These included successful actions by a driver whose delivery truck was wrecked after it stalled on the tracks and was struck by a train,[32] a pedestrian who caught her foot in a defective plank at a grade-crossing,[33] and a company whose horse-drawn brick truck was destroyed when hit by a train (one horse was killed instantly and the other was so severely injured it had to be shot by a policeman).[34]

The *Palsgraf* jury was drawn from the citizens of Kings County. It would not have included clergymen, lawyers, physicians, policemen, firemen, and editors, who were then exempt from service. It also did not include women. In 1927, New York was one of a majority of states that still barred women from jury service. Despite the efforts of groups like the League of Women Voters, the National Women's Party and the Brooklyn Women's Bar Association to pass a bill permitting women to be called for jury service, arguments that women were "temperamentally unfit," were ignorant of business disputes, or that their primary duty was to be the guardian of the home would prevail until 1937.[35]

Regardless of its composition, the jury was likely to favor Matthew W. Wood and Mrs. Palsgraf. Critics complained that railways could rarely win a negligence case, that juries were prejudiced against public corporations that attempted to raise fares, and that they favored sympathetic poor plaintiffs over wealthy defendants. Complaints of jury bias have been supported by research showing that in cases involving injured passengers, railroads rarely escaped liability.[36] One study of the late nineteenth century reported California cases where a trial verdict could be ascertained, showed plaintiffs won 111 verdicts and defendants only twelve.[37] The LIRR fared better than this in all types of negligence actions, but plaintiffs still won approximately 70% of jury verdicts from 1916 to 1927.[38] Although the railroad's attorneys would sometimes attempt to "stiffen" juries by appealing to a sense of fairness, if a case reached the jury, the railroad generally prevailed only when the facts were heavily in its favor, such as accidents where motorists were killed while crossing the tracks when the gate was down or the warning bell was ringing.[39]

More basic complaints about juries were that they allegedly could not understand legal principles, or remember them well enough to apply them even in simple cases. Critics claimed that juries did not apply the law to facts, could not evaluate witnesses or determine the quality of evidence, and draw logical inferences. Certain complaints about juries were especially relevant to the *Palsgraf* trial. It was charged that they were particularly unfit to decide case involving medical issues and negligence, "as well as in cases that are close or narrowly decided upon the evidence. . . . [C]ases [that] can be solved only after analysis, comparison and synthesis of minute circumstances, by logical methods that are strange or unknown to laymen."[40] Such sentiments were sufficiently widespread that during the 1920s the New York County Lawyers' Association considered resolutions calling for an amendment to the state Constitution that would abolish jury trials in both civil and criminal cases. In Brooklyn, Justice Edward S. Byrne asked the Kings County Bar Association to consider such a plan, but it received a cold welcome in Justice Humphrey's home borough, where the Queens County Bar Association expressed opposition.

Tuesday, May 25, 1927, the day of the *Palsgraf* trial, was cloudy with showers. Anyone at the Kings County Courthouse perusing the daily papers would have encountered articles related to Charles A. Lindbergh's successful flight to Paris a few days before. Fortunately for Mrs. Palsgraf, getting to the downtown Brooklyn courthouse did not involve any elaborate detours to avoid using the Long Island Railroad. The same BMT elevated line that had taken her to East New York on the day of the accident could, by taking it in the opposite direction, also get her to the trial. Her destination, the Kings County Courthouse, located on Joralemon Street, adjacent to Borough Hall, had been constructed at a total cost of $550,000, and opened with great fanfare in 1865. A three-story building, its main front was faced with marble and featured a portico supported by four marble columns. It was topped by a wrought- and cast-iron dome that brought the building's total height to 106 feet. Inside, was a fifty-three-foot rotunda, and two iron staircases that led to a balcony on the second floor. The dimensions of its several courtrooms were approximately 48 feet by 52 feet.[41]

A civil trial like *Palsgraf* would have attracted no press coverage, but the old courthouse had been the center of media attention during major criminal trials.

Only two years before, nationwide news coverage was accorded the murder trial of a Cincinnati nurse, Olivia M.P. Stone, who had fired five bullets into attorney Ellis Kinkead on a busy street in broad daylight. Brooklyn defense attorney Edward J. Reilly, who had built a reputation winning acquittals for sympathetic women defendants, described the victim, who had left Stone for another woman, as a roué and drug addict; his client was portrayed as an honorable woman who had suffered a "brain explosion." When the jury returned a not-guilty verdict, the defendant was showered with flowers and the crowd gathered in the courthouse rotunda cheered loudly. No such dramatics occurred during the *Palsgraf* trial. It was a relatively simple affair that lasted only two days. Wood's case was a model of what judges who complained about court congestion desired. His witness list consisted only of the three Palsgrafs, two independent eyewitnesses, Herbert and Grace Gerhardt, contacted shortly before the trial, Mrs. Palsgraf's personal physician, and his medical expert, Dr. Graeme M. Hammond, who examined Mrs. Palsgraf only two days before testifying. His chief concern going into the trial was probably not swaying the jury, but presenting a sufficiently compelling case so that Humphrey would not grant the LIRR's inevitable motion to dismiss.

In handling *Palsgraf*, Keany departed from his frequent practice of retaining one of the Brennans. Instead, he selected William McNamara, one of his least experienced staff members, to try the case. Keany probably decided he did not need one of the experienced and high-priced Brennan brothers since he viewed the railroad's potential liability as quite low, because the case was simplified by the absence of possible contributory negligence, and its apparent lack of both factual disputes and inconsistencies in witnesses' statements. In addition, the plaintiff's alleged injuries were psychological in nature, not the usual broken bones and internal injures where Doc Brennan's medical expertise was so valuable. There was also no need to present the photos and maps that were often used as exhibits in the more usual LIRR negligence cases.[42] This resulted in a defense effort that in financial terms has been characterized as "bargain-basement,"[43] involving an estimated expenditure of only $16.55, considerably less than the amount expended by Wood, who paid his medical expert $125,[44] and whose costs are given in the record as $142.45.[45] Judge Noonan estimates that McNamara spent only half of a day preparing the case, and describes his courtroom performance as "workmanlike."[46]

As in the typical contributory negligence case, McNamara's goal was to avoid a jury verdict by convincing Humphrey to grant a motion for dismissal. Failing that, the attorney's task was to establish key facts that would result in Humphrey setting aside a verdict for the plaintiff or that could form the basis of a successful appeal to the Appellate Division. In a not unusual railroad tactic that reflected Keany's maxim of often the less said the better, the railroad did not produce any witnesses, not even the two conductors who had assisted the passenger with the bundle.[47] This resulted not only from the apparent lack of any significant factual disputes (a disagreement over where the passenger was located when first assisted by the conductors did emerge at the Appellate Division level), but because railroad employees frequently fared poorly while testifying, often "giving away the store."[48] Thus, McNamara merely cross-examined the plaintiff's witnesses in a manner that may appear less than vigorous. However, it was not his intention to discredit their statements (he made only one objection during their testimony),[49] but to clearly establish that the agreed-upon facts simply did not make out a case against the LIRR.

The trial opened with Mrs. Palsgraf's testimony. After giving personal information,[50] she related her experiences at the railroad station, describing the day of the accident as "quite hot" and the train platform as very crowded. She also provided a description of the departing train's speed at the time of the accident, indicating that it was "just . . . creeping along."[51] Since she apparently never saw the running men or the falling package, and was taken completely unawares by the explosion, details about how the accident occurred were provided by her daughter Lillian, and two independent eyewitnesses, Herbert Gerhardt, a self-employed Brooklyn engraver, and his wife, Grace. The brief Wood later submitted to the Appellate Division would describe the Gerhardts as "disinterested witnesses," but they had a definite interest in the outcome of the case. In her testimony, Grace Gerhardt stated that she had been struck in the stomach by the fireworks package as the unknown passenger rushed past, and that she had fainted during the post-explosion excitement. Her husband testified that afterwards she was "in bad condition,"[52] adding that he had intended to put in a claim against the LIRR, which he did once the jury returned its verdict for Mrs. Palsgraf, engaging Wood as his attorney.[53]

Although the papers had described three running men, at the trial this number was reduced to two. Herbert and Grace Gerhardt claimed they saw two Italians,[54] while Lillian Palsgraf testified to having seen "two men running."[55] In his examination of the Gerhardts, Wood sought to prove the railroad's liability by establishing that their employees had knocked the package from under the man's arm, setting off a chain of events that led to Mrs. Palsgraf's injuries. Both Gerhardts stated that the package was dropped as the conductor on the train attempted to pull the man with the package aboard while the trainman on the platform tried to push him from behind. They also said that the package fell because the conductor on the platform grabbed or pushed the arm of the man holding it. As for the size of the package, Herbert Gerhardt described it as round and eighteen inches in diameter, adding that the man did not have his arm "fully around it."[56] Grace Gerhardt testified that it was oval in shape, and "quite a large bundle" — approximately fifteen to twenty inches in width;[57] both Gerhardts indicated that it was wrapped in newspaper.

The testimony of Lillian and the Gerhardts makes it clear that the package did not fall to the tracks, but instead became wedged between the edge of the platform and the side of the car and exploded as the train continued to move.

Herbert Gerhardt said that the package fell in the space between the platform and the train, and that "the train pulled it, like, between the train and the platform and exploded it."[58] His wife testified that the package "fell between the platform and the train and it like stuck there, and as the train kept right on moving, why, it caused it to explode."[59] Lillian provided a similar version, indicating that the package fell between the platform and the train "and as the train went along the bundle rubbed alongside the station and the train and it exploded."[60]

All the witnesses described a severe explosion. Mrs. Palsgraf stated that it "sounded like a lot of firecrackers going off."[61] She also reported flying glass and a ball of fire, and being in a mass of smoke. She concluded her testimony by stating: "The whole station seemed to be in a blaze to me. . . ."[62] Elizabeth Palsgraf also recalled thick smoke and a ball of fire. Herbert Gerhardt described the explosion as "very loud."[63] Grace Gerhardt also said that the first explosion was "very loud,"[64] and that it produced black smoke that "covered all the station."[65] Lillian testified that after the explosion "everyone was running and hollering."[66] With respect to the scale, Elizabeth said that it "flew apart,"[67] while Herbert Gerhardt described it as "blown right to pieces and knocked down."[68]

Mrs. Palsgraf's distance from the explosion was not directly provided, but from the testimony, the jury would have been able to conclude she was quite close. On cross-examination, she indicated how far she walked after mounting the platform steps by estimating it as the distance from the witness chair to where McNamara was standing;[69] she also estimated that the width of the platform was about twelve to fifteen feet.[70] During cross-examination, Lillian estimated her distance from her mother in terms of the dimensions of the courtroom, which the clerk interpreted her to mean twenty-nine feet, and Wood took to indicate thirty feet.[71] Herbert Gerhardt also provided relevant distances, when he testified that he was standing near the platform steps when the man with the bundle rushed past. As for how far they were from where the package was dropped, Grace Gerhardt's answer was interpreted by Wood to be six or seven feet, and by McNamara as "about seven feet."[72] Her estimate of the platform's width, was similar to Mrs. Palsgraf's — about twelve feet.[73]

In his cross-examination, of the Palsgrafs and Gerhardts, McNamara did not attempt to discredit their testimony. He did seek further details or clarifications, but his main goal was to elicit answers establishing that many persons that day had valises or bundles, since their ubiquity on the platform and the conductors' lack of notice of the contents of unknown passenger's package was the basis of his defense. As McNamara stated in his first unsuccessful motion to dismiss: "There is no evidence of negligence on our part. . . . We can't have everyone open their bundles when they come on the station platform."[74]

During the trial's first day, Mrs. Palsgraf testified about the bruising, trembling, and shaking that had immediately forced her to stop doing outside cleaning work, and that had finally caused her to give up her janitorial duties in June 1926. On the second day, Dr. Karl A. Parshall, her personal physician, appeared to confirm the nature of her injuries. Under cross-examination, he stated that she was suffering from traumatic shock, adding that since her injuries had not improved in almost three years, "I don't see where it is going to get much better."[75] However, Parshall did admit that he was not a neurologist, and had never personally treated a case like Mrs. Palsgraf's. When asked if he had suggested that she see a neurologist, the doctor said, "those people are very poor and they didn't take to it very much, and so I didn't do anything about it."[76]

When Mrs. Palsgraf finally did see a neurologist, it was one of the preeminent authorities in the field. If there was a star witness at the *Palsgraf* trial, it was Wood's medical expert, Dr. Graeme M. Hammond. Born in 1858, Hammond was descended from Sir John Hammond, the first British Ambassador to the United States, and was the son of Dr. William A. Hammond, also a noted neurologist, and a major figure of nineteenth century American medicine.[77] During the Civil War, before being forced out by Secretary of War Edwin Stanton, the elder Hammond served as Surgeon General of the Union Army. As a result, Graeme M. Hammond, as a young boy, became acquainted with Abraham Lincoln, sometimes accompanying him on visits to wounded men at the Washington Soldier's Home.

Dr. Hammond attended the Columbia School of Mines, was an 1881 graduate of New York University Medical College, and later earned a law degree. Besides neurology, he studied vascular diseases, movement disorders, poliomyelitis, and syphilis. He was a founder and past-president of the Neurological Association, a fellow of the American Psychiatric Association, and a member of the New York Psychiatric Society. He was also a professor of nervous and mental diseases at the New York Post Graduate Medical School, and was affiliated with several New York hospitals. During World War I, he had been in command of the Camp Upton hospital for nervous and mental diseases, and later was in charge of a hospital for returned officers with nervous and mental problems.

Dr. Hammond had co-authored with his famous father a treatise on nervous diseases,[78] and contributed papers to the medical community, including reports on the proper method of carrying out a hanging,[79] and the health benefits of bicycle riding.[80] His views also appeared in the popular press, where he was reported as saying that playing bridge whist was "largely responsible for the many nervous breakdowns among women,"[81] advocating the use of x-rays to sterilize habitual criminals,[82] maintaining that those who claimed to be "obsessed by spirits" were really afflicted by those of the alcoholic variety,[83] and theorizing that some psychic force may have aided track and field athletes who gained unexpected victories.[84] During World War I, he advocated a combat role for women, stating that he'd like to "see women marching shoulder to shoulder with men into the trenches."[85]

Members of the *Palsgraf* jury whose perusals of the sports pages went beyond baseball and football scores, might have recognized Hammond since his name frequently appeared there in connection with athletic activities. The doctor had been an accomplished athlete at Columbia, where he played football, wrestled, and set the American record for the quarter-mile. Later, he became a champion fencer, and was the last member of the American team eliminated at the 1912 Olympics. A great believer in amateur athletics, he once said that "when I get into the next world, if there is such a place, I'm going to start an athletic union."[86] Accordingly, the doctor helped organize the American Fencing League and served as its president until 1930. He was also president of the New York Athletic Club from 1915 to 1919, a member of the American Olympic Committee in 1922, and a prominent member of the New York Bicycle League.

At the time of the *Palsgraf* trial, Hammond was a physically-fit, sixty-nine-year-old, who ran three miles three times a week at the New York Athletic Club; he maintained an active medical practice at his old-fashioned Victorian-style office. He resided on West 40th Street in Manhattan, and had a country estate on Long Island Sound in the Green Farms section of Westport, Connecticut. Hammond was 6 feet, 1 inch tall, with ruddy features and a white mustache and goatee that gave him the appearance of a "traditional Southern colonel."[87] The doctor was well regarded by his colleagues; he was described being kindly and genial and having a "practical, sound, common sense point of view."[88] He was also reportedly known as a bon vivant, who was greatly disappointed when Prohibition became the law of the land.

Hammond was an experienced expert witness who had testified on numerous occasions about the competence of wealthy and/or prominent people. These included: William S. Wyse, a former advertising manager who had transferred all his property to his wife (1895); "Florrie" J. Sullivan, a Tammany Hall politician held in the Bellevue Hospital psychopathic ward (1907); D.H. Ernst, a wealthy coal merchant who paid $64 in nickels for 8,000 picture postcards (1909); Gertrude Pike, an alleged dipsomaniac, who once helped police apprehend Herbert J. Eaton, the notorious "Tango Burglar," whose specialty was blackmailing and robbing wealthy women; and Draper Daugherty, the alcoholic son of United States Attorney General Harry M. Daugherty (1923). His most notable appearance came in 1907 during the first trial of Pittsburgh millionaire Henry K. Thaw. To support their insanity defense at this "Trial of the Century," Thaw's attorneys engaged Hammond and several other noted alienists to testify. Like the other experts, Hammond agreed that Thaw had not been sane when he shot Stanford White, and suggested that he had suffered from "maniacal furor, psycho kilesia, and possibly nerve storms."[89]

Because he was busy with patients, Hammond was late in arriving at court, but Justice Humphrey, not wanting to deprive Wood of his testimony, called a short recess. Once on the stand, the doctor testified that Mrs. Palsgraf "stammered quite a good deal . . . had insomnia, depression of spirits and crying spells — headaches."[90] He added that she suffered from "early mental fatigue on reading; early physical fatigue on trying to do any work; loss of energy and trembling of the body."[91] Hammond also noted that "there was a tremor in her hands and a twitching of the muscles of her arms and legs at times — not always."[92]

A modern psychiatrist would be likely to diagnose a patient with such symptoms as suffering from post-traumatic-stress disorder, and might add that the difficult circumstances of Mrs. Palsgraf's life would have made her more susceptible to the condition.[93] Dr. Hammond's diagnosis was traumatic hysteria, which he defined as "a nervous disorder which is due to shock or fright, more than to physical injury."[94] The concept of traumatic hysteria had its origins with railroad wrecks in the mid-nineteenth century.[95] After such accidents, physicians in Victorian Britain began to encounter patients who suffered from a variety of complaints, although they had escaped injury in an accident and appeared to be healthy. Known as "railway spine," this condition was first blamed on spinal concussion and "chronic inflammation of the spinal cord and membranes."[96] Over time, medical views changed and the condition, now called "railway brain," was variously blamed on disruption of the nervous system or the psychological influence of fear. The term "traumatic hysteria" originated with Parisian physician John-Martin Charcot, who, during the 1880s, worked with railroad employees and passengers who had been in train wrecks.[97] Among the symptoms that he observed in his *traumatistes* were fatigue, insomnia, and trembling of the hands and legs — the same symptoms that Dr. Hammond reported in Mrs. Palsgraf.

Injury cases like Mrs. Palsgraf's can often arouse suspicions of "motivational malingering." Indeed, when railway spine cases began to appear, one railroad surgeon stated that the condition "is the ready refuge of the malingerer . . . and affords advantages for the scheming, avaricious claimant. . . ."[98] However, Dr. Hammond was confident of a physician's ability to correctly diagnose hysterical afflictions. In his treatise on nervous diseases, he stated: "Although almost every known disease may be simulated, . . . the counterfeit is never a good one. Attention to the symptoms of the several diseases [and] . . . careful observation of the case and with due inquiry into the antecedents of the patient, will prevent a mistake from being made."[99]

As for Mrs. Palsgraf's prognosis, he indicated that no improvement in her condition was likely until her mind was no longer disturbed by the litigation, and that "as soon as the worry of the trial is over . . . she should make a good recovery in about three years."[100] This statement could be given a cynical interpretation,[101] but here the doctor was merely stating the standard medical view on the effect the stress of litigation on traumatic hysteria patients. As another physician wrote earlier in a medical journal: "In regard to the disappearance of so-called 'litigation symptoms,' . . . my observation has been when a claim for damages has been settled, the mental condition improves very much. . . . After a while, however, I have seen the old mental condition partly reestablish itself while the physical condition has undergone no change save that which could be accounted for by the slow repair of time."[102]

During the Thaw murder trial, the prosecution had attempted to cast doubt on Hammond's credibility by bringing up a previous case where the doctor had allegedly incorrectly diagnosed a defendant. However, at the *Palsgraf* trial, there would be no Brennan-like impugning of a physician's diagnosis. Instead, McNamara merely asked a few perfunctory questions about possible other causes for her condition, the susceptibility of women her age to nervous problems, treatments, whether there should have been a recovery since the accident, and whether her infirmities were permanent.

After Wood rested, Humphrey asked McNamara if he had anything to rebut the plaintiff's testimony. Instead, McNamara rested and unsuccessfully renewed his motion that the case be dismissed. The summations of the attorneys are not preserved in the record, but the substance of what they must have said can be ascertained from their later Appellate Division briefs. Wood would have emphasized the negligent handling of the passenger by the conductors, the close connection in space and time between their actions and Mrs. Palsgraf's injuries, and the fact that the whole incident could have been avoided had the conductors simply prevented the man from attempting to board. McNamara must have stressed the large number of persons on the platform with bundles, and the conductors' lack of notice of the package's contents.

Humphrey's charge to the jury stated that there was no dispute regarding the facts. These included Mrs. Palsgraf's presence on the LIRR platform, the passenger's release of the fireworks as he boarded the moving train, and the resulting explosion that caused her injuries, described as a "nervousness that still persists."[103] Despite the testimony of three witnesses that the fireworks package had become wedged between the side of the platform and the railcar, Humphrey said that it had fallen either to the platform or the track, which may be the basis for Cardozo's later statement that the package "fell to the tracks below." He agreed with McNamara's position that the railroad had no duty to inspect passengers' packages, stating: "If every passenger was examined who was entering a railway or trolley car or subway train, and searched for what he might have upon him, none of us would be able to get anywhere."[104] He then explained to the jury that Mrs. Palsgraf's claim was based on the allegedly negligent handling of the passenger with the package by the trainmen. He phrased the issue in terms of the ordinarily prudent person: "Did these men omit to do something which ordinarily prudent and careful train men should not omit to do? Or did they do something which an ordinarily prudent and careful officer in charge of a railway train in the station platform should not have done?"[105]

After Humphrey finished, McNamara attempted to ensure that that the jury would have no choice but to find the LIRR not liable by requesting charges that the railroad could not be considered negligent unless it knew or should have known that the package contained fireworks, that no inference should be drawn from the railroad's failure to call witnesses, and that the acts of the trainmen were not the proximate cause of Mrs. Palsgraf's injuries. A year earlier, at a trial where the LIRR was found not liable for the death of Mary M. Kelly, a nineteen-year-old passenger who fell out of an open door on a moving train, the judge had agreed to Thomas J. Brennan's request to charge the jury that the passenger had assumed the risk when she attempted to move from one car to another.[106] However, McNamara had no success with Humphrey; only the request regarding the absence of railroad witnesses was granted. The case then went to the jury, which took only two hours and thirty-five minutes, including time out for lunch, to bring in a verdict in favor of Mrs. Palsgraf, awarding her damages of $6,000.

How the jury arrived at $6,000 can only be a matter of speculation. Personal injury verdicts against the railroad varied widely. In 1915, a child who lost a leg after being struck by train won $15,000.[107] In 1916, a girl was awarded $1,000 after she lost the hearing in one ear after a train collision. A year later, a young woman whose jaw was broken in a grade-crossing accident won $25,000.[108] In 1918, a jury awarded $2,500 to a woman who claimed that catching her foot on a defective grade-crossing plank caused foot and knee injuries as well as severe injuries to her nervous system.[109] In 1924, a jury awarded a LIRR bridge carpenter $20,000 for the loss of a foot.[110] Finally, a year and a half before the *Palsgraf* trial, a Nassau County woman injured in a grade-crossing accident, and who testified from a stretcher, was awarded $11,000.[111] As for the *Palsgraf* verdict, it may have resulted from calculating Mrs. Palsgraf's pre-accident annual income, the amount of time at work she had already lost, and Dr. Hammond's prognosis that she might make a recovery in about three years, with some extra for pain and suffering. The jury could also have inflated the award to factor in Wood's expected contingent fee, or the amount may merely have been a compromise between those who wished to be generous with the LIRR's money, and those who were less so inclined.

After the verdict, McNamara moved to set it aside all the grounds specified in § 549 of the Civil Practice Act — contrary to law, contrary to the evidence and against the weight of evidence and excessive. The standard for setting aside a verdict as against the weight of the evidence was that "it shall plainly appear . . . that the jury could not have reached their conclusion upon any fair interpretation of the evidence."[112] Such a motion was not necessarily a futile gesture. For example, a verdict against the LIRR was set aside in 1914 case where a passenger, who was familiar with the station, got off the train and walked directly in front of a steam locomotive where he was struck and injured.[113] Noting the plaintiff's claim that the train had started up without noise or warning, the fact that he had used that train before and realized that it was about to proceed, the trial judge concluded that even when "[c]onsidering the evidence most favorably to the plaintiff, the claim of the plaintiff is opposed not only to all the probabilities of the case but to natural and physical laws."[114]

However, stating that it "is a close question in my mind,"[115] Humphrey denied the motion and let the verdict stand. By denying McNamara's two motions to dismiss and refusing his request to charge that the railroad employees' actions were not the proximate cause of Mrs. Palsgraf's injuries, Humphrey had left the question of negligence and proximate cause to the jury, and as a professed believer in the jury system, he was probably reluctant to set aside its verdict. Also, as previously noted, since Humphrey was often described as a kindly person, it would not be surprising if sympathy for a poor woman injured through no fault of her own had a role in deciding a borderline question. Accordingly, he chose to leave to the Appellate Division the question of whether the verdict was against the weight of the evidence.

Chapter 6
THE APPELLATE DIVISION

The court where Joseph F. Keany would now take the railroad's case, the Appellate Division, was established by the New York Constitution of 1894. It was the product of a court reform proposal made by Elihu Root, a wealthy corporate lawyer who would later serve as secretary of war under William McKinley, secretary of state under Theodore Roosevelt, and win the 1912 Nobel Peace Prize. Root's plan targeted the perceived deficiencies of the previous intermediate appeals court, the General Term of the Supreme Court. Each of the five General Terms had only three members who also handled ordinary judicial tasks and tried cases. This heavy work load often resulted in brief and hurried hearings that left counsel dissatisfied. In some instances, the case under appeal had been decided by one of the three judges, meaning he had to retire from the bench leaving only a panel of two. This was another source of discontent, since it meant that appeals were heard by the colleagues of the trial judge.

The bar's solution was to greatly increase the number of supreme court justices, but Root believed that this would have an adverse affect on the stability of decisional law. Instead, his plan divided the state into four departments, each with an intermediate appellate panel. Although the justices from the different departments would never sit together, they were to be considered one court. Root's analogy was to the English Court of the King's Bench and its High Court of Judicature, a single court that never met together for any purpose. The members of the new court were to be supreme court justices chosen by the governor, serving five-year terms. The First Department, consisting of Manhattan and the Bronx, was to have seven justices, and the remaining three departments five each.

Another objective of Root's plan was to reduce the appellate jurisdiction of the Court of Appeals. Over the years, the legislature had expanded the availability of appeals as of right, overloading the Court of Appeals docket. Root's solution was to limit the jurisdiction of the Court of Appeals to the review of questions of law except in death penalty cases. As Root told the Convention: "There is no reason, no sense, in allowing parties to go on and contest, over and over again . . . ."[1] In addition, no unanimous decision of the Appellate Division would be reviewed. An exception was that the Appellate Division "could allow an appeal upon any question of law which, in its opinion, ought to be reviewed by the Court of Appeals."[2]

Appellate Division justices were not expected to produce brilliant exercises in jurisprudence, but were instead supposed to competently and expeditiously handle appeals from the lower courts. In 1927, the Second Department decided 1,828 cases, including *Palsgraf*, and wrote 127 opinions.[3] The justices also performed their task of keeping cases away from the Court of Appeals. In 1927, they denied 153 motions for leave to appeal, granted only twenty-seven, and, including *Palsgraf*, produced only ten cases with dissenting opinions. However, not all members of the bar were necessarily satisfied with the court. On one occasion, Presiding Justice Edward Lazansky felt compelled to defend the work of his colleagues, saying that "impatience with the Appellate Division is wholly unwarranted . . . cases are studied, the law searched, and all positions assumed and debated."[4]

During 1927, the membership of the now seven-member Appellate Division, Second Department, bench underwent significant change. In February, William F. Hagarty replaced the deceased Walter H. Jaycox. Presiding Justice William H. Kelly died in October, and Associate Justice Edward Lazansky was promoted to his position. Two more new justices joined the court in November when William B. Carswell was appointed to fill Lazansky's old seat and Albert H.F. Seeger was named to temporarily replace the ailing Daniel F. Manning. This meant that the court now had four Brooklyn Democrats, Lazansky, Carswell, Hagarty, and Isaac M. Kapper, and three Republicans, J. Addison Young from New Rochelle, Albert H.F. Seeger from Newburgh, and Adelbert P. Rich from upstate Cayuga County. Two members of the court, Seeger and Carswell, were foreign-born, and two others, Lazansky and Hagarty, were sons of European immigrants. Only two, Lazansky and Young were college graduates, and two, Seeger and Rich had not attended law school.

Like Burt Jay Humphrey, all the Appellate Division justices who heard the *Palsgraf* appeal owed their places on the bench to the decisions of local political bosses. The Brooklyn justices had obtained their positions through a nominating process controlled by the Kings County Democratic Party leader, John H. "Uncle John" McCooey. The rotund, white-haired McCooey was a former worker at the Brooklyn Navy Yard, where he helped build the ill-fated *U.S.S. Maine*. He became the Brooklyn Democratic leader in 1909 and kept the position until his death in 1936. Credited with turning formerly Republican Brooklyn into a Democratic stronghold, the soft-spoken political boss maintained his power despite many attacks by political rivals and reformers. His critics included Fiorello La Guardia, who once called McCooey and other Democratic leaders the "1929 Reincarnation of the Tweed Ring,"[5] and Judge Samuel Seabury who maintained that McCooey and his political ally, Boss John F. Curry of Tammany Hall, had produced "the grossest waste and mismanagement."[6]

Although the highest government office ever held by McCooey was chief clerk of the Kings County Surrogate's Court, a $9,000-a-year position, he died a wealthy man, leaving an estate of $719,288, including stocks, bonds, mortgages, real estate, insurance, and $105,949.88 in bank deposits.[7] Since the Brooklyn boss unabashedly viewed politics as a means to secure appointments and promotions for his supporters and family members, his sister, Margaret, was appointed to a $12,500-a-year position as assistant superintendent of schools, and the law firm of his attorney son, John H. McCooey, Jr., a Cornell Law School graduate, received a large number of appointments as guardians and referees. To soothe the feelings of County Register James A. McQuade after he was grilled by Judge Samuel Seabury's investigating committee about how he'd accumulated $510,000 in six years on an annual salary of $12,000,[8] McCooey arranged for him to be elected sheriff of Kings County.

A telling demonstration of Boss McCooey's control of the judicial selection process came in 1931 when he placed the utterly undistinguished John Jr. on the supreme court bench. In a deal that the *New York Herald-Tribune* called a "civic crime,"[9] and a *New York Times* editorial denounced as being of "the most sordid kind,"[10] Kings County Democrats were allotted three of twelve newly-created justiceships. After the McCooey organization nominated the Boss's thirty-one-year-old son, the judicial committee of the Brooklyn Bar Association disapproved the candidacy. However, their report was overridden by a vote of the membership, whose McCooey loyalists claimed to believe that youth should not be a bar to judicial office. Among those supporting the McCooey cause were Presiding Justice Edward Lazansky, who was running for reelection, and Justices Kapper, Carswell, and Hagarty. Not surprisingly, the Appellate Division subsequently refused a request for an investigation into the bench deal by the City Club, an organization dedicated to efficient city government, whose president, businessman and Fusion leader Joseph M. Price, had characterized the selection of McCooey's son for the supreme court as "a glaring affront to the intelligence of the community."[11]

The Second Department's presiding justice, Edward Lazansky, was a lifelong Brooklyn resident. Born in 1872, he was the son of Alois and Rosie Lazansky, a Jewish couple who had come to the United States in 1868 from Prague, then the capital of the Austrian province of Bohemia. He was educated at the Brooklyn Latin School and Boy's High School before enrolling at Columbia over the objections of his father who wanted him to take over the family paint and glass store. After receiving an A.B. in 1892, he entered Columbia Law School; he graduated and was admitted to the bar in 1897. Active at an early age in Democratic politics, Lazansky ran for the Assembly in 1892, losing by only fifty-three votes. He was later appointed an assistant corporation counsel for Brooklyn by

Mayor George B. McClellan, serving from 1906 to 1908. In 1910, he was elected secretary of state and served one term before returning to private law practice.

Lazansky was a loyal Brooklynite who advised his fellow citizens not to be blinded by the "brightness of Manhattan's sun."[12] Married but childless, he and his wife, Cora, lived at the Granada Hotel and had a vacation home in the eastern Long Island community of Hampton Bays. The justice was a Dodger fan, and a lover of mystery stories, dogs, pot roast and sauerkraut. He enjoyed golf, and in 1919, scored a hole-in-one while playing with Justice Kapper. He also liked fishing, and once, when hearing cases in Riverhead, in eastern Suffolk County, went on a fishing trip as the guest of a local attorney. Both Lazansky and his wife enjoyed travel; in 1927, he visited Bolshevik Russia and she took a 101-day voyage to South Africa. The justice was also very active on behalf of Jewish charitable organizations, including the American Joint Jewish Distribution Committee, the Brooklyn Federation of Jewish Charities, and the Jewish Hospital of Brooklyn.

In 1909, Lazansky was suggested for a state supreme court vacancy, but was turned down by Republican Governor Charles Evans Hughes. His next opportunity did not come until 1917, when he won a nomination by finishing third in a five-man primary contest. The primary election was tainted by vote fraud charges, and the losing candidates, Burt Jay Humphrey and George J.S. Dowling, demanded and received an inspection of the ballot boxes. The recount had little impact on the vote totals, and, in the ensuing general election, Lazansky won his seat on the supreme court bench by finishing third in a six-candidate race. His candidacy benefited from a landslide victory by Democratic mayoral candidate John F. Hylan, who routed the incumbent, Mayor John Purroy Mitchell, winning by the unprecedented margin of 158,459 votes.[13] In January 1926, after eight years as a justice, Lazanksy was named to the Appellate Division by Governor Alfred E. Smith; he became presiding justice in October 1927.

Lazansky's early judicial career included the legal aftermath of the Malbone Street crash. In 1921, he dismissed indictments against officials of the Brooklyn Rapid Transit Company after the Brooklyn district attorney determined that it would be almost impossible to obtain convictions. The next year he made headlines by denying a writ a mandamus that would have compelled the Kings County commissioner of jurors to include women on jury lists, declaring that "these considerations must be addressed to the legislature. . . ."[14] In a 1925 case with serious financial implications, he ruled that the election law did not require the Board of Elections to equip all polling places throughout the city with voting machines, a decision that saved New York City at least $2,700,000.[15]

Other Lazansky trials included a malpractice suit against a dentist accused of causing a woman's death by allowing an extracted tooth to lodge in her lung,[16] and a case arising from the death of a stevedore in a shipboard explosion allegedly caused by the use of an acetylene torch in the vicinity of cans of gasoline. Here, the defendant's unsuccessful effort to escape liability included having an expert witness demonstrate the effects of gasoline vapor in the air by placing two guinea pigs in glass jars in front of Lazansky. There were also the inevitable domestic relations cases, such as the separation action of the new wife of a retired police captain whose mother-in-law once locked her out of the house, forcing her to gain entry through a coal chute. Lazansky also encountered the LIRR in the courtroom, presiding at a trial in Suffolk County Supreme Court in Riverhead where Doc Brennan successfully defended the railroad in a suit arising from yet another fatal grade-crossing accident. In a less serious Riverhead incident, Lazansky asked court officers to stop a young couple from embracing. In doing so, he joked, "I don't know what it is, but there is something in this Riverhead air that induces spooning. . . . Spooning is all right in some places, but not in the courtroom."[17] An entirely different reaction to a breach of courtroom decorum took place in Nassau County Supreme Court in 1922, when Lazansky was so angered by the conduct of well-known admiralty lawyer Silas B. Axtell that he declared a mistrial and told the attorney he was "not fit to be practicing law" and was "very fortunate [he was] not in the county jail."[18]

Brooklyn Democrat William B. Carswell was the son of Scottish immigrants, David Bruce Carswell, a painter, and his wife, Ann Brown Carswell. Born in Edinburgh, Scotland, in 1883, he was brought to the United States at age four. After attending Brooklyn public schools, Carswell worked as a bookkeeper, and received his legal education at St. Lawrence University's Brooklyn Law School, receiving an L.L.B., *cum laude*, in 1908, and an L.L.M., *summa cum laude*, in 1909. After graduation, he practiced law as a member of the firm of Carmody & Carswell; he belonged to numerous organizations including the University Club of Brooklyn, the Elks, and Clan MacDonald, No. 33, Order of Scottish Clans. He and his wife, Charlotte, had three sons, including one who died of pneumonia at the age of two months in 1926.

Like Lazansky, Carswell was active in the Brooklyn Democratic organization. He had particularly close ties to Boss McCooey, and in 1912 his party connections resulted in a nomination for state senator and a easy victory in the general election. As a senator, Carswell took part in struggle between the legislature and newly-elected Governor William "Henry Clay" Sulzer. When Sulzer was impeached on charges of campaign finance irregularities in 1913 and removed from office, Carswell was one of the senators voting for impeachment. The Sulzer affair was widely viewed by the public as Tammany leader Charles F. Murphy's revenge for the governor's refusal to agree to patronage demands, and, in 1914, the voters' backlash caused the defeat of many of Carswell's anti-Sulzer colleagues. Despite the opposition of the *Brooklyn Daily Eagle*, Carswell was reelected, but only after a recount that left him with a majority of only sixteen votes and an unsuccessful court challenge by his opponent that reached the Appellate Division.[19]

His vote for Sulzer's impeachment would continue to haunt Carswell. In 1916, he was the McCooey nominee for Brooklyn district attorney. However, in an election surprise, he was decisively beaten in the primary by an independent candidate, Assistant Corporation Counsel James T. O'Neill. McCooey then threw his support to O'Neill in the general election, and when Carswell did likewise, the *Brooklyn Daily Eagle*, caustically commented, "regularity is the breath of life to the political machinist."[20] Carswell returned to public office in 1919 as assistant corporation counsel in charge of the Brooklyn office, an appointment that resulted from his ties to newly-elected Mayor John F. Hylan, a McCooey ally. In 1921, Hylan backed Carswell for a supreme court nomination, but he was passed over by Kings County organization regulars, who selected prominent Brooklyn attorney William F. Hagarty. A year later, Hylan again backed Carswell for the court, praising his role in blocking a proposed Brooklyn Rapid Transit fare increase. This time, Carswell was nominated, and won election as part of gubernatorial candidate Alfred E. Smith's landslide victory in New York City.

While on the supreme court bench, Carswell authored an eight-page instructional pamphlet for jurors that proved so popular that it was reprinted in the *ABA Journal*, and eventually had a total printing of over 500,000. Among his few reported negligence decisions was the case of a seven-year-old boy injured when he voluntarily dropped from a rope tied to a telephone pole. Holding that the doctrine of attractive nuisance did not apply, Carswell set aside a $1,000 verdict for the plaintiff and dismissed the complaint.[21] Perhaps his most notable case came in April 1926, when he denied incorporation to the "Colonial Association of Workers and Peasants of America." Reflecting the widespread hostility to foreign ideologies, he lectured the applicants on "their lack of Americanism," adding that "[t]here are no such persons as a matter of class distinction, known as peasants in the United States. Such class distinctions are foreign to our soil. . . ."[22]

The third Brooklyn resident on the *Palsgraf* panel was the man who had displaced Carswell from the 1921 Democratic judicial ticket, William F. Hagarty. The forty-nine-year-old Hagarty was born in Dayton, Ohio, and came east at age eleven, when his father, Irish immigrant Cornelius E. Hagarty, relocated his iron-and-wire-fence business to Brooklyn. Hagarty attended Boy's High School, playing football, baseball, and other sports. As an adult, he retained his interest in athletic pursuits, serving as the president of the Crescent Athletic Club, playing golf, and frequently riding a horse in Brooklyn's Prospect Park. Known for his sense of humor and robust health, the justice reportedly never missed a day in court because of illness. Although he was a bachelor, his advice to attorneys was to marry at a young age.

After graduating from New York Law School, Hargarty went into private practice in Brooklyn, concentrating on business and estate matters. In Hagarty's one reported negligence action, he successfully represented an employer against an injured employee.[23] His most newsworthy case came in 1904, when he served as co-counsel for Morris C. Mengis, a broker who allegedly had a $1,000,000 oral contract to provide General Louis Fitzgerald, Vice-President of the Coney Island and Brooklyn Railroad Company, with data and information related to the prospective purchase of the Western Maryland Railroad. Mengis was awarded $1,112,000, then the largest civil award in Brooklyn history, but the judgment was reversed and a new trial ordered by the Appellate Division.[24]

In 1921, after being selected for a supreme court nomination over Carswell by the Kings County Democratic organization, Hagarty was defeated by District Attorney Harry E. Lewis, despite the landslide reelection victory of Mayor Hylan.[25] A year later, he received a second chance, and was elected as part of the same lop-sided victory of Democrat Alfred E. Smith that helped elect Carswell.[26] Fittingly for the athletically-inclined Hagarty, one of his earlier decisions involved a sporting event. In September 1923, the manager of a black heavyweight contender, Harry Wills, the Brown Panther of New Orleans, sought to block a bout scheduled to take place at the Polo Grounds between Jack Dempsey and Argentine fighter, Luis Angel Firpo, the Wild Bull of the Pampas. Wills' manager hoped to compel the State Athletic Commission to substitute his fighter for Firpo, but Hagarty refused to issue a writ of mandamus stopping the fight.

A more serious controversy arose later that year, when Hagarty issued an order blocking police action against slot machines, prompting New York City Assistant Corporation Counsel M. Martin Dolphin to claim that the supreme court was protecting slot machine manufacturers. An angry Hagarty demanded an apology for what he regarded as a slur on the court, and within a week Dolphin sent the justice a three-page letter apologizing and denying any intent to "assail the integrity of the court."[27] Hagarty's appointment to the Appellate Division in February 1927, meant that he did not preside over what would have been the most notable case of his career — the three-week, nationally-publicized murder trial of Queens housewife Ruth Brown Snyder and her lover, corset salesman Henry Judd Gray, for the murder of Snyder's allegedly dull husband — an event he later said he was "very glad to miss."[28]

The Second Department's senior Republican was J. Addison Young of New Rochelle. Born in the Suffolk County community of Aquebogue on the Long Island's North Fork, he was the son of farmer James Halsey Young and his wife Lucy. Young attended the local Franklinville Academy, and graduated from Williams College in 1888. After graduation, Young joined his cousin's law firm in the Westchester County community of New Rochelle and attended Columbia

Law School. Like many other students he left after two years without a degree, unwilling to complete the new three-year course of study. Married with two children, Young was a trustee of the First Presbyterian Church of New Rochelle and a member of the Masons. He also served six years on the New Rochelle Board of Education and was a founder and director of the New Rochelle Trust Company.

Young would have been familiar with the LIRR. Its Greenport line ran near his boyhood home in Aquebogue, and it would have been the primary means for him to travel to Manhattan. Young was also no stranger to railroad accidents. In January 1902, just after he took office as Westchester County district attorney, New Rochelle was shocked when the Park Avenue tunnel disaster killed fifteen residents and injured over twenty. Speaking before a mass meeting of Westchester County residents, Young denounced the New York Central's management for thinking only of its stockholders. He later helped represent the estates of Alfred W. Perrin, president of the Union Bag and Paper Company, who left a widow and four children, and Henry G. Dimon, assistant general manager of the American Bridge Company and father of five. Juries awarded damages of $75,000 for Perrin and $60,000 for Dimon; both verdicts were affirmed by the Appellate Division and the Court of Appeals.[29]

During Young's six years as Westchester County district attorney, he successfully prosecuted twenty of twenty-eight accused murders. Other notable convictions included the butler of a wealthy manufacturer, who claimed to have been given doped Vichy water by burglars before he stole $2,500 in valuables, and Frank E. Xavier, the editor of the *Yonkers Herald*, for criminal libel, after he printed an article stating that Manhattan District Attorney William T. Jerome had agreed with financier J.P. Morgan and his partner, George W. Perkins, that in exchange for the gubernatorial nomination, he would not indict certain New York Life Insurance Company executives. Young also appeared before the Court of Appeals, successfully arguing for the affirmation of a misdemeanor conviction of a member of the Christian Catholic Church of Chicago whose adopted daughter died of whooping cough after he failed to get her medical attention.[30]

Like his colleagues from Brooklyn, Young owed his place on the bench to the decisions of a political boss. For Young, it was veteran Westchester County Republican leader William L. Ward, a former congressman and a wealthy nuts-and-bolts manufacturer from Port Chester, who made his fortune supplying the burgeoning automobile industry. Known as the "amiable autocrat" and a "benevolent despot," he was elected chairman of the Westchester Republican Party in 1896 and tenaciously held the position until his death, thirty-seven years later.[31] In 1915, Ward chose Young and Albert H.F. Seeger of Orange County to run for two newly-created Ninth Judicial District supreme court justiceships. Since no state-wide offices were at stake in 1915, the judicial contest became the focus of attention. Democrats charged that the law creating the new justiceships was merely a Ward Machine ploy to gain places on the court for loyal Republicans, and urged voters to defeat both Young and Seeger. Despite Democratic efforts, Young easily defeated his opponent, State Senator John C. Taylor, winning by 5,000 votes.[32] However, in a much closer contest, Seeger lost to Democratic Westchester County Judge William P. Platt by 969 votes.[33]

There was more controversy when Republican Governor Nathan L. Miller appointed Young to the Appellate Division in 1922. Young only had four year's experience on the supreme court, and many Republicans had favored Justice Arthur S. Tompkins of Nyack, a fifteen-year veteran of the court. They believed that Ward had influenced Miller to pass over Tompkins because he had opposed the 1915 Ward-backed law that added the two new justice positions. Noting Ward's influence in Albany, one Republican observed, "Judge Tompkins may be close to the governor, but Ward is closer."[34]

Young is estimated to have written 3,000 opinions while on the bench.[35] His decisions included granting a divorce to the wife of actor Douglas Fairbanks, and setting aside a $24,896.15 verdict in favor of a woman whose husband had died of an infection after being treated by a dentist. His most publicized and controversial opinion came in July 1918, when he upheld a Mount Vernon ordinance banning the sale of all Hearst and German-language newspapers within the city for the duration of World War I. The city's common council had voted the ban, citing editorials in the Hearst-owned *New York Journal* and *New York American* that were "obstructive to America's aims in the war."[36] In his decision, Young stated: "The well-established rule that equity will not interfere to prevent the enforcement of the criminal law applies to the facts of this case."[37] Mount Vernon alderman William G. Dawson, who had introduced the ordinance, hailed Young's decision, saying "there is no doubt that the ordinance which we have passed represents the patriotic sentiment of the people of this city."[38] However, the Appellate Division wasted little time in reversing, holding: "It is clear that such a ban on a newspaper by a city or municipality is beyond its powers, as it would thereby invade the constitutional rights of a free press."[39]

Young also had at least one courtroom encounter with the LIRR. In May 1918, he returned to Suffolk County to preside at the trial of the case of Greenport shipbuilder George H. Hammond, who, along with two other men, had been killed on the windy and snowy evening of January 21, 1917, when a wagon in which they were riding was struck at a grade-crossing. After hearing testimony that no train whistle had sounded, that the crossing bell could not be heard, and that the locomotive's headlight had been covered with snow, the jury returned a verdict of $13,077 for the plaintiff. Young denied Doc Brennan's motion for a new trial, a decision that was later affirmed by the Appellate Division.[40]

The court's oldest member was Albert H.F. Seeger. Born in 1859 in Stuttgart, then in the German Kingdom of Wuertemburg, Seeger was brought to the United States a year later by his parents, John and Louisa Seeger. The elder Seeger was a cabinetmaker who settled first in Goshen, and then in Newburgh, a small Orange County city located on the banks of the Hudson River. The future judge graduated from Newburgh Free Academy in 1875, went to work at a local law office, and was admitted to the bar in 1880; he established his own firm in 1889.

In 1884, Seeger married May E. Riker of Newburgh; they had one son, John A. Seeger. A member of the Presbyterian Church, he also belonged to a large number of organizations, including the Masons and Odd Fellows, the Newburgh Wheelmen (a trotting horse racing group), and two German-American groups, the Newburgh Turnverein and the Newburgh Mannerchor. Seeger's chief non-legal avocation was trotting horses, and reports of his races appeared in the newspapers almost as often as stories about his cases.[41] Rated as one of the "most skillful amateur reinsman in Orange County,"[42] he regularly engaged in match races with Justice Arthur S. Tompkins, events that continued almost until Tompkins' death in 1938.

Seeger gained a reputation in Orange County by winning a reversal of the fraud conviction of a Newburgh banker,[43] and for a successful lawsuit against a state senator who had arranged for the arrest of a man whom he'd sued for malicious prosecution. Seeger subsequently served as Orange County assistant district attorney, and was elected to the district attorney's position in 1903. In 1905, he single-handedly confronted an angry crowd of 300 striking brickworkers who were armed with cordwood and carrying a red flag. Seeger reportedly seized a double-barreled shotgun from one striker and successfully ordered the men to disperse.

In 1906, Seeger was elected county judge. An episode during this period illustrated another side of his personality. Making an unexpected Saturday visit to his chambers, he discovered a group of law students, invited there by his clerks, lounging about and smoking. When he asked to what he owed the honor of so many visitors, the youngest of the group responded, "[t]o your absence, sir."[44] As a reward for his truthfulness, the judge reportedly put him on the payroll the following week. During this period, he continued to represent clients, including two plaintiffs in supreme court negligence actions against railroads, one arising from a grade-crossing accident where the jury awarded damages of $25,000, and the other involving the death of a New York Central employee where the widow received a judgment of $10,000.[45] He was also involved in the aftermath of the Thaw murder trials as one of the attorneys representing the eccentric millionaire in his unsuccessful attempt to be allowed private visitations from his mother and his lawyers while incarcerated as a mental patient at the Matteawan State Hospital.[46]

Seeger easily won reelection as county judge in 1912, defeating both the Democratic and Bull Moose candidates. In 1915, as previously noted, Seeger was defeated when he ran for the supreme court. Two years later, he was nominated again, and this time was elected. As a county judge and a supreme court justice, Seeger ruled on the expected variety of cases. None involved negligence actions against railroads; instead, they included granting an injunction against striking members of the United Hatters of America, and denying a request to enjoin the Yonkers American Legion post from sending the second-place finisher in the "Miss Yonkers" contest to an Atlantic City beauty pageant. Seeger's most high-profile criminal case involved Walter S. Ward, the son of a wealthy businessman, who was accused of killing an alleged blackmailer. Seeger dismissed the charges, finding that there was no evidence that the killing was a crime.[47] Another controversial decision occurred in 1925 when he enjoined the Mount Vernon School Board from allowing children to be released from school forty-five minutes early once each week to attend religious instruction.[48]

Many of Seeger's most newsworthy cases involved domestic relations. He presided over the divorce action of a woman whose traveling salesman husband had claimed to be a federal judge, and the alimony case of the former wife of a Socialist cabinet maker who accused him of being "inclined toward anarchism and free love."[49] On another occasion, he set aside a divorce issued to a woman as part of a fake divorce mill scheme conducted by a New York City attorney. Less seriously, Seeger once issued an order forbidding a mother-in-law from gossiping about the marital affairs of her daughter and son-in-law. His ultimate domestic relations case was the nationally-publicized 1927 separation trial of Edward West "Daddy" Browning, a wealthy fifty-two-year-old real estate man, and his teenaged bride, Frances "Peaches" Heenan. Frantic crowds mobbed the Carmel, N.Y., courthouse, sitting on window ledges, and even tearing a heavy oak door from its hinges in an effort to hear such testimony as Peaches' claim that her husband kept a honking goose in their bedroom and disturbed her sleep by sanding his shoe trees. At the close of the trial, Seeger denied Peaches a separation on the ground of cruel and inhuman treatment. Instead, he granted Browning a separation on the ground of abandonment. He concluded that charges of Browning's abnormality were baseless, holding: "The plaintiff may be a man of peculiar character, tastes, and ideas," but that Peaches had failed to justify abandoning him.[50]

Chapter 7

THE FIRST APPEAL

On May 27, 1927, Justice Humphrey denied McNamara's motion for a new trial, and four days later a judgment of $6,142.45 (including costs) was entered against the railroad in the Kings County clerk's office.[1] Keany filed his notice of appeal to the Appellate Division, Second Department, on June 14, beginning *Palsgraf*'s journey through the New York State appellate courts. As one of the relatively few LIRR passenger-injury cases to reach the appellate level, *Palsgraf* now added this unusual element to its already unlikely set of facts.[2] However, it is not surprising that once tried, *Palsgraf* became an appellate case. Although Wood has been criticized for not settling after the verdict,[3] any post-verdict settlement offer, if made, would probably have been too low to seriously consider. Moreover, it is unlikely that there was any offer since Keany's department was adamant about the railroad's lack of liability. It is also possible that Keany followed a similar policy to that of the New York Central Railroad after the Park Avenue tunnel disaster, where victims were told that they if they did not accept a pre-trial settlement offer, they could expect the railroad to contest their cases all the way to the Court of Appeals.

Keany would certainly not have been surprised by the jury's verdict, and probably viewed a review by the more dispassionate appellate justices as the railroad's real day in court. Between 1916, when he became general solicitor, and 1927, the Appellate Division had reversed approximately 50% of trial court judgments for LIRR negligence plaintiffs, including the $29,364.68 verdict for the death of socialite S. Osgood Pell in the Wreck Lead grade-crossing accident, set aside as being against the weight of the evidence.[4] However, the Appellate Division was not necessarily a safe harbor for the LIRR. In 1923, it reversed in the case of Myra Paige Wiren, the passenger injured while getting off a train, where Doc Brennan had obtained a dismissal immediately after opposing counsel's opening argument.[5] In 1926, it ruled that the case of Thomas V. Brick, the deckhand who drowned after falling from a LIRR tug, should have been allowed to go to the jury.[6] Later that year, it deprived the railroad of yet another apparent courtroom victory when it ordered a new trial in the case of Frank D'Aurio, the trackwalker killed by a train.[7] Only a few days before the *Palsgraf* trial, the LIRR lost again when the court ordered a new trial in the case of Mary M. Kelly, the girl who had fallen from a moving train, holding that the trial judge had incorrectly charged the jury.[8]

The oral argument took place on Friday, October 21, 1927, at Borough Hall in downtown Brooklyn. Opened in 1848 as Brooklyn City Hall, Borough Hall was the Second Department's home from 1903 to 1938. It is a Greek Revival-style building, topped by a cast iron cupola, whose marble-faced front features a large stone staircase leading to an entrance under a portico supported by six fluted Ionic columns. The courtroom was located in the old Brooklyn Common Council chamber, which had been restored and reconfigured for the court's use in 1902–03 after the walls and ceiling were badly damaged in 1895 by a serious fire. The restored room was designed in the beaux arts style with a domed ceiling, carved wood paneling, and ornate plasterwork.

Palsgraf appears to have been William McNamara's first appellate argument, and sending him to Borough Hall was another indication of the low importance Keany accorded the case, an effort to hold down costs by using in-house counsel, or an expression of confidence in the young attorney's abilities and the desire to give him some appellate experience. In contrast, the Appellate Division courtroom would have been familiar to Matthew W. Wood, who had argued here several times before. In addition to the *Wensley*, *Day*, and *Richter* cases, his pre-*Palsgraf* appearances included a failed effort to prevent an attorney's disbarment,[9] and successful appeals in a 1913 mechanics lien action,[10] and a 1919 demurrage case.[11] Wood had also won an appeal there on his own behalf. After a 1915 traffic accident, the attorney was sued by all five occupants of the other vehicle, while his sister, Hazel Borst, who was his passenger, brought an action against the other driver. The parties suing Wood subsequently orally agreed to a settlement of $1,500 if he could persuade Hazel to drop her suit. After initially agreeing, she changed her mind. The court then ordered Wood not only to pay the $1,500, but also ruled that he would have to indemnify the other driver for any settlement or judgment paid to Hazel. However, on appeal, the Appellate Division ruled since his sister was not his client, he was not obligated to pay anyone anything.[12]

Wood's appellate brief initially stressed that the facts were not disputed at the trial and that the court had so charged the jury. He noted Mrs. Palsgraf's status as a passenger by mentioning that she had purchased a ticket, but did not elaborate further on this point. The running men were connected to Mrs. Palsgraf by stating that they were "also passengers."[13] He stressed the large size of the bundle, and that it was "forcibly knocked" from under the man's arm by the railroad's employees, causing an explosion that filled the station with "dense black pungent smoke."[14] He characterized the trainmen's conduct as a series of affirmative actions — deliberately holding the door open so that the man with the bundle could board, and then taking hold of him to pull him onto the train. Mrs. Palsgraf's injuries were attributed to being "forcibly and violently" struck by the falling scale.[15] They are described as "a permanent affliction of the vocal cords or muscles controlling the power of speech so that the plaintiff has continuously stuttered or stammered when endeavoring to talk."[16]

The railroad's brief contained a shorter recitation of the facts. It noted that Mrs. Palsgraf intended to take a train to Rockaway Beach, but omitted any mention of her status as a fare-paying passenger. Those waiting on the platform with Mrs. Palsgraf were not described as passengers, but particular note was made of how many of them were carrying packages and bags. The brief also attempted to cast the actions of the conductors in the best light by claiming that they did not attempt to assist the passenger until he had jumped onto the train, and then took hold of him only so he would not fall. It then related how the package became wedged between the train and platform and acknowledged that the resulting explosion caused Mrs. Palsgraf's injuries. No information about the explosion's severity is provided. Mrs. Palsgraf's injuries are described as "slight bruises to her left side but . . . principally . . . nervous shock that 2 or 3 days later caused a stuttering and stammering in her speech which lasted up to the trial."[17]

In his approach to the negligence issue, Wood followed the standard analysis of first arguing that the railroad's employees were negligent and then asserting that this negligence was the proximate cause of Mrs. Palsgraf's injuries. He maintained that the railroad's negligence was supported by undisputed proof, contending that the trainmen were derelict in their handling of passenger with the package. He suggested that the accident "could have easily been avoided if the guard had closed the door instead of holding it open or had in some other way blocked the passage of the intending passenger or if the platform man instead of grabbing and pushing the passenger had prevented his progress so that he could not gain access to the train."[18] To establish proximate cause, Wood described the ensuing events as "contemporaneous and continuous," adding that "[t]here was an unbroken connection between the act and the injury."[19] He dismissed the railroad's argument that lack of notice of the package's contents exonerated it from blame, maintaining that there would be no doubt as to its liability if the package had contained a heavy plumber's tool that struck Mrs. Palsgraf, if the passenger had fallen against her, injuring her, or if the passenger himself had suffered injury by falling between the train and the platform.

As authority on the proximate cause issue, Wood cited three famous opinions: the *Squib Case*,[20] where a defendant who threw a lighted squib into a crowd was held liable for the plaintiff's injuries although the squib had subsequently passed through several hands before exploding and injuring the victim; the *Negro Boy Case*,[21] where the defendant was held liable for spilled wine when a youth he chased with a pick-axe fled into his employer's store and knocked the faucet from a wine cask; and the *Balloon Case*,[22] where a balloonist who made a forced landing in the plaintiff's garden was found liable for damages caused by those seeking to assist him. He also provided the court with several favorable definitions of proximate cause, including one by Judge William S. Andrews, author of the future *Palsgraf* dissent, who once wrote: "Generally, . . . the question is one of whether the act of the defendant gave rise to the stream of events which culminated in the injury."[23] Finally, although at trial Humphrey had charged the jury to draw no inference from the railroad's failure to call any witnesses, Wood asserted that this meant that any inferences of negligence should be construed against the defendant.[24]

The railroad's brief maintained that the jury's verdict was contrary to law and the evidence. It stressed at the outset that nothing in the package's appearance indicated that its contents were dangerous, and that its employees had no reason to suspect that the package contained explosives, noting that Humphrey had charged that the railroad was under no obligation to examine each passenger's package. Also stressed was that the trainmen's handling of the passenger in no way threatened injury to anyone on the station platform. It then reiterated the LIRR's basic argument on negligence and proximate cause: "Not knowing the contents of the package defendant's employees could not reasonably foresee or anticipate that it might explode. Such an occurrence is not a natural and probably consequence of assisting a man to board a train. Their action therefore was not negligent or the proximate cause of plaintiff's injures."[25]

Among the authorities cited by the LIRR was *Perry v. Rochester Lime Co.*, where Cardozo had written: "[defendant] became answerable . . . for those consequences that ought to have been foreseen by a reasonably prudent man."[26] Also cited was Cardozo's opinion in *Adams v. Bullock*, where he wrote: "We think that ordinary caution did not involve forethought of this extraordinary peril."[27] Also stressed was the fact that Mrs. Palsgraf's injuries *were only made possible by the intervening act* of the passenger carrying the explosives upon the train."[28] Cited as authority on this point was Chief Judge Frank H. Hiscock's opinion in *Saugerties Bank v. Delaware & Hudson Co.*, where he stated, "if the consequences were only made possible by the intervening act of a third party which could not have reasonably been anticipated then the sequential relation between the act and results would not be regarded as so established as to come within the rule of proximate cause."[29]

In a reply brief, the LIRR disputed Wood's allegations that trainmen had attempted to propel the man from the platform to the train, instead claiming that he jumped onto the train after it had started to move, and that the conductors did not touch the man until after he had jumped upon the train; it also denied that he was roughly handled or that the package was forcibly knocked from under his arm. The reply brief also pointed out that the Gerhardts were not disinterested witness, having sued the railroad after the *Palsgraf* trial. It charged that Wood's account of the events was unsupported by the testimony, and was intended to mislead the court into believing that the man was forced onto the train against his will and that his package was "forcibly and wantonly knocked from under his arm."[30] Also rejected was Wood's contention about a presumption of negligence because the LIRR presented no evidence at trial. It maintained that the facts of the accident were completely explained by Mrs. Palsgraf's witnesses, and stated that Humphrey had been correct when he charged the jurors that they should draw no inferences from the railroad's failure to present any witnesses.

In an opinion delivered on December 9, the Appellate Division ruled for Mrs. Palsgraf by a vote of 3–2. The majority opinion was written by trotting horse enthusiast Albert H.F. Seeger, with two Brooklyn Democrats, Hagarty and Carswell concurring. *Palsgraf* was only Seeger's second reported Appellate Division opinion, and one of only eight that he would author during his brief service with the court.[31] Seeger's description of the facts was relatively short. It failed to indicate the real severity of the explosion, the extent of the physical damage it caused, the injuries to other bystanders, and the pandemonium on the platform. The opinion did provide the date and location of the incident, and described Mrs. Palsgraf as a passenger intending to take a train. It then related how the two men with the package attempted to board the moving train and that the trainmen knocked the package from under the passenger's arm. Like Humphrey and Cardozo, he inaccurately positions the fallen package, stating that if fell "under the train."[32] However, Seeger does correctly note that the scale was large, and that Mrs. Palsgraf's injuries were severe.

The Orange County justice accepted the jury's finding that the railroad was guilty of negligence and ignored the issue of where the passenger was when assisted by the conductors. He adopted the position taken in Wood's brief: "Instead of aiding or assisting the passenger . . . they might better have discouraged and warned him not to board the moving train."[33] Like Wood, he cited as favorable authority the *Squib*, *Negro Boy*, and *Balloon* cases. Seeger rejected the LIRR's claim that the lack of notice that the package contained explosives relieved it of any liability, and he concluded by noting that Mrs. Palsgraf's status as a passenger entitled her to "the highest degree of care required by common carriers."[34]

Edward Lazansky, joined by J. Addison Young, dissented. In an opinion that has been praised for its "admirable brevity,"[35] Lazansky merely stated that the trainmen's negligence had caused the package to be thrown between the train and platform. He did not mention the scale, noting only that the explosion "caused injury to the plaintiff."[36] On the negligence issue, he cited no precedents; he maintained that the jury may have been warranted in finding the act of assisting a passenger to board a moving train was negligent, and agreed with Wood that the door should have been closed before the train started, adding that the jury was also justified in finding the defendant's negligence caused the package to fall and then to explode. However, he did not believe that the negligence of the conductors was the proximate cause of Mrs. Palsgraf's injuries. Instead, he agreed with the LIRR's contention that the passenger's negligence in attempting to board the train while carrying explosives intervened between the railroad's negligence and Mrs. Palsgraf's injuries, concluding with: "Defendant's negligence was a cause of plaintiff's injury, but too remote."[37]

Chapter 8

THE COURT OF APPEALS

Palsgraf's final destination, the New York Court of Appeals, was one of the nation's most influential state appellate courts. Established by the New York Constitution of 1846, it replaced the state's former highest court, the Court of Supreme Judicature and Correction of Errors. That court, established in 1784 and modeled on the English House of Lords, was an unwieldy body consisting of four judges and the entire thirty-two member state Senate. In contrast, the new court, when first established, consisted of only four elected judges and four supreme court justices appointed by the governor and serving one year terms. From the outset, the court was engaged in a losing effort to keep up with its docket. It quickly fell behind and never caught up; by 1865, it took unpreferred cases four years to reach the judges.

In 1869, a constitutional amendment was adopted changing the court's membership to seven elected judges serving fourteen-year terms. When the revamped court began hearing cases in July 1870, a temporary five-member Commission of Appeals took on the backlog to give the new judges a fresh start. However, the court quickly fell behind again, eventually requiring the establishment of a Second Division which disposed of 2,093 cases between 1889 and 1892. These continuing calendar problems resulted in another constitutional amendment in 1899, authorizing the governor to designate up to four additional judges.[1] It was this provision that enabled three judges on the *Palsgraf* panel, Benjamin Cardozo, William S. Andrews, and Frederick E. Crane to first become members of the court.[2]

Although the court was highly regarded by the 1920s, only a decade earlier it had been the subject of intense criticism from social progressives. The chief cause was a 1911 decision, *Ives v. South Buffalo Railway Company*,[3] holding that New York's new workmen's compensation law, the Wainwright Act,[4] was an unconstitutional taking of property without due process. *Ives* pleased those who saw workmen's compensation as a dangerous example of creeping socialism, but it was denounced by many, including a future Court of Appeals judge, political reformer Samuel Seabury, then a state supreme court justice, who characterized the decision as "reactionary."[5] Another notable critic was former-President Theodore Roosevelt. During his 1912 Bull Moose Party challenge to President William Howard Taft, he attacked *Ives* as being "against human rights,"[6] and proposed that the electorate be given the power to recall judicial decisions.

Another threat to the court's image was partisan politics. Although the state's politicians were fond of spouting pieties about a non-partisan Court of Appeals, party interests often took precedence over the supposed sanctity of the state's highest court. The political bosses were always involved in the nomination process, and such factors as religion and geography, and even a judge's previous decisions could be critical criteria when they considered candidates. This occurred in 1913, when Murphy of Tammany Hall and McCooey of Brooklyn sensed that many voters were still angry over the *Ives* opinion, and denied a bipartisan nomination for chief judge to the opinion's author, Republican William E. Werner. Instead, they nominated Associate Judge Willard Bartlett, who narrowly defeated Werner. A less serious example of previous decisions as a campaign issue came three years later when eccentric millionaire Harry K. Thaw, the acquitted killer of Stanford White, briefly reappeared in New York to urge the electorate to vote for Republican Frank H. Hiscock over Democrat Almet Jenks, claiming that Jenks had treated him unfairly during and after his murder trial.

In 1928, the Court of Appeals consisted of three Democrats, Benjamin N. Cardozo, Irving Lehman, and John F. O'Brien, and four Republicans, William S. Andrews, Cuthbert W. Pound, Frederick E. Crane, and Henry T. Kellogg. As a group, they came from a higher socio-economic level than the Appellate Division justices who had considered *Palsgraf*. Andrews and O'Brien were the sons of former Court of Appeals judges; Kellogg's father had served as an Appellate Division justice, and Cardozo's had been on the old General Term. None came from poor backgrounds; Cardozo, Andrews, and Kellogg came from very affluent families, and Lehman was extremely wealthy. All the judges had attended college; only Pound had not attended law school, but he had been a law school professor. All were native-born citizens, and only one, Irving Lehman, was the son of a European immigrant. Like the Appellate Division panel, the court had undergone recent changes in personnel; Kellogg had joined the court in 1926 and O'Brien in 1927. Three judges, Cardozo, Pound, and Lehman, were regarded as "liberals." Socially, the seven members of the court were a collegial group who all stayed at Albany's Ten Eyck Hotel while the court was in session, usually having breakfast and dinner together in the hotel dining room.[7] Professionally, according to Irving Lehman, no one judge could dominate their discussions, although Cardozo "wielded a mighty influence."[8]

The court's chief judge, Benjamin N. Cardozo, was regarded as one of nation's leading jurists and legal scholars. Already known for such landmark decisions as *MacPherson v. Buick Motor Company*[9] (1916), *Wood v. Lucy, Lady Duff-Gor-*

don[10] (1917), *Jacob & Youngs v. Kent*[11] (1921), and *Allegheny College v. National Chautauqua Bank of Jamestown*[12] (1927), he had also authored *The Jurisdiction of the Court of Appeals of the State of New York* (1909), *The Nature of the Judicial Process* (1921), *The Growth of the Law* (1924), and, most recently, *The Paradoxes of Legal Science* (1928). Born in Manhattan in 1870, he was the younger son of Albert and Rebecca Cardozo, members of New York's Sephardic Jewish community.

When Cardozo was born, his father was an affluent, well-regarded New York supreme court justice. Until 1872, Albert Cardozo's life was a success story. He was born in Philadelphia and educated in the New York public schools. In 1854, he married Rebecca Nathan, a member of a prominent and affluent Sephardic family whose presence in New York City dated from the 1700s. He entered the legal profession after studying in the office of noted attorney Archibald Hilton. Cardozo then became active in the Tammany Hall organization, and in 1863, was elected to the court of common pleas as its candidate. In 1867, he won election to the supreme court, and was appointed to its general term in 1870. However, unlike his Court of Appeals colleagues whose fathers' judicial service was surely a source of pride, for Benjamin Cardozo his father's career as a judge was a family disgrace that he wished to "work away."[13]

Characterized by Professor Andrew L. Kaufman as "'a good family man' [with] a weakness in his public character,"[14] Albert Cardozo became a target of members of the Association of the Bar who were determined to reform the Tammany-tainted court system. Their investigation focused on Cardozo and two other Tammany judges, George Barnard and John H. McCunn. In 1872, the Association forwarded reports on the three judges to the state legislature's judiciary committee. Cardozo faced five charges, most notably assisting financiers Jay Gould and Jim Fisk in efforts to reduce their losses after a failed attempt to corner the gold market, and nepotism in awarding referee appointments to his nephew, Gratz Nathan. Worse, a check of Cardozo's bank account revealed twenty-seven deposits made between 1869 and 1871 that corresponded closely to withdrawals made by his nephew.[15] When the judiciary committee recommended his impeachment, Albert Cardozo resigned.[16]

Although there was strong antipathy towards Albert Cardozo among some members of the Association of the Bar, they did not press for his disbarment and he was able to resume practicing in partnership with another Tammany-connected lawyer, Richard S. Newcombe. After giving up his judgeship, reduced financial circumstances forced Cardozo to move the family to a smaller home. However, by 1877, his finances were sufficiently recovered to permit a resumption of the family's affluent lifestyle.[17] At his death in 1885, he left an estate consisting of the family's Manhattan brownstone, a house in Long Branch, New Jersey, a life insurance policy, and "amounts to about $100,000."[18]

Benjamin Cardozo led a sheltered life as a youth. After his mother's death in 1879, he was largely cared for by his older sister Nellie, and possibly governesses.[19] He apparently was educated entirely at home, never attending a public or private school.[20] He entered Columbia College at age fifteen after being prepared for the entrance examinations by Horatio Alger. Cardozo earned top grades at Columbia; after graduating in 1889, he enrolled in Columbia Law School. Like many of his classmates, he did not remain for the third year of instruction. Instead, he joined the firm of his elder brother, Albert, and was admitted to the bar in October 1891.

Like many members of his family, Cardozo never married.[21] In fact, there is no convincing evidence that he ever had a romantic involvement of any kind, and his chief biographer, Professor Kaufman, states that it is likely that he led a celibate life.[22] Cardozo lived in a brownstone on West 75th Street with his older sister Nellie, who, by the mid-1920s, was an invalid. He was hardly a social recluse, sometimes going to discussion group dinners, dining out with friends, or seeing an occasional play, but most of his evenings were spent at home reading and working on legal matters. His personal manner has been described as kindly, courteous, and self-effacing. According to Samuel Seabury, who served with the court from 1914 to 1916, when cases were under discussion, Cardozo was "very tactful in his arguments and discussions, and in consultation, rarely taking an uncompromising position on the subject."[23]

Although Cardozo retained his membership his family synagogue, the historic Congregation Shearith Israel founded in 1730, he was not particularly observant — once describing himself as a "heathen" — and only occasionally participated in synagogue affairs.[24] He belonged to the General Committee of the American Jewish Committee, the Board of Governors of the American Friends of Hebrew University, and the Jewish Welfare Board, but unlike his colleague, Judge Irving Lehman, he did not assume a leadership role in the Jewish organizations to which he belonged. Cardozo's law-related extra-judicial activities included serving on committees of the New York County Lawyers' Association and participation in the American Law Institute.

As Cardozo became known in the profession, other attorneys brought him their most difficult cases. His practice included both trial and appellate work, and consisted primarily of contract and commercial debt collection cases. Cardozo did handle some negligence cases; in 1906, he won a verdict for a bystander injured by dynamite unlawfully stored on a public street, only to have it overturned by the Appellate Division.[25] In 1910, he failed to convince the Court of Appeals than an employer's negligence was the proximate cause of injuries to worker injured by a brick that fell down a construction chute.[26] A few cases handled by Cardozo's firm involved public figures. In 1907, he successfully argued the appeal of Lee Shubert after the theater-owner had lost a $25,000 verdict in a breach of contract case.[27] Cardozo then won a second trial, and prevailed again at the appellate level.[28] He also represented producer Florenz Ziegfeld in an unsuccessful action against an actress who had allegedly violated an injunction against appearing on stage except under Ziegfeld's management.[29] The firm also had some experience with libel actions. One of Cardozo's last cases as an attorney was the defense of the Commercial Advertiser Association, publisher of the New York *Globe and Advertiser*, against a $25,000 libel suit by Old West gunslinger-turned-sportswriter, Bat Masterson. The jury awarded Masterson $3,500 in damages, but on appeal, Cardozo was able to get the amount reduced to $1,000.[30]

Cardozo's opportunity to run for supreme court justice came as a result of the anti-Tammany backlash that followed the impeachment of Governor William Sulzer. The Fusion forces were looking for a Jewish candidate to oppose the incumbent, Democratic and Hearst Independence League candidate, Bartow S. Weeks, a Columbia Law School graduate and former district attorney, recently appointed by Governor Sulzer to fill a vacancy. Their first choice was attorney Julius Frank, but they were advised that what they needed was a "real" (i.e., Sephardic) Jew, not a member of a reform synagogue like Frank.[31] At first, some Republicans refused to back Cardozo's candidacy since they had expected to nominate noted attorney and Harvard Law School graduate William H. Wadhams. However, having promised Cardozo the nomination, the Fusionists refused to reconsider. After a week, the Republican relented and ratified the nomination.

Cardozo's candidacy was endorsed by 125 leading New York City attorneys.[32] This support was noted by Fusion, which extolled Cardozo, noting that he had "almost the unanimous support of the bar" and claimed "that not for years has there been such an exceptionally fit nomination for Supreme Court Justice in this county."[33] Like several of the other judges who would hear *Palsgraf*, Cardozo's election was facilitated by a landslide victory at the top of the ticket. Reformer John Purroy Mitchell crushed Tammany's lackluster candidate, Edward E. McCall, citywide by 233,919 votes. Weeks received 20,000 more votes in Manhattan and the Bronx than McCall, and outpolled Cardozo in Manhattan. However, a heavy Fusion vote in the Bronx more than offset the Manhattan results and provided Cardozo with a margin of 2,264 votes.[34] In later years, Cardozo claimed that he won because Italian-American voters thought he was one of them. However, a careful examination of voting patterns by Professor Kaufman revealed that Cardozo fared poorly in Italian-American districts, and instead received a heavy vote from Bronx anti-Tammany Irish-American Democrats.[35]

Cardozo served on the supreme court for one month and heard only five cases, including one jury trial, where a plaintiff who had been thrown from a street car won a $500 verdict.[36] On February 2, 1914, he was named by Governor Martin H. Glynn to a vacancy among the designated Court of Appeals judges. Samuel Seabury was said to be in line for the postion, but he had angered the court's judges with his criticisms of their anti-labor decisions. The court twice requested that the governor appoint Cardozo, but the offer was made only after yet another candidate, Justice Samuel Greenbaum, turned the offer down for financial reasons.[37] Cardozo's opportunity to run for a full term came in 1916, when two vacancies occurred on the court; Samuel Seabury had resigned to run for governor, and Frank H. Hiscock had moved up to the chief judgeship. When newly-elected Governor Charles S. Whitman offered Cardozo the old Seabury seat, the Judiciary Committee of the Association of the Bar urged him to accept, stating: "we are firmly convinced that it is our duty to urge your acceptance on the ground that you can thereby render a public service that will tend to strengthen the court."[38] Knowing that if he accepted the appointment he would have to stand for election the following November, and unwilling to give up his supreme court seat with its fourteen-year term, Cardozo initially turned the offer down, only accepting reluctantly after party leaders agreed to a bipartisan endorsements for himself and upstate Republican Chester B. McLaughlin.[39] Publicly, Cardozo characterized the appointment as "a call to duty which cannot be ignored . . . [and] an honor which makes acceptance easy."[40]

A similar bipartisan deal permitted Cardozo to become chief judge. When Frank H. Hiscock was about to retire in 1926, the Republicans received a commitment from Governor Smith to support a bipartisan nomination for Cuthbert W. Pound, whose election as a regular Court of Appeals judge predated Cardozo's by one year. The deal was viewed favorably by many Democrats since the resulting associate judge vacancy would be filled by a member of their party. However, when Smith, who admired Cardozo and felt complimented when the judge treated him as if he were a member of the bar, was informed that Cardozo had eighteen months more service on the court than Pound, he switched sides. After some political maneuvering, an agreement was reached between the governor and Republican leaders for a bipartisan judicial ticket with Cardozo for chief judge and upstate Republican Henry T. Kellogg for associate judge.

Unlike his colleagues on the Court of Appeals who had lengthy experience as trial judges, hearing first-hand tales of domestic discord, and sitting in the same courtrooms as injured accident victims and accused criminals, Cardozo's encounters with the seamier and more sordid side of life came through his appellate cases.[41] The subjects of his domestic relations opinions included a fraudulent divorce,[42] child custody,[43] a husband seeking to annul his marriage to an insane woman,[44] and a wife who refused to co-habit with her husband.[45] Cardozo's criminal opinions dealt with such offenses as arson,[46] robbery,[47] forgery,[48] and obtaining money under false pretenses.[49] He also wrote opinions in a series of murder cases, including three where the defendants were eventually executed.[50] One was the sensational case of Father Hans Schmidt, convicted of murdering a former rectory maid, Anna Aumuller, dismembering her body, and dumping it into the Hudson River. Schmidt appealed his conviction on the grounds that he'd confessed to murder and feigned insanity to conceal the fact that the girl had died after an illegal abortion. After holding that a defendant who had committed a fraud on the court was not entitled to a new trial, Cardozo used his opinion as a vehicle for a lengthy discussion of the *M'Naughten* insanity rule.[51]

Before hearing *Palsgraf*, Cardozo authored several opinions in cases where persons were injured by public carriers. Here, he showed no general propensity to favor large corporate defendants. He did deprive a victim of a $1,150 judgment by reversing the Appellate Division and granting a new trial in *Adams v. Bullock*, the case of a twelve-year-old boy who was severely shocked on Good Friday 1916, when a wire he was swinging about made accidental contact with an overhead power line used by a Dunkirk trolley company.[52] However, a majority of his decisions involving common carriers favored the plaintiffs, including a fatal grade-crossing accident,[53] a boy killed by falling high tension electric wires,[54] and a pedestrian run down by a trolley car.[55] His most famous holding for a plaintiff was *Wagner v. International Railway Company*, the case of Buffalo upholsterer Arthur Wagner who fell through the ties of a trestle while searching for his cousin, Herbert Wagner, who had just been thrown off a trolley car platform.[56] The Appellate Division, Fourth Department, had affirmed the trial court's refusal of the plaintiff's motion for a new trial, but Cardozo, maintaining that "danger invites rescue," reversed and granted Wagner another day in court.[57]

Another "liberal" Court of Appeals judge who, like Cardozo, enjoyed a reputation as a legal scholar was Republican Cuthbert W. Pound. When comparing Pound to Cardozo, one reporter noted that they shared "a scholarly paleness."[58] Another observed that Cardozo was "austere and gentle, while Pound was lenient and gentle."[59] His Court of Appeals colleague, Judge Crane, credited Pound with having a mind of a "practical bent" that "saved him from becoming merely academic,"[60] while Karl Llewellyn wrote that he had "earthy common sense."[61]

A cousin of Harvard Law School professor Roscoe Pound, Judge Pound was born in 1864 in Lockport, a small Niagara County city on the Erie Canal, near Buffalo. He was the son of Alexander Pound, originally from Ontario, and Almina Pound from nearby Orleans County. Alexander Pound was an early Lockport resident who earned a respectable living as a farmer, butcher, and foundryman. Pound's older brother, John, almost twenty years his senior, was a prominent Lockport attorney whose public offices included membership on the county board of supervisors, state assemblyman, assistant United States attorney, United States Circuit Court commissioner, and president of the board of education. He also served as Lockport's mayor in 1879 and 1880.

After graduating from Lockport Union School in 1883, Cuthbert Pound attended Cornell, but left without graduating to work in his elder brother's law office. He was admitted to the bar in 1886, practiced law with his brother and served as Lockport city attorney. In 1887, Pound married Emma White of Lockport; they had three children. The Pound family experienced tragedy in 1903, when his younger son, Cuthbert W. Pound, Jr., accidentally killed himself with a rifle. By 1928, the judge's wife had died and he was a widower. Like Cardozo, Pound's interests outside the law were limited. Although he was said to enjoy poetry, gardening and concerts, Pound once claimed that his life was one-sided and incomplete, saying, "I have no hobbies. I don't play golf. I do not drive a car. I do not play bridge. I do not sing."[62] His non-legal activities included serving as a trustee of Cornell University, and belonging to a Lockport Masonic lodge; he was also a member of Lockport's Grace Episcopal Church.

As a young attorney, Pound became involved in Niagara County Republican politics, and was elected to the state Senate in 1893. There, he was an active supporter of women's suffrage, and served as a member of the Lexow Commission investigating corruption in New York City. Pound left the Senate after one term and returned to Cornell as a law professor, teaching constitutional law, evidence, corporation law, and criminal law. His stature there was such that when Cleveland businessman Hayward Kendall, an 1898 Cornell graduate, when offering the university $1,000,000 in 1928 if it would abolish coeducation and fraternities, excluded only Pound and another professor when denigrating the faculty members he had encountered as a student.

While in Albany, Pound developed a close association with Theodore Roosevelt, and in 1900, the then-governor appointed him a member of the Civil Service Commission. In 1904, he was made president of the Commission by Governor Benjamin B. Odell, but resigned the position the next year to become counsel to Governor Frank W. Higgins. Two years later, Higgins appointed Pound to the vacancy created by the death of Henry A. Childs, a supreme court justice for western New York's Eighth Judicial District. Endorsed by both the Republicans and Democrats, he had no difficulty winning election to a full term the following fall.

Pound's most notable supreme court opinion was the precursor to the notorious Court of Appeals decision, *Ives v. South Buffalo Railway*.[63] When Buffalo railway switchman, Earl Ives, who sprained his ankle while on the job, claimed $70 in damages under New York's new workmen's compensation statute, his employer challenged the constitutionality of the statute. Pound, however, ruled the employer lacked standing stating, "it does not lie in the mouth of the defendant to raise this objection to the statute."[64] The Court of Appeals ruling that reversed Pound was itself overturned by a constitutional amendment, permitting the enactment of a new workmen's compensation law.[65] In an earlier case, Pound demonstrated his sympathy for disadvantaged married women when he declined to follow a referee's award granting custody of her children to a clearly adulterous father. Instead, he ruled that the mother should have the opportunity seek a modification by presenting "proof of the wishes of the children and additional proof as to their future interests. . . ."[66]

In 1915, Pound was appointed to the Court of Appeals as a temporary judge by Governor Charles S. Whitman. Nominated by the Republicans for a full term the following year, he was endorsed by the Association of the Bar and the Lawyers Nonpartisan Committee. In the general election, he benefited from the statewide Republican sweep, defeating Democrat John T. Norton of Rensselaer, formerly a deputy state attorney general and advisor to Governor Martin

H. Glynn. On the Court of Appeals, Pound wrote opinions that favored the rights of the less privileged, including married women, members of organized labor, and accident victims.[67] These included negligence actions against common carriers. In two grade-crossing cases, he reversed Appellate Division decisions that had deprived plaintiffs of jury verdicts on the grounds that they had been guilty of contributory negligence as a matter of law.[68] In a case involving a railroad passenger, Pound affirmed an Appellate Division ruling ordering a new trial for a plaintiff who claimed his satchel, containing clothing and a diamond scarf pin, had vanished because of the negligence of a sleeping car porter.[69]

Brooklyn's representative on the Court of Appeals was Frederick E. Crane. Born there in 1869, he was the son of Frederick W.H. and Mary G. Crane. His father, the son of Ethan Crane, a Congregational minister from Old Saybrook, Connecticut, played one season of professional baseball with the Brooklyn Atlantics,[70] and later became the president of the Robert Hoe Press Manufacturing Company. Crane received his primary and secondary education at Adelphi Academy, a private Brooklyn school founded in 1863. He graduated from Columbia Law School in 1889 and was admitted to the bar the following year.

Crane served briefly as a Kings County assistant district attorney, but resigned in 1896, citing the demands of private practice, the small salary, and his being ignored by District Attorney Foster L. Backus when important cases were prosecuted. As an attorney, he handled several murder cases, defended city officials against corruption charges, and represented the plaintiff in a negligence suit against the Nassau Electric Railway Company after the man had been thrown from his carriage when a streetcar frightened his horse. In 1901, Crane was the Republican-Fusion candidate for one of the two county judgeships, running against the Democratic incumbent, Judge William B. Hurd. The *Brooklyn Daily Eagle*, disturbed that the Republican-Fusion forces had refused to endorse an incumbent judge with a good record, published instructions for voters on how to split their tickets;[71] their effort was in vain as Crane easy defeated Hurd, benefiting from a citywide Fusion sweep, highlighted by a victory in the mayoral race, where Seth Low, President of Columbia University, defeated Tammany candidate Edward M. Shepard. As a trial judge, Crane proved popular with the bar and was known for his "plain manner of delivering decisions."[72] In 1906, he received one of eight Republican nominations for the supreme court in the Second Judicial District, and won a seat on the bench by finishing third in a twenty-three candidate field.

Crane's courtroom experiences as a county judge and supreme court justice included the usual variety of civil suits, occasionally interrupted by such unusual actions as a doctor's lawsuit against the New York Zoological Society demanding $1,000 for treating a rhinoceros, and the trial of the so-called "Rock and Rye Case," where a longshoreman who was served alcohol instead of seltzer as a "chaser" won a $200 verdict from a Brooklyn saloonkeeper. Crane's docket was also filled with cases involving domestic discord, marital failures, and a seemingly endless succession of accused bigamists. In 1915, faced with yet another bigamist, the exasperated judge remarked: "Swapping wives and husbands has become as common as swapping horses. . . . If we want polygamy, why don't we come out bravely and establish it as the Mormons did in Utah."[73]

The majority of Crane's cases deemed newsworthy by the press were criminal trials. Between 1902 and 1916, he passed sentence on petty thieves, bookmakers, burglars, and murderers. The trial that attracted the most sensational press coverage was that of T. Jenkins Hains in January 1906. The son of a retired general, Hains was accused of preventing onlookers at the Bayside Yacht Club from interfering while his brother, army officer Captain Peter C. Hains, Jr., shot to death a man he suspected of having an affair with his wife. After multiple ballots, the jury acquitted Hains, leading to such a celebratory uproar that Crane was forced to clear the courtroom. Less fortunate was the defendant in another widely-publicized case, ex-servant Joseph Hanel, convicted of strangling his former employer, a wealthy Brooklyn woman, during a burglary. Crane sentenced him to death; Hanel went to the electric chair on September 1, 1916.

Crane resided in the Park Slope section of Brooklyn and had a summer home in the Suffolk County community of Bellport. His wife was the former Mary Gertrude Craven whom he married in Montreal in 1893; they had two children, a son and a daughter. Known for his wit, he was a devotee of classical music and enjoyed attending concerts. In addition to his judicial duties, he served as a trustee of the Brooklyn Institute of Arts and Science, and lectured for six years on medical jurisprudence at Long Island College Hospital. Of the seven Court of Appeals judges, he would have had the most personal experience with the Long Island Railroad. During his supreme court service, the LIRR would have been the most convenient way to reach courthouses in Queens, Nassau, and Suffolk Counties. Crane also appears to have been the only judge who heard *Palsgraf* to have any personal experience with railroad accidents. In 1906, he was among the passengers who were shaken up when a New York to Bar Harbor, Maine, passenger train, the Maine Central's Knickerbocker Limited, collided head-on with a runaway freight car near Pittsfield, Massachusetts, killing an engineer.

In January 1917, Crane was appointed a temporary judge of the Court of Appeals by Governor Whitman, filling the place of Cuthbert W. Pound who had been elected to an associate judge's position. In 1920, Crane was nominated by both the Republicans and Democrats for one of two court vacancies. The Democrats opted to nominate Crane not only because of an existing policy to nominate temporary Court of Appeals judges who had "made good," but also as an effort to get Republican votes in Brooklyn. Crane was sufficiently prominent in Republican circles that in 1924 he was mentioned as a possible choice for United States attorney general, and then as a potential candidate for governor. In 1925, he visited The Hague, and on his return home, advocated United States membership in the Permanent Court of International Justice.

During the 1920s, Crane's Court of Appeals cases included a decision reversing the juvenile delinquency conviction of a Buffalo youth because his confession had been obtained after police threats to punch him in the nose,[74] and a married actress's libel action arising from a false report in a New York City paper that she planned to marry comedian Roscoe "Fatty" Arbuckle.[75] He wrote several opinions involving common carriers and the alleged contributory negligence of the accident victim. In 1923, he reinstated a $15,000 verdict for a Cohoes widow whose husband, a $33-per-week employee of a knitting company, had been killed in a grade-crossing accident,[76] and held that a trial court had incorrectly dismissed a Buffalo policeman's action against a trolley company.[77] However in 1922, he reversed three Appellate Division decisions that had affirmed verdicts for plaintiffs — $7,110.50 for the death of a twenty-one-year-old woman killed by a Manhattan trolley,[78] $6,500 for a Niagara County fruit farmer injured when his car was hit by a New York Central freight train,[79] and $10,115.31 for the death of Adolph Castle, a Buffalo stationery salesman, killed by another New York Central train while using a North Tonawanda grade-crossing after making a sales call.[80] Only one Crane Court of Appeals opinion dealt in any way with the LIRR. In 1927, he ruled that a Suffolk County woman should have had the opportunity to present evidence that her chauffeur was acting outside the scope of his employment when the car he was driving was involved in a grade-crossing accident that injured two child passengers — good news for the car owner, but a holding that deprived the injured children of a verdicts of $15,001.75 and $4,002.[81]

The wealthiest member of the court in 1928 was Irving Lehman, one of three sons of Mayer Lehman, a founder of the Lehman Brothers firm, and Babette Newgass Lehman, a member of a well-to-do New Orleans family. Born near the Bavarian city of Wurzburg in 1830, Mayer Lehman came to the United States at the age of thirty and went into business with his two brothers in Montgomery Alabama, making a career as a cotton broker. During the Civil War he strongly supported the Southern cause, and was active in attempts to help Confederate prisoners held in the North. Finding life in Reconstruction-era Alabama distasteful, he and his brother, Emmanuel, relocated their business to New York City in 1867, where Mayer Lehman helped found the New York Cotton Exchange. However, the profits of the Lehman Brothers firm were not just based on cotton trading. Emmanuel Lehman was also active in the petroleum, coffee, and sugar markets; the brothers also had railroad, mining, and industrial interests.

Like his brother, future New York governor Herbert Lehman, Irving Lehman received his early education at the Sach's School for Boys, established by Dr.

Julius Sachs, a stern taskmaster and one of the leading figures in American secondary education. He then earned bachelor's and master's degrees at Columbia before graduating from Columbia Law School, where he won the Tappan Prize in constitutional law. Lehman was admitted to the bar in 1898, and practiced with the firm of Marshall, Moran, Williamson & Vicker, and later with Worcester, Williams & Lehman. He reportedly handled his legal affairs with such honesty and candor that an experienced attorney once told him, "young man, if you want to get along at all as a lawyer in this town, you've really must learn to be more shifty."[82] In 1901, he married Sissie Straus, the daughter of department store mogul and philanthropist, Nathan Straus.

Lehman was a member of Temple Emanu-el, a Manhattan reform congregation founded in 1845 by Western European Jews, which rose to prominence as the prosperity of its members increased. During the 1880s, the synagogue provided charitable assistance for Eastern European Jews fleeing pogroms and poverty. Lehman himself served as a volunteer social worker at the Henry Street Settlement House between his college graduation and his election as a judge. He took a keen interest in Jewish education, encouraging members of his faith to learn more about their religion and deploring the tendency of many toward indifference and ignorance. His leadership positions included membership on the executive board of the American Jewish Committee, and the presidencies of the Young Men's Hebrew Association, the Jewish Welfare Board, and Temple Emanu-el.

In 1908, Lehman was nominated for supreme court justice by Tammany Hall, then headed by Charles F. Murphy. Known for his inscrutable manner, it was said of "Silent Charlie" that he would not sing the Star-Spangled Banner, lest he commit himself.[83] The taciturn boss was a former shipyard worker, amateur baseball player, and saloon owner who gained control over the Tammany organization after scandals and electoral defeats led to the retirement of former boss Richard Croker. Often attacked by critics and political enemies, he shrugged off their harsh words, once saying, "[i]t is the fate of political leaders to be reviled. If one is too thin-skinned to stand it one should never take the job."[84] Murphy led Tammany Hall from 1902 until his death in 1924, successfully electing three New York City mayors, George B. McClellan, William J. Gaynor, and John F. Hylan; three New York governors, John Alden Dix, William Sulzer, and Alfred E. Smith; and one senator, Robert Wagner. At his death, he left a net estate of $1,992,987,[85] said to have been derived from speculating on contracts.

Lehman received the supreme court nomination when Tammany's expected candidate, Manhattan attorney Emanuel Blumenstiel, was discarded because he'd been the subject of unsuccessful disbarment proceedings and was reportedly unpopular with certain Jewish voters. Lehman's father-in-law, Nathan Straus, was active in Democratic affairs, and the judge later acknowledged that his selection was facilitated by Straus' large donations to the New York Democratic Party. Before the election, there were also reports that Straus, in exchange for the nomination of his son-in-law, had agreed to arrange for newspaper publisher William Randolph Hearst's Independence League to field a candidate for surrogate who would draw votes away from Republican incumbent Charles H. Beckett. Straus, however, maintained that he'd never made a deal with any party. As for contributions to Tammany Hall, he stated, "I have not contributed as much this year [1908] as usual."[86]

Ultimately, Tammany Hall needed no political assistance from Straus. Although 1908 was a presidential election year, and Republican William Howard Taft narrowly took the city vote, the unsuccessful Democratic gubernatorial candidate, Lewis Stuyvesant Chanler, won a city-wide majority of over 60,000 votes and the Tammany organization won all the local races.[87] Its candidate for surrogate, John P. Cohalan, brother of Tammany Hall sachem Daniel F. Cohalan, defeated Beckett by 25,004 votes, while Lehman won by an even wider margin, defeating the Republican incumbent, former Lieutenant Governor M. Bruce Linn, by over 32,000 votes.[88]

Lehman's judicial career began inauspiciously when the courtroom roof sprang a serious leak on his first day, dripping copious amounts of rainwater between the bench and jury box. Under more normal circumstances, his judicial activities included a ruling that a bull terrier belonging to a banker's wife must be muzzled, issuing an injunction against use of intimidation and threats by striking cloakworkers, and dismissing a breach of contract suit by heavyweight champion Jess Willard against two ex-managers. He also had his share of domestic disputes, including a man who admitted to spanking his wife, and another who denied biting his.

Since his court was located in Manhattan, Lehman heard several cases involving large sums of money. These included a ruling that the New York Disposal Company must pay the city $400,000, a reduction of the assessment on the Equitable Building that saved the owners $2,000,000 in taxes, and a decision that the city could not recover $1,990,000 from the Interborough Rapid Transit Company. Lehman was also the presiding judge in the $28,000,000 suit by Dick Brothers & Company, minority LIRR shareholders, which alleged that the railroad was run for the benefit of its parent company, the Pennsylvania Railroad. He dismissed the suit, holding that he could find that cooperation between the LIRR directors and the Pennsylvania Railroad "was for the best interest of both."[89]

Lehman's election to the Court of Appeals in 1923 was relatively uncomplicated. Although upstate Democrats wanted John E. Mack, the former district attorney of Dutchess County, and Boss McCooey indicated an early preference for Appellate Division, Second Department, Presiding Justice William J. Kelly, Lehman was the choice of Tammany Hall leader Murphy to succeed retiring Syracuse Democrat, John W. Hogan. Republicans had threatened to withhold support from any candidate "hand-picked" by Murphy, but relented when the choice turned out to be Lehman. He received the party's nomination at the September convention and won easily in November, opposed by only the Socialist candidate, New York City Magistrate Judge Jacob Panken.

By 1928, Lehman had already written Court of Appeals opinions in several
noteworthy cases. In 1924, he upheld the state theater brokers license law,[90] an
anti-scalping measure intended to end the resale of tickets at extortionate
prices,[91] and in 1928 lifted an injunction preventing four labor leaders from
inducing workers to join their new union and leave the employ of the Interborough Rapid Transit Company.[92] He also wrote opinions in several death
penalty cases, granting new trials to a Bronx woman accused of killing a
wealthy contractor,[93] an Essex county farm wife convicted of murdering her husband,[94] and Anthony J. Pantano, convicted of participation in the cold-blooded
shooting of two Brooklyn bank messengers.[95] Less fortunate were Ruth Snyder
and her former lover, Henry Judd Gray, convicted of the murder of Snyder's husband at the trial Justice Hagarty was glad to miss. In his opinion, Lehman
rejected the defendant's claims that a joint trial had violated their rights, and
upheld their death sentences.[96] In his one personal injuries case involving a
common carrier, he affirmed a verdict in favor of a street car company, holding
that the issue of an infant's contributory negligence was properly submitted to
the jury.[97]

William Shankland Andrews, the author of the *Palsgraf* dissent, was a Republican from Syracuse. He was the son of Charles Andrews, who served on the
Court of Appeals for twenty-seven years, and Marcia A. Shankland, the daughter of William H. Shankland, a former supreme court justice who was a member of the Court of Appeals during 1849. Born in 1827, Charles Andrews served
as Onondaga County district attorney from 1854 to 1857, Mayor of Syracuse in
1861–62 and 1868, and as a trustee of Syracuse University from 1879 until his
death in 1918. Elected to the reconstituted Court of Appeals in 1870, he temporarily served as chief judge in 1881–82, but was defeated for the position in
the 1882 election by his next-door-neighbor, William C. Ruger. Reelected as an
associate judge in 1884, when he defeated Democrat Charles A. Rapallo, he
again served as chief judge in 1895, and retired in 1897. Known as the "First
Citizen" of Syracuse, the vigorous Andrews continued horseback riding until
shortly before his death.

Born in 1858, William S. Andrews grew up in a large mansion in Syracuse. He
received his early education at St. John's Military Academy in Manlius, N.Y.,
graduated from Harvard College in 1880 and from Columbia Law School with
honors in 1882. After being admitted to the bar in 1884, he practiced law in
Syracuse with the firm of Knapp, Nottingham & Andrews. In 1884, Andrews
married Mary Raymond Shipman, who would author numerous books, most
notably *The Perfect Tribute*, the story of Abraham Lincoln and a dying Confederate soldier, which sold over 600,000 copies. They had one son, Paul Shipman
Andrews, who later became Dean of Syracuse University Law School. The family lived on estate called Wolf Hollow in the Syracuse suburb of Taunton. Dog

lovers who enjoyed walks in the woods, Andrews and his wife vacationed annually at a rustic camp 100 miles from Quebec City.

In 1899, Andrews won the nomination for supreme court justice in the Fifth Judicial District after a multi-ballot convention struggle. Endorsed by the *Albany Law Journal* as "a brilliant young member of the bar,"[98] he easily defeated Democrat Howard Wiggins of Rome in the general election; he was reelected in 1914 with a bipartisan endorsement. During his career on the trial bench, Andrews reportedly handled 2,000 cases. Most of these were strictly of local interest, such as issuing an injunction against one street railway company using the rails of another, ruling that a local association still owed money on a $580 cash register that had been destroyed by fire,[99] a determination that tribal law should be applied when determining the right to occupy the land of an Onondaga Indian,[100] and a trial where a man was convicted of manslaughter for killing his father-in-law. A case of more far-reaching consequences was his enforcement of a new state law protecting the mineral springs at Saratoga by issuing an injunction against the extraction of carbonic gas from the area's mineral waters.[101] The ban sent the million-dollar National Carbonic Gas Company into receivership; the gas company eventually took the issue to the United States Supreme Court, which upheld the law.[102]

Andrews was thrust into the national spotlight when he presided at the 1915 libel action of state Republican leader William Barnes against former President Theodore Roosevelt. Barnes, a Taft supporter, sued for $50,000 after Roosevelt published an article alleging that he had entered into corrupt bipartisan political deals with Tammany Hall's Boss Charles F. Murphy. The trial lasted over four weeks and featured testimony by Roosevelt, Assemblyman and future Governor Alfred E. Smith, former Governor Benjamin B. Odell, and the former treasurer of the National Democratic Finance Committee, millionaire financier and sportsman August "The Younger" Belmont who traveled all the way from his Kentucky horse farm to be there. During the proceedings, Andrews made key rulings, deciding newspaper articles impugning Roosevelt's credibility were not admissible, and that the term "corruption" as used in the Roosevelt article might not mean "anything more than an impropriety and not pecuniary corruption at all."[103] After the jury returned a verdict in favor of Roosevelt, the former president enthusiastically shook hands with each juror before returning to his hotel, a trip that rapidly turned into a triumphal parade.

Andrews enjoyed trial work, and reportedly declined promotions to the Appellate Division. However, less than two years after the Roosevelt-Barnes trial, he accepted Governor Whitman's appointment as a temporary Court of Appeals judge. While serving in this capacity, he authored the controversial and unpopular decision striking down a recent New York law providing $45,000,000 for World War I veterans' bonuses.[104] The law, which had been overwhelmingly approved in a referendum, provided for bonuses of up to $250 for each veteran, many of who were jobless, homeless or poverty-stricken. Characterizing the bonus as a gift since it was not payment for any state obligation, Andrews ruled that the law was unconstitutional because it lent the credit of the state for the benefit of individuals.

Andrews' decision in the veterans' bonus case immediately became an issue within the Republican Party. Court of Appeals Judge Emory A. Chase had died in June, and Andrews was the leading candidate to fill the vacancy. However, his unpopular bonus decision gave many Republicans second thoughts. Other party veterans disliked Andrews, blaming his rulings for the failure of state leader Barnes' lawsuit against Theodore Roosevelt. As a pretext, some began to object to his candidacy on geographic grounds, claiming that since Governor Nathan L. Miller, Republican state leader, George A. Glynn, and two Court of Appeals judges, Frank H. Hiscock and John W. Hogan, were also from Syracuse, that city would be accused of "trying to 'hog' everything. . . ."[105]

Ultimately, the delegates to the Republican state convention disregarded attacks on the Andrews' candidacy, instead heeding the arguments of a prominent New York lawyer, William G. Guthrie, who in his speech supporting Andrews' nomination said, "I can conceive of no more destructive assault upon our rights and liberties or of a more fatal blow at the high traditions of the courts of justice of our State, than to have the Republican Party deny a nomination to an able, upright and fearless judge as a punishment for the conscientious and courageous performance of his plain duty to decide according to his conscience."[106] Similar sentiments were expressed by the *New York Times* which editorialized: "It will be an evil day for this State when Judges are punished for interpreting honestly fundamental law against the clamor of interested minorities or majorities, punished for upholding the Constitution against the whims of the Legislature or popular passion."[107]

There was never any question of the Democrats giving Andrews a bipartisan endorsement. Convinced that they had an excellent chance of winning, they nominated Townsend Scudder, a well-regarded former supreme court justice from Nassau County who had been defeated for reelection in the 1924 Republican landslide victory of President Calvin Coolidge. Although the Democratic organization cited Scudder's long experience on the bench and the fact that two Court of Appeals judges were already from Syracuse, Andrews drew support from many prominent Democrats in the state's legal community. On Election Day, although there was a heavy vote for Scudder in New York City, Andrews swept all but two upstate counties, emerging victorious by over 65,000 votes statewide.[108]

The summer after his election victory, Andrews pleased foes of censorship (but not the Society for the Suppression of Vice), when he affirmed a $2,500 judgment for malicious prosecution against the Society for arranging the prosecution of a bookstore clerk who had sold a copy of Thomas Gautier's allegedly obscene 1836 novel *Mademoiselle de Maupin*. In an opinion in which Cardozo and Pound concurred, he held that it was best that a jury "in close touch with currents of public feeling" determined whether the clerk had a reasonable ground to believe that the book was obscene or indecent.[109] (In his dissent, Judge Crane maintained that "literary ability is no excuse for degeneracy.")[110]

Among Andrews' other notable pre-*Palsgraf* Court of Appeals opinions were two 1927 decisions related to labor issues. In May, he ruled that the a state education law prohibiting discrimination in teachers' salaries based on sex did not prevent the Syracuse School Board from paying male teachers more than women under a contract made before the enactment of the statute.[111] Later that month, he dismissed an injunction against peaceful picketing by a few waitresses on strike against a small Manhattan bakery/restaurant.[112] Negligence cases against common carriers included reinstating a $51,608.48 verdict in favor of a Syracuse steel company against the New York Central, whose fifty-four-car freight train had blocked the fire department's route to the plaintiff's burning factory,[113] granting a new trial to a pedestrian struck by a trolley,[114] and finding the New York Central not liable for the death of a child although it had failed to fence its property.[115]

The northern New Yorker on the Court of Appeals was Henry T. Kellogg, a resident of Valcour, a Clinton County town on the shores of Lake Champlain, just south of the city of Plattsburgh. Like Judge Andrews, he enjoyed the advantage of coming from a locally prominent family. The Kelloggs were one of the oldest families in the Clinton County, having moved there from Massachusetts around 1800. While still in Massachusetts, family members participated in major historical events; Daniel Kellogg took part in Benedict Arnold's failed attack on Quebec City in 1775, dying of exposure and disease during the army's retreat; Elijah Kellogg was with Ethan Allen during the capture of Ft. Ticonderoga. The judge's grandfather, Lorenzo Kellogg, and great-grandfather, Henry Ketchum Averill, both fought in the War of 1812, serving with the militia forces that opposed the September 1814 invasion of northern New York by more than 8,000 British troops.

Henry T. Kellogg's father, S. Alonzo Kellogg, was a graduate of Middlebury College who then read law and started a private practice. His mother, Susan Elizabeth Averill, was also from a prominent local family; she was a descendant of Zephaniah Platt, the founder of Plattsburgh. S. Alonzo Kellogg's eventful career began in 1860 when he moved to Utah Territory and began practicing law in the area that became Nevada. After Nevada achieved statehood, the elder Kellogg was elected to the state Senate as a member of the Union Party. However, in 1866, he left Nevada, returned to Clinton County, and opened a law office. He then served two terms as district attorney, and two as county judge before being elected a supreme court justice in 1890. In 1894, Kellogg was backed by Republican state party boss Thomas C. Platt for the Court of Appeals, but the nomination went instead to Albert Haight of Buffalo. He then continued serving as a trial judge until January 1900, when he was named to the Appellate Division, Third Department, by Governor Theodore Roosevelt.

Born in 1869 in Champlain, a town just south of the Canadian border, Henry T. Kellogg attended Rock Point Military Academy in Burlington, Vermont; he graduated *cum laude* from Harvard College in 1889, and from Harvard Law School in 1892. After practicing law in Plattsburgh and serving as a bank-ruptcy referee, Kellogg was elected county judge in 1902. The March of the fol-lowing year, he married Katherine Weed, a daughter of Smith M. Weed, a Harvard Law School graduate, and a prominent Plattsburgh lawyer, legislator, and businessman; they had no children.

In June 1903, S. Alonzo Kellogg was forced to retire because of ill health, but not before he was able to arrange for Governor Benjamin B. Odell to appoint his son to finish the few months remaining in his term. Despite feelings among some Republicans in other Fourth Judicial District counties that the nomination should go to one of their residents, the party convention nominated Henry T. Kellogg for a full fourteen-year term; at age thirty-four, he was the youngest man ever nominated for the supreme court in northern New York. Despite his relative youth, he garnered such editorial plaudits as "a young man . . . of remarkable ability,"[116] and was elected. His subsequent performance on the bench was well received, and when he ran for reelection in 1917, he was endorsed by the bar associations of all eleven Fourth Judicial District counties and had no Democratic opponent.

While on the supreme court, Kellogg traveled all over the sprawling Fourth Judicial District, hearing cases that involved the same disputes, mishaps and human failings as those of his fellow judges in far more densely populated areas. His most notable criminal cases were the 1905 trial of a St. Lawrence County man acquitted of conspiring with the wife and son of the victim to fatally poison him with whiskey laced with lye, and the well-publicized habeas corpus proceeding brought by a burglar who had been sentenced to thirty years in Dannemora Prison. More mundane legal affairs included the appointment of receivers for the bankrupt railroads, a dispute over the construction of a munic-ipal lighting plant in Potsdam, and a $1,000 lawsuit over a horse that ran away after being frightened by an automobile.

Major civil actions where Kellogg presided were a $100,000 alienation of affections action brought by the wife of a millionaire Port Henry race track owner, and a trial where another Port Henry woman won a $15,000 verdict from the Northern Iron Company after her husband was killed in a crane acci-dent. Perhaps Kellogg's most publicized case, one reported by the *New York Times*, was the conspiracy and false imprisonment action of Father Alexander Klauder, a Catholic priest who had been removed from his pastorate and placed in a mental institution by the Bishop of Ogdensburg. After six weeks of incar-ceration, Klauder won his release and sued the bishop, the diocesan vicar gen-eral, and two doctors. In May 1914, a $15,000 judgment against the defendants was reversed by the Appellate Division,[117] resulting in a second trial with Kel-logg presiding. After listening to a series of defense witness describe Klauder's erratic behavior, he put an end to the long-running litigation by refusing to allow the case to go the jury.

Kellogg could have moved up to the Appellate Division as early as 1913, but he told Governor Sulzer that he preferred to remain on the trial bench because he felt an obligation to those who had elected him to the supreme court. In 1915, he again declined a promotion, refusing an offer from Governor Whitman to become the presiding justice for the Third Department. However, in 1917, when Whitman offered an associate justice position, Kellogg finally accepted. His next opportunity for advancement came in 1926 when Court of Appeals Associate Judge Chester B. McLaughlin retired. Early suggestions for the vacancy included two Democratic judges from Troy and Republican Justice Charles B. Sears of Buffalo. However, geography and politics favored Kellogg's candidacy. Since McLaughlin was a resident of Port Henry, there was strong sentiment that his seat should go to another northern New Yorker. Once selected by the Republicans, Kellogg was able to run unopposed thanks to the same bipartisan deal that made Cardozo chief judge — in exchange for the nomination of Cardozo by the Republicans, the Democratic nomination for associate judge went to Kellogg.

While serving with the Appellate Division, Third Department, Kellogg wrote several opinions in negligence cases involving railroads and members of the public, including reversals of judgments for plaintiffs in four grade-crossing accidents,[118] a barn fire,[119] and for a pedestrian struck by a train.[120] In two cases where the judgment had been for the defendant railroad, he authored an affirmance,[121] and once granted a plaintiff a new trial.[122] As for the LIRR, soon after joining the Court of Appeals, Kellogg ruled against it in the *Maiorano* grade-crossing case, holding that the deceased motorist was not contributorily negligent as a matter of law despite crossing the tracks when the signal bell was sounding; he reversed the trial court and Appellate Division, and ordered a new trial.[123]

The newest member of the Court of Appeals was John F. O'Brien, appointed in January 1927 to fill the vacancy caused by Cardozo's election as chief judge. Although he was a long-time New York City resident, O'Brien was originally from Watertown, a small city in Jefferson County, thirty miles from the Canadian border. A paper manufacturing center, Watertown is known for its heavy annual snowfalls, and as the place where millionaire F.W. Woolworth first conceived the concept of a five-and-dime store.

O'Brien was the son of a former Court of Appeals judge, Denis O'Brien, who served on the court from 1889 to 1907, and Margaret Cahill O'Brien. Denis O'Brien was born in Ogdensburg in 1837 to Irish Catholic immigrants from County Clare. The son of a farmer, he was educated at the local common school, studied law, and was admitted to the bar in 1861. He moved to Watertown the following year; after Watertown was incorporated as a city, he served three terms on the common council and then was elected mayor. Elected an assemblyman in 1869, he became a member of the Democratic state committee in 1880. In 1882, O'Brien was elected New York attorney general. After two terms, he was elected to the Court of Appeals in 1888, defeating Albert Haight of Buffalo, thanks to a large margin of victory in Manhattan and Kings County. He was reelected in 1902 with bipartisan support, and retired on account of age in 1907.

Born in 1874, John F. O'Brien was educated in local schools and graduated from Watertown High School in 1892. He is reported to have taken an early interest in the law, spending time as a youth at the Jefferson County Courthouse. After graduating from Georgetown College, he joined the New York City corporation counsel's office as an assistant, attended New York Law School, and graduated in 1898. In 1914, he married Hilda Le Grand Lockwood, the daughter of wealthy New York banker Le Grand Lockwood, Jr., and great-granddaughter of Clark Bissell, the former governor of Connecticut, chief justice of the Connecticut Supreme Court, and Kent Professor of Law at Yale. Their family consisted of a son and a daughter.

Of all the judges who heard the *Palsgraf case*, O'Brien had the most in common with the members of the Long Island Railroad legal department. Before joining the Court of Appeals, his entire legal career was spent with the New York City corporation counsel's office. After serving as a junior assistant, he was placed in charge of appeals, becoming involved with a large number of cases that went to New York's highest court.[124] Many of these were the same kind of cases Keany and his staff handled for the LIRR. However, O'Brien's reported negligence cases were generally less serious than those facing the railroad. These included slips on ice and snow,[125] injuries allegedly caused by defective pavements or sidewalks,[126] and an incident where a city-owned horse collided with a car.[127] One negligence action had at least a superficial resemblance to *Palsgraf* in that it involved a woman pedestrian injured when struck by a falling object — a lamppost knocked over by a city-owned truck.[128] O'Brien cases that involved fatalities included a pedestrian killed by a falling scaffold,[129] a wagon driver killed when a culvert collapsed,[130] and a nineteen-year-old girl struck and killed by a city-owned truck operated by a driver making an unauthorized private trip.[131]

O'Brien's selection to the Court of Appeals was unexpected; when Governor Smith called to inform him of his appointment, he reportedly believed he was being "kidded."[132] In fact, Smith only chose O'Brien after Justice Victor J. Dowling of the Appellate Division, Third Department, declined the nomination. O'Brien received his surprise nomination after he was recommended to the governor by the Court of Appeals judges because they had been very impressed with his appellate work. Also in O'Brien's favor was the fact that he was

Catholic, and the general consensus was that a Catholic should be added to a court that then consisted of four Protestant and two Jewish judges.

Although O'Brien was a Democrat who was not active politically, and had not been proposed for the court by Tammany Hall, it proved difficult for him to secure a bipartisan nomination for the November 1927 election. In June, the Republican state executive committee refused to recommend him, claiming he was merely a political appointee filling out an unexpired term. A war of words between the governor and the Republican leadership then began. Smith charged their failure to endorse O'Brien was petty partisan politics. In turn, they called Smith's remarks "non-partisan bunk,"[133] and cited numerous instances where the governor had replaced Republican judges with Democrats. By September, however, there were reports that Republican state committee leader George K. Morris would back O'Brien. He also benefited from endorsements from leading Republicans, such as Nicholas Murray Butler, who stated that "by inheritance, by temperament, by training, he possesses exceptional fitness for the position he now admirably fills."[134] More pragmatically, Butler pointed out that the previous year Democrats had backed Kellogg for the court with the understanding that Republicans would support a Democrat once Cardozo moved up to chief judge. Among other Republicans who backed O'Brien were retired Chief Judge Frank H. Hiscock, Albert H.F. Seeger's perennial horse racing opponent, Justice Arthur S. Tompkins, and former Governor Nathan L. Miller. All Republican opposition to O'Brien reportedly ended when Tammany Hall agreed to endorse a Republican for the court of general sessions, clearing the way for a bipartisan nomination and his election to a full term on the court.

Mrs. Helen Palsgraf

Courtesy of Grace White Lohr.

East New York LIRR station as it appeared in the 1920s.

LIRR car of the type most likely involved in the Palsgraf incident.

**Penny scale at a train station,
a common sight on station platforms.**

From the collection of Bill & Jan Berning,
www.pennyscale.com.

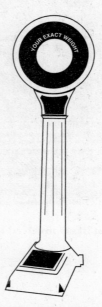

**Lollipop-style penny scale, the type
most likely to have been involved
in *Palsgraf*.**

PALSGRAF v. LONG ISLAND RAILROAD CO., 248 N.Y. 339
"The door was open and a guard reached forward to help him in while another guard, standing on the platform, pushed him from behind."

Joseph Keany, LIRR General Solicitor

YALE SHINGLE.

MATTHEW WILLS WOOD

"Woodie"

After a little preparatory work, viz.: University of Pennsylvania, 1901, LL.B. New York Law School 1903, decided he would like to take a room in Divinity and remove the dust from certain odd volumes in the library. He has succeeded. Good boy!

Matthew W. Wood in the 1904 Yale Shingle.

Courtesy of Yale University Archives.

MATTHEW W. WOOD,
Attorney and Counselor at Law,
WOOLWORTH BLDG.,   NEW YORK.
GENERAL PRACTICE IN ALL STATE AND FEDERAL COURTS.
SPECIAL ATTENTION GIVEN TO THE INTERESTS OF NON-RESIDENT HEIRS.
COMMERCIAL DEPARTMENT. BANKRUPTCY MATTERS.
DEPOSITIONS TAKEN. NOTARY IN OFFICE.
REFERENCES.—Irving Trust Co., N.Y.; Hubbell Publishing Co., N.Y.; J. H. Day Co., Cincinnati, Ohio; Walter H. Lipe, Treasurer of Beechnut Packing Co.; Mallouk Bros., N.Y., Montreal and Chicago.
Other references furnished on request.

Business card of Matthew Wills Wood,
Mrs. Palsgraf's attorney.

From the Hubbell's Legal Directory.

**Dr. Graeme M. Hammond, Mrs. Palsgraf's
medical expert**

Courtesy of the New York Athletic Club.

Justice Burt Jay Humphrey

Courtesy of the Long Island Division, Queensboro Public Library.

REGULAR
DEMOCRATIC NOMINATION,

FOR COUNTY JUDGE,

BURT JAY

HUMPHREY.

Political ad for Justice Humphrey's
1903 campaign for County Judge.

Presiding Justice Edward Lazansky of the Appellate Division

Courtesy of St. John's Law Library.

Justice Albert H.F. Seeger of the Appellate Division.

Courtesy of New York County Lawyers' Association Library.

COURT of APPEALS

Frederick E Crane
ASSOCIATE JUDGE

William S Andrews
ASSOCIATE JUDGE

Cuthbert W Pound
ASSOCIATE JUDGE

Benjamin N Cardozo
CHIEF JUDGE

Irving Lehman
ASSOCIATE JUDGE

Henry T Kellogg
ASSOCIATE JUDGE

John F O'Brien
ASSOCIATE JUDGE

Judges of the Court of Appeals

Chapter 9
THE SECOND APPEAL

Because Edward Lazansky and J. Addison Young had dissented in the Appellate Division, the LIRR was able to take *Palsgraf* to the Court of Appeals on an appeal as of right.[1] Matthew W. Wood must have known that he would have to argue his case in Albany. Keany would certainly not forego the opportunity to appeal, and with the case being handled by a member of his own legal department, the additional cost to the LIRR would not be particularly great. Thus, the LIRR's notice of appeal that arrived shortly after Christmas was certainly expected. Wood was already well acquainted with the Court of Appeals. His experiences there included the 1909 subway financing case, the 1918 *Chapman* appeal, the 1922 demurrage case, the 1923 *Day* appeal, and most recently, an unsuccessful attempt to convince the court that it should hear an appeal of the *Hild* Navy Yard injury case. Wood had been on the winning side only in the 1922 demurrage appeal, and he would have been hopeful of bettering his record before the state's highest court.

In contrast, the LIRR legal department had fared well in the few pre-*Palsgraf* negligence cases that had reached the Court of Appeals during Keany's tenure as general solicitor, getting favorable opinions in six out of seven cases decided since 1916. Recently, it had won a reversal in the case of drowned tugboat crewman Thomas V. Brick, where Cardozo wrote: "The mariner on the dizzy mast has this at least in common with his sheltered brother in the harbor, that the work of each is on the waves. One who would shun their perils wholly, should stay upon the land."[2] Its lone defeat came in early 1927, when Judge Kellogg reversed the Appellate Division and granted the plaintiff a new trial in the *Maiorano* grade-crossing case.

The LIRR's case was again argued by William McNamara in what was his first appearance before the Court of Appeals. The oral argument was held on the afternoon of February 23, 1928; each attorney was allotted one hour to present his case. The weather that day was cold and partly cloudy, and if Wood or McNamara perused the Albany papers that morning, they would have seen a report announcing the arrest of the dreaded "Jack the Hugger" who had been harassing Albany women for the past two months. Their destination was Court of Appeals Hall, a Greek Revival building completed in 1842 for use as a state office building. The court had moved there in 1916 from its old home on the third floor of the State Capitol. The courtroom was and is an imposing facility that largely duplicates the appearance of the court's old home in the State Capitol building. It features an elaborately carved wooden bench for the seven judges,

wood-paneled walls, a high ceiling with hanging chandeliers that offer sub-
dued lighting, a large bronze-marble-and-onyx fireplace, and a distinctive tall
clock. On the walls are oil portraits of John Jay, Chancellor James Kent, and
past Court of Appeals judges.

The brief submitted to the Court of Appeals by the LIRR legal department
was virtually the same as that used for the Appellate Division. Its only significant addition was one paragraph addressing Justice Seeger's comment that
Mrs. Palsgraf's status as a passenger entitled her to the highest degree of care.
On this point, it stressed that she had not been "injured by any defect in the
cars, roadway, or other appliances of the defendant." In contrast, Wood's brief
sought to take advantage of the Court of Appeals lack of jurisdiction over factual questions by arguing that the LIRR's appeal was based on the facts, i.e., the
actions of its employees, and whether their actions were the proximate cause of
Mrs. Palsgraf's injuries. Wood argued that the LIRR's employees' conduct was
clearly a factual question, and that their negligence was now "indisputably
fixed," noting that they had been found negligent by the jury and all five Appellate Division justices.[3] On the proximate cause issue, he maintained that the
Court of Appeals had previously held that it was one of fact, not law.[4] Wood also
added another hypothetical situation aimed a refuting the railroad's argument
that it was exonerated by its lack of notice of the package's content — a scenario
suggested by an Appellate Division justice during oral argument — where a
driver whose car struck a pedestrian with a bottle in his pocket would be liable
for injuries caused by the broken glass, despite ignorance of the bottle's
presence.

Both briefs competently argued the standard opposing views on proximate
cause and liability for unforeseen consequences, but they would have no influence on the outcome of the case. Instead, the determinative event was Cardozo's
attendance at an American Law Institute discussion of the *Restatement of
Torts*, Tentative Draft No. 18-R on negligence, held on October 23, 1927, about
six weeks before the Appellate Division decided *Palsgraf*. There, he reportedly
discussed with Warren A. Seavey, Francis H. Bohlen (the Reporter for the ALI's
Restatement of the Law of Torts), Professor Leon Green, and Philadelphia attorney Robert Dechert a hypothetical involving a driver whose negligently driven
car endangers passerby A. The car then strikes a box containing dynamite,
which explodes causing debris to strike a window-washer working ten stories
above the street, who falls onto A. Cardozo is said to have expressed the opinion that the driver would be liable to A.[5] Professor Kaufman believes that this
discussion either took place in an informal setting or represents a composite of
views expressed on different days, or even that this discussion took place four
years later, at the meeting of February 20–21, 1931.[6]

The actual conference minutes for the October 1927 meeting indicate that Cardozo did debate with Learned Hand, Francis H. Bohlen, and Professor Edward Thurston of Yale Law School, another hypothetical where a driver ran over an ordinary-looking paper box containing explosives that then exploded, wrecking a house. Cardozo's position was: "If I run down the box the only interest invaded is the ownership in that box. I run the risk of causing any damage to that box which may happen. . . . But I have not been negligent towards any other interest, that is, to the adjoining property."[7] This, as Professor Kaufman observes, is the position taken in *Palsgraf*,[8] indicating that Cardozo was doctrinally committed to denying recovery to the unforeseeable plaintiff. Thus, the professor concludes that Cardozo brought a "fully developed doctrinal analysis" to his consideration of *Palsgraf* and "fit the case into the theoretical framework."[9] In addition, since Cardozo was aware of the work of the ALI advisers on the issue, he would have seen *Palsgraf* as an opportunity to establish a definitive precedent that resolved the duty/foreseeability issue.[10] As a result, there was no real chance, as Matthew W. Wood may have hoped, that the Court of Appeals would merely issue a memorandum or per curium opinion affirming Justice Seeger with little or no comment.

Ever since the publication of Dean William L. Prosser's 1953 article, *Palsgraf Revisited*,[11] a story has circulated that Cardozo, between the Appellate Division and Court of Appeals decisions, inappropriately discussed the case at an ALI advisers' meeting.[12] However, Professor Kaufman's study of the meeting minutes found that neither *Palsgraf* nor any other railroad hypothetical was discussed on October 23rd. He also indicates that the only meeting of the ALI advisers between the Appellate Division decision on December 9, 1927, and the Court of Appeals decision on May 29, 1928, was on December 12 and 13, 1927, making it highly unlikely that the opinion could have been discussed.[13] He adds that Cardozo could not have attended that meeting since he was then hearing arguments in Albany.[14] Professor Kaufman's statement that it was unlikely the case was discussed seems well founded since December 9, 1927, was a Friday. There was a short *New York Times* article on the decision that appeared on Sunday, December 11, but it appeared on page 29 and provided only one-sentence summaries of the majority and dissenting opinions.[15] The only venue for full publication was the *New York Law Journal*, but the only mention of the case on December 10 was in a listing along with approximately forty-three other decisions, stating merely: "Judgment and order affirmed with costs."[16] There was also no full publication on any day early the following week.

The parties had to wait three months for the court to hand down its decision. When it did so on May 29, 1928, LIRR was presented with a victory on grounds that it never argued. Cardozo once said that after certain cases had traveled around the court's consultation table, they become something "its own mother wouldn't recognize. . . ."[17] This was the situation with *Palsgraf*, which had been argued as strictly a proximate cause action. Now, Cardozo, joined by Pound, Lehman, and Kellogg, maintained that "the law of causation, remote or proximate, is . . . foreign to the case before us."[18] Noting that there was "nothing in the situation to suggest to the most cautious mind that the parcel wrapped in newspaper would spread wreckage through the station,"[19] he declared that Mrs. Palsgraf was beyond "[t]he range of reasonable apprehension." Cardozo reasoned: "The conduct of the defendant's guard, if a wrong in its relation to the holder of the package, was not a wrong in its relation to the plaintiff"[20] and that what she needed to show was a "'a wrong' to herself; i.e., a violation of her own right, and not merely a wrong to some one else, nor conduct 'wrongful' because unsocial, but not 'a wrong' to any one."[21] He then concluded: "The risk reasonably to be perceived defines the duty to be obeyed; and risk imports relation; it is risk to another or to others within the range of apprehension."[22]

Of the cases provided by the briefs, only three of the twenty-two decisions cited by Wood, and only three of the seventeen cited by the LIRR, appeared in Cardozo's opinion. These were *Scott v. Shepard*,[23] (the *Squib Case*) (cited by Wood and the LIRR); *Paul v. Consolidated Fireworks Co.*,[24] (cited by Wood and the LIRR); *Parrott v. Wells Fargo & Co.*,[25] (cited by the LIRR); and *Adams v. Bullock*,[26] (cited by Wood). Instead of other cases referred to by the brief writers, Cardozo cited a string of opinions supporting the proposition that there must have been a duty to the complaining person, and that negligence in the abstract is not tortious. He also cited numerous secondary authorities, none of which appear in the briefs, including *Pollock on Torts*, which was the source of the famous quote: "Proof of negligence in the air, so to speak, will not do."[27]

Cardozo's legal arguments were accompanied by a recitation of facts that has been characterized as "highly abstract"[28] and "elliptical."[29] Mrs. Palsgraf and the LIRR were not mentioned by name, nor were any details provided about them.[30] Omitted was any indication of the force of the explosion or the nature of Mrs. Palsgraf's injuries. The opinion mentioned that she had purchased a ticket for a trip to Rockaway Beach, but refrained from explicitly identifying her or the men with the fireworks as passengers. The train involved in the events is described as merely "bound for another place."[31] Cardozo accurately notes that the package was covered with newspaper, but then describes it as "small,"[32] although newspaper accounts all said that it was large, and trial witness Grace Gerhardt described it as "quite a large bundle."[33] He gave the length of the package as fifteen inches,[34] although the Gerhardts had stated that it may have been as large as eighteen or twenty inches in diameter.[35] When describing the attempts of the two passengers to board the moving train, Cardozo did not explicitly characterize the efforts of the trainmen to assist them as negligence. Instead, like the railroad's brief, he stated that the passenger with the bundle appeared to be in danger of falling. The record does not explicitly support this claim, although Herbert Gerhardt, when cross-examined by McNamara, stated that the man with the bundle was afraid of losing his balance.

On the critical issue of Mrs. Palsgraf's distance from the explosion, Cardozo declined to provide any estimated distances measured in feet. Instead, he placed Mrs. Palsgraf at the "other end of the platform many feet away."[36] Although Lillian and Elizabeth used the phrases "other end of the platform," and "other end of the station" in describing the location of the newsstand,[37] this surely meant only that part of the platform located on the other side of the stairway entrance from where they were standing. His use of the term "many feet away" ignored the clarification of Lillian's estimate of her distance from her mother that set it at only twenty-nine or thirty feet,[38] and shows he made no connection between Mrs. Palsgraf's testimony on how far from the steps she went after reaching the platform, and Herbert Gerhardt's statements as to his location near those steps and his wife's testimony about their proximity to the accident. Cardozo also used the terms "far away," "distant," and "far removed," to describe Mrs. Palsgraf.[39] Presumably, he is speaking figuratively here, meaning that since Mrs. Palsgraf was outside the zone of foreseeable harm, she was "far" or "distant" from the alleged negligent act. As for the package, Cardozo maintained that it "fell upon the rails," an occurrence reported nowhere in the trial testimony, and that moved the site of the explosion even farther from wherever Mrs. Palsgraf was standing.[40]

The affidavit accompanying Wood's motion for reargument explained Cardozo's factual inaccuracies by suggesting: "The learned Chief Judge has most certainly confused [Mrs. Palsgraf] with . . . [her] little daughter Lillian. . . ."[41] Judge Posner states that it is impossible to say whether Cardozo's factual inaccuracies in *Palsgraf* were conscious,[42] while Professor Kaufman's position is that "sometimes, as in *Palsgraf* . . ., [Cardozo] left out some facts that now seem important to a full understanding of the problem, especially from the perspective of the losing party. This situation did not happen often, and I see no evidence that Cardozo was being manipulative."[43] He maintains that Cardozo's famous remark in *Law and Literature* that "one must permit oneself, and that quite advisedly and deliberately, a certain margin of misstatement,"[44] related not to deliberate misstatements, but to the omission of extraneous facts that would overload the opinion.[45] He also explains Cardozo's treatment of the facts as an "unintended consequence of his literary style."[46]

As Professor Kaufman observes, a simplification or recasting of the facts has been noted in other Cardozo opinions. One commentator notes that in *MacPherson*, "Cardozo overstates the simplicity and clarity of the plaintiff's proof,"[47] resulting in a case that was "more factually compelling than it actually was," making the rejection of privity "necessary and appropriate."[48] A second example is *Murphy v. Steeplechase Amusement Co.*,[49] where the plaintiff had been injured on a ride called the "Flopper." Here, another commentator examined the trial transcript and concluded that "Cardozo's opinion is inaccurate and misleading. . . . [T]he Flopper was more dangerous than the opinion implies."[50] He added that the result in *Murphy* is a "compelling tale, . . . insinuat[ing] that the legal standard is as compelling as the tale."[51]

As in *MacPherson* and *Murphy*, it is difficult not to conclude that the inaccuracies and embellishments in the *Palsgraf* facts were crafted to support the result. As Judge Posner concludes, Cardozo's version of the event was "schematic"[52] and "slanted."[53] Once Cardozo determined that Mrs. Palsgraf was not in the "range of reasonable apprehension," he selectively utilized the record to present a simplified account of the event that exaggerated its unforeseeability — a task made easier by imprecise testimony (most notably Lillian's statement that the newsstand "was at the other end of the platform" and Elizabeth's testimony that the newsstand was "at the other end of the station") and Humphrey's inaccurate description of where the package fell. Cardozo's choice of language also enhanced his position. In addition to the use of "far" or "distant" to describe Mrs. Palsgraf's proximity to the explosion, such phrases as "bound for another place" and "many feet away" portray "a disjointed series of unrelated incidents . . . [providing] no basis . . . for tracing any chain of causality among events,"[54] that effectively eliminated the issue of proximate causation.

Judge Andrews's dissent, like that of Lazansky in the Appellate Division, contained little factual information. However, as one commentator has noted, unlike Cardozo, Andrews did "narrate a simple chain of consecutive events."[55] He began with the passenger's attempt to board the train and stated that the package fell between the platform and the cars, and that the concussion broke some scales. Unlike Cardozo, he noted that the explosion was "violent."[56] However, as Judge Posner has observed, he effectively conceded the facts to Cardozo, failing to point out the factual inaccuracies in the majority opinion, particularly the critical issue of Mrs. Palsgraf's distance from the explosion.[57] Apparently mistaking or assuming that Lillian's estimate of her distance from her mother was also Mrs. Palsgraf's distance from the explosion, Andrews initially stated that the distance was "considerable,"[58] and later speculated that it may have been "25 or 30 feet, [or] perhaps less,"[59] still sufficiently distant to place her far outside Cardozo's zone of foreseeable risk. Whether Andrews actually did not bother to read the record, as Judge Posner has suggested,[60] cannot be determined, but his error on such an important question certainly suggests that he did not read it carefully.

In his dissent, Andrews accepted that the LIRR employees were negligent, and that the railroad was liable for the proximate consequences of that negligence. However, unlike Wood's brief, he did not cite precedents such as the *Balloon Case*. Instead, he discussed the nature of negligence, concluding, "every one owes to the world at large the duty of refraining from those acts that may unreasonably threaten the safety of others."[61] Andrews then presented a hypothetical proposed by "a distinguished and helpful writer on the law of torts,"[62] where a chauffeur collides with another car filled with dynamite, causing an explosion, killing A who is on a nearby sidewalk, and injuring B and C who are sitting at windows — B in a building opposite, and C a block away. The noise also startles a nursemaid ten blocks away causing her to drop a baby. The scenario's author suggested that A could recover, but that C and the baby could not because the chauffeur had no reason to think his conduct placed either the baby or C at risk. As for B, that was regarded as a question for the jury. The use of this hypothetical may be another example of the influence of the Restaters on *Palsgraf* since, as one commentator has suggested, the "distinguished and helpful writer" may have been *Restatement* Reporter Francis H. Bohlen.[63]

Andrews' conclusion regarding the hypothetical was that if C and the baby were to be denied recovery, it was because the chauffeur's negligence was not the proximate cause of their injuries. However, as to proximate cause, he concluded that the law's reluctance to trace a sequence of events past a given point is "indicative on our notions of public policy,"[64] and a "question of expediency,"[65] adding that there is little guidance in how far to go "other than common sense."[66] With regard to *Palsgraf*, he posed the question of "what might ordinarily be expected to follow the fire or explosion," and concluded, "it needed no great foresight to predict that the natural result would be to injure one on the platform at no greater distance from its scene than the plaintiff."[67] He also used against the LIRR the statement in its brief that "it cannot be denied that the explosion was the direct cause of the plaintiff's injuries."[68] Citing the direct and continuous sequence of events, he concluded that it "cannot [be said] as a matter of law that the plaintiff's injuries were not the proximate result of the negligence."[69]

Wood waited until early September to file a motion for reargument. The affidavit accompanying the motion stated that "there was an apparent error in the understanding of the facts of the case,"[70] and, as previously noted, suggested that Cardozo must have mistaken Mrs. Palsgraf's position on the platform for that of Lillian. Complaining about the use of such terms as "far" and "distant," it grouped together all the allusions to distance in the trial transcript, and concluded that Mrs. Palsgraf was likely the passenger nearest to the site of the explosion — even closer than the Gerhardts, who were six or seven feet from where the package was dropped.[71] It also stated that both the man with the fireworks and the train were moving toward Mrs. Palsgraf and that, after the package was dropped, the force of the moving train brought it even closer to her, with the result that she was standing "immediately at the spot where the explosion took place."[72]

The affidavit alluded to Andrews' hypothetical about victims A, B, and C who were at different distances from an explosion. It noted that Andrews believed that only C might be unable to recover, and claimed that Mrs. Palsgraf, who was surely in the position of A or B, was erroneously placed in the distant "C" class. It also complained about the characterization of the package as small, and objected to the imposition of costs, adding that seven of the thirteen judges who had heard the case had found for the plaintiff. The affidavit also claimed that Cardozo's opinion was "so analytical and metaphysical and so finely drawn that it is not operable as a basis of sound justice. . . ."[73] It added: "I feel that an incorrect rule of law has been promulgated . . . which not only deprives [Mrs. Palsgraf] of [her] rights but will also deprive others in the future. . . ."[74]

On September 26, the railroad filed an answer to Wood's motion, stating that Cardozo's opinion accurately stated the facts of the case. Both sides must have known that the chances for a reargument were remote. The court rarely granted such motions; in 1927 and 1928, there had been sixty-seven denials. Only one motion was granted, and this was in a case where Judge Andrews had handed down a brief opinion only three weeks after oral argument,[75] not for a major exercise in tort theory by the court's foremost judge. Moreover, Cardozo was notably hostile to requests reopen a case. According to Judge Samuel Seabury, "the loser who asked him to reopen a decision once made, found a cold welcome."[76] Cardozo himself once remarked about a request for a rehearing, "I will give it my most biased consideration."[77] Thus, he would hardly have been receptive to motion for reargument stating that his opinion was incorrect on the law and facts, and was not the basis for sound justice. Not surprisingly, the court wasted little time in rejecting Wood's motion. A memorandum opinion that Professor Kaufman believes was written by Cardozo, stated: "If we assume that the plaintiff was nearer the scene of the explosion than the prevailing opinion would suggest, she was not so near that injury from a falling package, not known to contain explosives, would be within the range of reasonable prevision."[78]

Chapter 10
THE CASE RECONSIDERED

When it replied to Wood's motion for reargument, the LIRR claimed that Cardozo's opinion disclosed a "correct understanding of the facts"[1] was based on the fact that Mrs. Palsgraf and Elizabeth did not see anyone attempt to board the moving train, and because the Gerhardts, who did witness the explosion, did not see Mrs. Palsgraf or the scales until after the explosion had taken place.[2] However, neither of these points is necessarily convincing. As the overhead photo of the East New York Station shows, anyone standing by the entry steps might not be able to see a person located eight to ten feet away in the corner formed by the enclosure around these steps. In addition, even if Mrs. Palsgraf was in the Gerhardts' line of sight, they would have had no reason to notice her. As for Elizabeth Palsgraf, at the critical moment she could easily have been directing her gaze in a different direction.

As for Mrs. Palsgraf's actual distance from the explosion, although she may not have been quite as close as alleged by the affidavit, she was most certainly far closer than suggested by Cardozo or Andrews. Even though the record provides no direct indication of what Mrs. Palsgaf's position was relative to the site of the explosion, as noted previously, a comparison of the statements of Mrs. Palsgraf, her daughter, Lillian, and Herbert Gerhardt regarding distances and their respective positions on the platform provides clear evidence that she was quite close to the blast. In her affidavit that accompanied the motion for reargument, Mrs. Palsgraf claimed that after purchasing tickets she and Elizabeth went up to the platform, turned right, and walked only eight to ten feet from the entry steps.[3] Herbert Gerhardt indicated that he and his wife were standing where passengers came up to the platform from the ticket office when the men with the bundle rushed past, striking Grace Gerhardt in the stomach with the package. This places him as few as eight feet from Mrs. Palsgraf, meaning that the two men were also not very far from her when they began their dash for the train. According to Grace, she and her husband were six or seven feet away when the package was dropped, and Herbert stated that the package exploded five or ten feet from where it fell, meaning that as the train dragged the package along, it was taking it closer to Mrs. Palsgraf. As for Lillian, after climbing the steps, she turned left to go to the newsstand, and her distance from her mother at the time of the explosion was only twenty-nine or thirty feet. However, there is nothing in Lillian's testimony or in her 1978 *Harvard Law Record* recollections that indicates that she was in close proximity to the actual explosion. Thus, Mrs. Palsgraf may have been about thirty feet from Lillian, but she would have been considerably closer than that to the Gerhardts and the exploding fireworks, easily within the approximately ten-foot range suggested by Judge Posner,[4] which is about the same distance the newspapers reported that the scale was from the explosion.

Further support for an estimate of ten feet is provided by evidence regarding the width of the platform. The most likely location for a scale would be at the rear of the platform, against the wooden wall separating it from Atlantic Avenue. If the explosion took place directly in front of Mrs. Palsgraf, her distance from the blast would have been approximately that of the platform's width. A visual comparison of the width of the platform as shown in the station photographs with the space between the track rails[5] shows it to have been ten to twelve feet wide, again confirming newspaper accounts that the scale was about that distance from the explosion.[6] The overhead photo also helps illustrate another aspect of Mrs. Palsgraf's testimony, revealing that just east of the entry steps was a shed-like structure that would have provided the "corner" by which she said she was standing, and where she and Elizabeth were pushed by the panic-stricken crowd seeking to exit the station.[7]

As for the train, one of its most important features relating to Cardozo's fact pattern is the size of the gap between the side of the cars and the station platform. This distance for the two types of electric coaches then in use, the MP-41 and the larger MP-54, was approximately six inches.[8] The fireworks package, as described by the Gerhardts, was an oval-shaped bundle fifteen to twenty inches in diameter. Thus, the comparative dimensions of the package and the space between the train and platform indicate that the bundle simply could not have fallen to the tracks unless it was dropped between the cars. These dimensions also lend support to the testimony of Lillian Palsgraf and the Gerhardts that the bundle became wedged (or at least partially wedged) between the side of the car and the edge of the platform and then was dragged and crushed until its contents exploded.[9]

It has been suggested that the explosion could not have knocked over the scale since "these were ordinary fireworks, and not bombs."[10] Efforts to explain the force of the explosion have even included the fanciful suggestion that sticks of dynamite used by the railroad caused the explosion.[11] However, ordinary fireworks are quite capable of causing considerable damage, serious injuries, and even death.[12] Regardless of their potential explosive power, the *Palsgraf* fireworks were likely to explode if dropped or mishandled. Shells containing flash powder are more sensitive to shock and friction than those made from ordinary black powder;[13] this sensitivity to friction makes pyrotechnic explosives more hazardous than high explosives. Increasing the possibility of an explosion was the common use in 1920s fireworks of a volatile chlorate compound as an oxidizer.[14] Thus, it would hardly be surprising that a package containing such materials would quickly explode if caught between a moving train and the station platform.

There has been speculation that the exploding fireworks included a Roman candle.[15] However, if the *Palsgraf* fireworks were in fact similar to those in a package abandoned by the would-be passengers, this can be ruled out, since those fireworks were described as being three or four inches in diameter, and Roman candles are generally only fourteen to sixteen millimeters wide.[16] Although there are Roman candles that are up to three to four inches wide, these were rare in the 1920s, and candles of such width were two or three feet long. In addition, Roman candles, with one open end designed to eject stars, have far less explosive power than shells.

If one assumes, as did some of the first newspaper accounts, that the contents of the exploded package were similar to those in the package left behind at the scene — six fireworks, approximately eighteen inches in length and three to four inches in diameter — this strongly suggests that they were four-break Italian-style shells, each consisting of one shell (or break) to cause the loud "salute" and three additional shells to produce the white, green, and red colors of the Italian flag.[17] These breaks consist of short cylinders of equal diameter and length joined together with fuses projecting into the adjoining section.[18]

Even if more were definitely known about the contents of the bundle, it would still be difficult to calculate precisely the explosive power of the fireworks. Although each firework would have contained a black powder lifting charge, the most important consideration in estimating the strength of any explosion is the contents of the four breaks.[19] Of the four breaks in each firework, the "salute," containing flash powder consisting of fine aluminum powder and an oxidizer, would have had the greatest explosive power.[20] The explosive power of such salutes has been estimated at 0.4 to 0.6 sticks of TNT.[21] In contrast, the breaks, designed to produce the colored star display, contain only a small black powder explosive charge along with selected chemical compounds that produce the desired color when they oxidize.[22] The explosive power of each of these color breaks could have been anywhere from 0.2 to 0.4 sticks of TNT.[23]

Regardless of the amount of explosive material contained in the fireworks, their strength would have been enhanced by being contained and compressed within a hard paper casing.[24] Although newspaper articles described the fireworks casing as cardboard, the packaging was actually made of layered paper and glue, with a patterned wrapping of string known as "spiking," that produced a hard, lightweight, and strong casing; the resulting appearance often caused the shells to be called "salamis." Such fireworks could weigh three to four pounds, meaning that any package containing several shells would be relatively heavy, helping to explain why the package was dropped.

As for the strength of the blast wave actually produced by the explosion, even if the exact amount and composition of the materials in the *Palsgraf* fireworks were known, this would still be difficult to estimate since air blasts are subject to too many variables to allow for more than a rough estimate of the energy released.[25] In addition, fireworks produce an unequal blast wave, so the amount of force directed in a given direction can vary.[26] If all the explosive material possibly contained in the fireworks had detonated simultaneously, the blast from the *Palsgraf* explosion could have been sufficient to kill or cause serious injury at close range. However, the sequential explosions described in the newspapers would have created a pulsating blast effect, with each pulse having less explosive force than a simultaneous explosion.[27]

When estimating the force of the blasts, other factors to consider are how far persons or objects are from the explosion, since the blast effect of explosions diminishes rapidly with distance,[28] and is reduced by the presence of intervening objects. The force of the explosions might also have been reduced because a blast wave from a platform-level explosion would be moving toward the scale at an upward angle, and because the edge of the platform could have partially shielded persons and objects from its effects. Finally, the nature of the injuries suffered by those on the platform may not be a good indicator of the severity of the blast. Injuries from explosions depend not only on the strength of the blast, but also by the body's orientation,[29] and it is reportedly not uncommon for those near exploding fireworks not to be hit by flying debris or be injured by the blast wave.[30]

At the trial, Mrs. Palsgraf testified that she was choked in smoke and that there was a ball of fire and flying glass, all before the scale struck her.[31] Dean Prosser, in *Palsgraf Revisited*, finds in this interval support for the theory that the crowd, not the explosion, knocked down the scale.[32] However, her testimony is not inconsistent with the scale being toppled by the explosion. Newspaper reports indicated that the fireworks did not explode all at once. Thus, there could have been smoke and a ball of fire from explosions of the colored star shells, accompanied by a blast wave sufficiently strong to break glass, before more powerful explosions toppled the scale. Thus, the scenario described by Mrs. Palsgraf closely matches the effects of a sequential explosion of multi-break fireworks shells.[33]

In addition to blast waves moving directly across the platform, another consideration is the effect of shock reflection. Some of the shock waves from the explosions would have been directed perpendicularly against the unyielding steel side of the car and then would have been reflected directly back across the platform in a kind of soundboard effect.[34] Waves would have also reflected back from the wooden wall at the back of the platform. Thus, a pulsating blast wave created by sequential explosions would have also included weaker blast reflected back from both the side of the steel rail car and the back of the platform.[35] Another factor could have been the construction of the platform. Concrete transmits shock waves more effectively than wood, and if the scale were resting on such a surface, this too could have helped destabilize it.

The key object against which the blast wave was directed is described in the newspapers as a penny scale. Herbert Gerhardt's testimony that "the glass was busted and blown" after the explosion,[36] and Mrs. Palsgraf's description of its height, suggests that the scale involved in *Palsgraf* was the then-common lollipop type, so called because of its shape.[37] A typical lollipop scale was made of cast iron with a porcelain finish.[38] They weighed approximately 250 pounds and were about six feet tall.[39] At the top of such scales was a large clock-like glass face, covering the dial and the mechanism.[40] The bases, narrower than the glass face, ranged from twelve to fourteen inches wide and twenty-six to twenty-eight inches from front to back, so the scales could be regarded as top-heavy.[41] Considering the height of such a scale, and the narrowness of its base, it is entirely possible that a sufficiently powerful blast wave could have immediately knocked it down, or more likely, considering the absence of truly major damage and serious injuries, weaker pulsating waves could just have destabilized it, and then rocked it until it fell over.[42]

Two other suggested explanations for the scale's fall are possible, assuming that it was not knocked over by the explosion. One proposal is that the scale was really tipped over by the stampeding crowd, not the force of the explosion.[43] Since the Palsgrafs were not far from the platform entrance, and Elizabeth described how, after the explosion, the crowd pushed her and her mother into a corner, it is not inconceivable that this surging mass of people could have toppled the scale in its attempt to flee the platform. This scenario also draws support because nobody ever reported seeing the explosion knock over the scale. Instead, both the newspaper reports, and trial witness Herbert Gerhardt, described the condition of the scale only after the explosion. In her 1970s interview, Lillian Palsgraf Farmer was very definite about the explosion toppling the scale,[44] but, considering her distance from her mother and the black smoke that instantly covered the platform, it is likely that she was merely repeating what her mother and sister had once told her.

The other alternative suggestion is that damage to the platform somehow caused the scale to tip.[45] Since the newspaper stories described damage to the platform, it is also not impossible that the platform under the scale buckled, either causing it to fall or making it more vulnerable to being knocked over by subsequent explosions or by the crowd. If, at the time of the explosion, the main part of the platform, like the far end shown in the Prosser casebook photo, consisted of planks running at an angle from the outer edge to the rear wall or partition,[46] those planks directly impacted by the explosion might have been the same ones that ran beneath the scale, meaning any buckling would have helped tip it over.

Of the many scenarios explaining the fall of the scale, those that can definitely be ruled out are the versions provided by Cardozo and Andrews. As previously noted, a package with the dimensions described at the trial could not have fallen to the tracks unless it fell between the cars. However, this was not the scenario described in the trial testimony, and, since the package was dropped by one of the railcar doors, presumably straight down, it would not have fallen into the space between the cars. Furthermore, even if the bundle had somehow fallen to track level and exploded either from the impact of the fall or from being run over by the wheels, anyone and anything on the platform would then have been shielded from the blast by a multi-ton steel passenger coach.[47] Even more unlikely is that Mrs. Palsgraf and the scale were at the other end of the station as described by Cardozo, or even the twenty-five to thirty feet as speculated by Andrews. At either distance, any blast wave likely to be produced by fireworks in a package the size of the one described would have mostly dissipated.[48] Also, since the platform was described as being crowded, a blast wave traveling thirty feet or more would have been largely blocked by the crowd of persons that would have been between the site of the explosion and the scale. More importantly, any explosion capable of knocking down a heavy scale located at a distance of thirty feet or one that was literally "at the other end of the station," would have wreaked havoc on anything or anyone that was much closer.

When it found the trainmen had been negligent and awarded Mrs. Palsgraf $6,000 in damages,[49] the jury set the stage for the endless debate and commentary that are now part of the history of *Palsgraf*. Despite the jury's verdict, speculation over what really happened on August 24, 1924, includes the question of whether there was really any negligence at all on the part of the railroad. At the trial, Humphrey allowed the jury's decision to stand, but his doubts about the strength of the plaintiff's case are indicated in the statement that his decision on the motion to set aside the verdict was "a close question in my mind."[50] Others have had similar doubts. In his opinion, Cardozo stated: "The man was not injured in his person nor even put in danger. . . . If there was a wrong to him at all, *which may well be doubted*, it was a wrong to a property interest only, the safety of his package."[51] Thirty years later, Judge Henry J. Friendly agreed, stating, "there is little evidence of negligence of any sort" in *Palsgraf*, and adding: "How much ink would have been saved over the years if the Court of Appeals had reversed Mrs. Palsgraf's judgment on the basis that there was no evidence of negligence at all."[52]

In evaluating the various grounds proposed for finding the railroad negligent, those advanced in Wood's initial complaint are the most easily dismissed. Since Mrs. Palsgraf's injuries did not result from being pushed off an overcrowded platform, his claim of negligence based on allowing large numbers of people to gather on the platform, or for failing to promulgate rules for such situations, can be characterized as the type of hyperbolic boilerplate common to negligence complaints. As Wood must have known, along with anyone else familiar with New York area commuter rail travel, the standard that he sets here for the LIRR is utterly unrealistic. Similarly unfounded is his claim that the railroad could be regarded as negligent for failing to recognize the potentially dangerous contents of the newspaper-wrapped package; this was not near the Fourth of July, nor was it the date of any festival that men who appeared to be Italians might be expected to be carrying fireworks.[53]

Initially, the question of the railroad's alleged negligence centers largely on the manner in which the man with the package actually boarded the train. As previously noted, Wood claimed that the conductors, instead of closing the door or barring his path, propelled him from the platform to the car. The LIRR, of course, denied any negligence, claiming that "it does not appear [that the conductors] had the opportunity to prevent the man from boarding the train or to prevent the men from boarding the train or to warn them against such an action"[54] It added: "Faced with such an emergency they cannot be charged with negligence because they elected to assist the man rather than stand idly by and leave him to his fate."[55] Cardozo accepted the railroad's version of the facts by stating that the passenger had already jumped aboard and seemed about to fall when the conductors assisted him, noting that "the purpose of the act, as well as its effect, was to make [the man's] person safe."[56] In contrast, Andrews did not attempt to specify the location of the passenger when the conductors intervened, and stated that the act of knocking the package from the passenger's arms was negligent.[57]

Unfortunately, evidence regarding the conductors' conduct ultimately derives from only a few lines of testimony by the Gerhardts that are lacking in detail, and that can be regarded as contradictory. When questioned by Wood, both Gerhardts stated only that the conductors were trying to help the man with the bundle onto the train. When cross-examined by McNamara, Herbert Gerhardt said that the man with the bundle had already gotten onto the train when the trainmen tried to push and pull him aboard. He added that the man "got on himself any way because he went with a running start."[58] In contrast, when McNamara cross-examined Grace Gerhardt, he phrased his question so that an affirmative answer would indicate that the passenger had not yet boarded the train when the guards attempted to assist him. He asked: "And the second man was about to get on when he dropped the bundle; is that right?" Grace Gerhardt answered that the man was about to get on when he dropped his package while being assisted by the guards. She also stated that the conductor on the train had held the door open, but provided no further details that would support assertions as to whether the trainmen could or could not have prevented the men from attempting to board the moving train. If the conductors did not in fact have a real opportunity to prevent the running men from attempting to board, the question of their negligence then logically rests on whether the man with the package was already aboard when they attempted to assist him. If that were the case, then, as the railroad's brief asserts, the trainmen would really have had no choice about helping him.

Even if the conductor did hold the door open and encouraged the men to board the train, this in itself, under the standards of the 1920s, should not have been conclusive as to the railroad's negligence. Although the *Palsgraf* affidavit claims that it was negligence as a matter of law to board a moving train, or to assist such an attempt, by the 1920s this statement was debatable. In 1886, the Court of Appeals had ruled that such attempts constituted negligence per se,[59] but in 1897 in a case arising from an accident at the East New York Station, the court noted: "It is a matter of common knowledge that it is a daily occurrence that ordinarily prudent persons safely board a train or car moving at two or three miles an hour."[60] A standard negligence treatise of the day agreed. The sixth edition of Shearman and Redfield's *Law of Evidence*, published in 1913, contains the statement: "An attempt to get on or off even a steam train in motion is not negligence *per se*, incapable of justification. . . ."[61] Thus, if it was not necessarily negligent for a passenger to make such an attempt, it would be difficult to argue that to facilitate the attempt would also always constitute a negligent act. This would be particularly true if, as in *Palsgraf*, there was a raised platform, eliminating the chance of tripping on, or falling from, the car's steps. Accordingly, if the conductor held the door open to assist an attempt to board the moving train, the strongest argument for his negligence was that he was doing so for an individual encumbered with a package, who was less likely to be able to board safely.[62]

However, it was not necessarily the practice of LIRR trainmen to encourage persons to board moving trains. In an incident at the Jamaica station in 1923, a man was prevented from boarding a train that was either leaving or about to leave; an argument ensued, and the would-be passenger was arrested for disorderly conduct. In any case, it is possible that with the train involved in *Palsgraf*, the doors were not left open because the conductors wished to afford the running men an opportunity to board the train. LIRR electric cars in 1924 had side doors providing entry and exit through enclosed vestibules, rather than directly into the seating area as is the case with contemporary passenger cars. The doors were operated with manual controls, and when opened, slid back into pockets in the side of the car body. Since the doors were manually operated, it would not be surprising if some were still open when a train started in motion. Furthermore, during the 1920s, LIRR regulations did not mandate that the side doors be closed at all times when trains were in motion. Although a 1917 Public Service Commission order instructed the railroad to institute a rule against leaving the station with the doors open,[63] as late as 1926 the railroad rule book contained no explicit bar against starting to move or even departing the station with doors still open.[64] Instead, they were only required to be shut when approaching and passing through tunnels, on through trains, and on locals making infrequent stops, or in cold weather.

The rationale for finding the railroad negligent because the train started moving with the side doors open, as argued in Wood's briefs and Lazansky's dissent, was that this not only facilitated the attempts of latecomers to jump aboard the train, but also because the cars lacked gates that could be pulled across open doorways to prevent those inside from falling from the train, as did clergyman John C. Whiting in 1921.[65] However, as with instances of persons seeking to board slowly-moving trains, there was no New York precedent establishing that an open door was negligence as a matter of law.[66] Open doors on trains starting to depart and moving at very slow speeds was a common practice in the 1920s, and a railroad's liability generally depended upon the facts of the particular case.[67] In *Palsgraf*, the fact that the train was moving very slowly and had not yet cleared the station would both weigh in the LIRR's favor.[68]

The dimensions and weight of the typical 1920s penny scale are relevant to another possible basis for finding the railroad negligent, one that was not utilized by Matthew W. Wood. One modern torts casebook includes the remark: "anything on a railroad platform so easily knocked over as this scale obviously did not belong there."[69] Another speculates about the outcome of the case if the basis of the *Palsgraf* cause of action had been "the defective scales, which any of the normal shocks and bumps of railroading might have caused to break and fall."[70] The allegedly misplaced and/or defective *Palsgraf* scale was one of hundreds of thousands of such scales placed in public places. They were extremely common in the United States during the 1920s and 1930s, with their popularity peaking in the 1930s, when there were more than 750,000 in the United States;[71] they could be quite profitable, with one at a good location capable of generating an income of $1,000 a year.[72] The leading coin-operated scale company, Peerless Weighing & Vending Machine Corp., had thousands of route men, and, in 1929, was reportedly worth over $50 million.

It was also not a common practice of Peerless and other companies to secure their scales, since their size and weight prevented theft. Despite this large number of unsecured scales, the case reporters provide no evidence that they presented a major safety problem because they fell on people. Instead, reported negligence cases involving scales almost entirely concern passersby who tripped over them.[73] In one published case where a scale fell over, it was a machine placed on a sloping floor of a store vestibule between two entry/exit doorways, and knocked over by a man running for a bus.[74] Even here, the plaintiff's case was dismissed by the trial court, and it took a ruling from the Massachusetts Supreme Judicial Court that such an occurrence was reasonably foreseeable to get a new trial. It is hard to imagine the court making such a ruling in the case of a scale unobtrusively placed at the rear of a level railroad platform, and blown over by a major explosion. Although it has been suggested that Wood did not think of an action based on the negligent placement of the scale,[75] he displayed no inability in his other reported cases to recognize possible grounds for a negligence cause of action. Thus, it is entirely possible that this approach did occur to him, but being aware of size, weight, ubiquity, safety record, and typical placement of such scales, he did not think that such a claim would be any more convincing than the charges in his complaint that the railroad failed to promulgate rules for crowded platforms.

After reviewing the evidence, one can easily understand why Humphrey regarded as a close call his decision on whether to grant the railroad's motion to set aside the verdict, and why Cardozo was skeptical about the case against the railroad. If one applies Cardozo's statement in *Palsgraf*, that "the risk reasonably to be perceived defines the duty to be obeyed,"[76] or the formula of Judge Learned Hand that the extent of duty is determined by the probability of an accident, the gravity of the injury, and the burden of precautions,[77] an examination of the actual facts favors the LIRR. If one accepts the railroad's claim that the conductors had no choice but to aid the man with the bundle, it is clear that preventing him from falling outweighed the risk to a package. Even if one rejects the railroad's version of the conductors' actions, preventing a passenger from missing his train appears to outweigh the apparent risks. The danger to a passenger boarding a very slow-moving train was minimal, particularly when he was young and seemingly able-bodied, and was entering from a raised platform, level with the door of the car. In addition, as has been pointed out so often in the past, there was nothing in the appearance of a bundle wrapped in newspaper that indicated that it was either of any great value or posed any particular danger.

However, assuming that the railroad employees were indeed negligent in their treatment of the passenger with the fireworks, the question remains how the case might be decided under a more plausible fact pattern than the one offered by Cardozo. Here, a scenario featuring a more powerful explosion and putting Mrs. Palsgraf no more than ten or twelve feet away does not change the result under Cardozo's own unforeseeable plaintiff standard. Since Wood's motion for reargument, based on claims that Mrs. Palsgraf was the closest person to the explosion, was rejected, Cardozo would require Mrs. Palsgraf to have been virtually next to the conductors when the package was knocked loose in order to belong to the class of persons to whom a duty of care was owed. Thus, a more accurate rendition of the facts does not adversely affect his position. In fact, an accurate description of the force of the explosion strengthens his argument since it is hardly foreseeable that such a powerful blast could result from the innocuous-looking package described in the testimony.

Equally unpromising for a plaintiff like Mrs. Palsgraf is the *Restatement (Second) of Torts*. As Professor Epstein observes, the *Restatement* appears to accept Cardozo's position regarding classes of persons to who duty is owed when it states:

> If the actor's conduct creates a recognizable risk of harm only to a particular class of person, the fact that it causes harm to a person of a different class, to whom the actor could not reasonably have anticipated injury, does not render the actor liable to the persons so injured.[78]

Thus, again, given Mrs. Palsgraf's lack of immediate proximity to the explosion, and the unforeseeability of the events, more accurate facts would not affect the outcome of the case.

An altered version of the facts, however, certainly strengthens the position of Andrews' dissent. By creating a general duty of care to the world at large,

Andrews extends the range of potential liability to unforeseeable plaintiffs. As one commentator has observed, this then "throws the issue . . . back into the morass of 'proximate cause,' and the search for some reasonably close connection between the defendant's conduct and the injury."[79] However, even though the injury to Mrs. Palsgraf involved direct causation, acceptance of Andrews' view that she should recover founders on the nature of the chain of events. As Dean Prosser states: "What did happen to her is too preposterous. Her connection with the defendant's guards and the package is too tenuous. . . . She is too remote."[80] This argument loses its force if the explosion is portrayed as a powerful platform-level blast that caused both injuries to others and extensive physical damage, and if Mrs. Palsgraf is placed considerably closer to the site of the event. Conversely, Andrews' position becomes far more persuasive when it no longer relates to a wildly improbable fact pattern that makes the event seem highly unforeseeable.[81]

Increasing the persuasiveness of Andrews' position also benefits the unforeseeable plaintiff since ultimately determining the issue on the basis of proximate cause, absent special circumstances, leaves the decision to a jury, not a judge,[82] and juries can, given sufficient evidence, award damages to an unforeseeable plaintiff. This, of course, is exactly what happened at the *Palsgraf* trial. As Judge Noonan observes, the Brooklyn jurors were not likely to be sympathetic to railroads,[83] and, when presented with a modicum of evidence alleging negligence by the railroad's employees, and with a direct chain of causation, they took the opportunity to return a verdict in favor of a poor working-class woman.

Finally, a more accurate rendition of the facts could only help Mrs. Palsgraf under the standard set by the discussion draft of the *Restatement (Third) of Torts: General Principles*, which, as one commentator has noted, "kill[s] the *Palsgraf* analysis."[84] Section 6 of the draft would make findings of no duty unusual, and such findings would have to be "based on judicial recognition of special problems of principle or policy that justify the withholding of liability."[85] Not only would she benefit from this greatly broadened concept of duty, but her status as a fare-paying passenger injured while in close proximity to a powerful explosion negligently caused by railroad employees would ensure that she would not find her case falling into any of the exceptions to the general duty rule.

It has been noted that there were possible social and economic implications in the choice of negligence doctrine made in *Palsgraf* — a choice between the welfare of the traveling public and the need to relieve railroads, a critical component of modern life, of undue liability for some of the inevitable accidents that their operations produced.[86] Cardozo's standard would protect common carriers from suits by unforeseeable plaintiffs, while the Andrews approach with its broader concept of duty, and its frank acknowledgment of policy factors in determining liability, would appear to be more adverse to large and wealthy corporate defendants. Although this question properly belongs to the controversial topic of the influence of economics on the development of tort law during the nineteenth and early twentieth centuries, when the focus is narrowed to the New York Court of Appeals and common carriers, there is little evidence of an overly solicitous attitude for the economic well-being of large corporations.

In 1858, when a passenger was injured because a train derailed after striking a cow, the court set a very high standard for railroads, calling for the "utmost foresight as to possible dangers and the utmost prudence in guarding against them. . . ."[87] A few years later, it set an extremely high standard for latent defects in passenger cars, approving the lower court's ruling "that [the railroad] must be held accountable, in every event, to furnish a road-worthy coach; and that, if the event proved it not to have been so, he must suffer the consequences."[88] Concerns about excessive liability did influence the Court of Appeals decision in *Ryan v. New York Central Railroad*,[89] the case that established the "first burning" rule, and the determination five years later, that railroads were "not held to an absolute warranty that the passengers shall not be injured, rendering them liable in any event, in the absence of negligence."[90] However, in 1876, it left them vulnerable to pro-plaintiff juries in lawsuits arising from the all-too-common grade-crossing accidents — actions that could and did result in large verdicts — when it ruled that the question of contributory negligence in such cases "is ordinarily one of fact for the jury."[91]

As noted in chapters 5, 6 and 8, the thirteen judges who heard *Palsgraf* also had demonstrated no particular past propensity for favoring the financial interests of the railroads over passengers and members of the public. As for Cardozo, Professor Kaufman maintains that "[e]ven when the conduct was attributable to large corporate business, his focus in negligence cases was on the individual actors. He did not socialize the issue into broader protection."[92] In any case, his standard holding that defendants were not liable to persons beyond the zone of foreseeable harm did nothing to protect railroads from liability for injuries and deaths caused by derailments, collisions, grade-crossing accidents, and for hitting pedestrians. Those suing after such events were invariably foreseeable victims. This is demonstrated by the fact that *Palsgraf* has been cited in only a handful of reported New York opinions involving railroads; only one case, *Marenghi v. New York Transit Authority*,[93] where a passenger was knocked down by another who was rushing for an open car door, has similar elements of proximate causation, unforeseeability, and intervening negligence. Thus, an underlying economic motive in *Palsgraf* can be discounted. When the court discarded proximate cause when deciding liability to unforeseeable plaintiffs, it was narrowly focused on legal doctrine.

Since Cardozo was an affluent childless bachelor with virtually no trial court experience, it has been suggested that his decision in *Palsgraf* represents insensitivity to the less fortunate. It may be true as Judge Noonan suggests that "[t]he childless and *a fortiori* the unmarried will have an approach to a chain of calamities in a case like *Palsgraf* different in outlook and emotional context from that of a reflective spouse and parent,"[94] but there was no pattern to how such life experience influenced a judge's position. Judges Andrews and Crane, who both had children, agreed that Mrs. Palsgraf should recover, but family men like J. Addison Young and Cuthbert W. Pound (who had lost a young son in a tragic accident), held for the LIRR. The childless were also on both sides of the issue, with Henry T. Kellogg concurring with Cardozo, and bachelor William F. Hagarty with Seeger.

In response to the charges of insensitivity, a Cardozo defender has written: "In *Palsgraf*, as in every case with which he dealt, Cardozo . . . thoroughly considered the complex humanity of the litigating parties," adding that if Cardozo were to consider the personal aspects of Mrs. Palsgraf's fate, he should then have kept in mind the possible fate of the railroad employees if their handling of the package resulted in liability for the LIRR.[95] Certainly, Cardozo could have had no real knowledge of the socio-economic plight of people like Mrs. Palsgraf, but Professor Kaufman's research of the Court of Appeals internal case reports has uncovered written evidence of an awareness of the adverse impact his decisions might have on the losing party. In two of these he wrote: "This is a hard case, but I see no escape from an affirmance of the judgment";[96] and, "[t]he result seems to me unfortunate, but I think the statute makes it unavoidable."[97] Cardozo was also aware of the feelings of the losing attorneys, once saying, "I have not been so long away from the bar as to forget what it means to lose a case — the precious judgment won with so much toil reversed and nullified. . . ."[98] Particularly appropriate for *Palsgraf,* is another of his remarks: "We are handing down decisions in closely balanced cases where the patient and careful work of months and even years of conscientious members of the bar is shattered overnight."[99]

In any event, decisions that deprived sympathetic plaintiffs of hard-won verdicts were an unavoidable part of an appellate judge's role. Many are understandably distressed by the *Palsgraf* result because a poor woman lost what certainly was badly-needed money, but it should kept in mind that Mrs. Palsgraf was just one of many who shared that plight. For example, in the *Castle* grade-crossing case, Frederick E. Crane, a *Palsgraf* dissenter, authored an opinion that took a $10,115.31 judgment from the unemployed widow and two small children of the deceased Buffalo stationery salesman, Adolph Castle (money that the New York Central would never have missed). It should also be noted that an appellate judge's appearance of sensitivity or insensitivity may depend on what case is under consideration. In *Hynes*, where a youth was killed by falling electric wires, the allegedly insensitive Cardozo rejected the New York Central's trespass argument and granted a new trial.[100] However, in the veterans' bonus case, Judge Andrews, who would have allowed Mrs. Palsgraf to keep her $6,000 judgment, prevented badly needed money from reaching thousands of needy war veterans. Here, Pound, a member of the *Palsgraf* majority, with Cardozo concurring, wrote a dissent, finding that the payment the bonus was for a public purpose.

More pointed criticism on the insensitivity issue focuses on the award of costs to the LIRR. Here, critics make the same point as Mrs. Palsgraf did in her affidavit: "This is so large a sum to me that I have been and will be unable to pay it, except at great sacrifice after a long time."[101] Judge Noonan states that this awarding of costs was the result of "severe impartiality," and that "[o]nly a judge who did not see who was before him could have decreed such a result."[102] According to another critic, "[f]orcing Palsgraf to pay the railroad's costs displayed insensitivity to her poverty. Cardozo's best defense is that he may have been unaware of [her] plight."[103] When considering Cardozo's alleged insensitivity, it should be noted that Lehman and Pound, both regarded as liberals, with a demonstrated record of sympathy for the less fortunate, concurred in Cardozo's opinion. Similarly, at the Appellate Division level, the dissenters, Lazansky and Young would have awarded costs to the LIRR. Furthermore, a survey of both Appellate Division and Court of Appeals cases of the period shows that in an overwhelming majority of instances, costs were awarded to the prevailing party.

The number of cases where losing negligence plaintiffs were assessed with costs are too numerous to mention. It will suffice to describe a case argued by Judge John F. O'Brien while he was an assistant corporation counsel. Here, Anna Cohen, a poor illiterate immigrant widow whose nineteen-year-old daughter was run down and killed by a New York City garbage and ash truck brought an action against the city. At trial, the widow Cohen testified that she had depended her daughter's $20 per week salary as a hat trimmer, and now lived on only $10 per week sent by a son. In reversing a $17,925 verdict for the plaintiff, Justice Victor J. Dowling, Governor Smith's first choice for the Court of Appeals in 1927, awarded costs to the City of New York. There is nothing in Dowling's background — an experienced jurist and prominent Catholic layman with a wife and two daughters — that suggests he was an insensitive man. Like Cardozo and Lazansky in *Palsgraf*, he was just following a routine practice. Thus, if there was insensitivity present in awarding costs to a large corporation, it was on the part of the system, and not that of any individual judge. In any event, it is a virtual certainty that the railroad did not attempt to collect costs from Mrs. Palsgraf, either because it followed a general policy of not attempting such recoveries, or because it realized, that given her lack of means, it would be utterly futile to do so.[104]

Cardozo's lack of trial judge experience is another consideration. Except for Judge O'Brien, all of his colleagues had spent years on the trial bench interacting with flesh-and-blood plaintiffs and defendants. As veteran New York supreme court Justice Francis B. Delehaunty once told a jury: "Twenty-four years upon the bench in this City have made me more human as the days go by."[105] However, experience as a trial judge was no sure predictor of how a judge would vote in *Palsgraf*. Cardozo may have had virtually no such experience, but other judges with this background voted for the LIRR.

Other forms of life experience and personal levels of affluence were also not telling factors; extremely wealthy Irving Lehman, affluent Henry T. Kellogg, and middle class Edward Lazansky all voted against Mrs. Palsgraf; Andrews, who wrote the dissent, was the affluent son of an affluent judge. One might expect involvement in charitable causes to produce sympathy for a poor plaintiff, but Lazansky and Lehman, both very active in this area, favored the railroad. Despite the fact that his hometown of New Rochelle was once devastated by the effects of a railroad's negligence, J. Addison Young voted for the LIRR, but John F. O'Brien, who had spent his legal career defending the City of New York, voted for the plaintiff. Finally, Mrs. Palsgraf's fellow Brooklynites, Crane, Carswell, and Hagarty would have let her keep her judgment, but not the borough's biggest judicial booster, lifelong resident and Dodger fan Edward Lazansky.

Chapter 11

EPILOGUE

After the accident, Mrs. Palsgraf reportedly never again rode the Long Island Railroad. As for losing her case, according to Lillian, she was upset over it for the rest of her life, and if Cardozo was right about who bore the blame for lost cases in the minds of losing parties, he was the target of her resentment.[1] By 1930, Mrs. Palsgraf had become one of the women the LIRR legal department head, Joseph F. Keany, once said were in short supply — those willing to take in children. The census for that year lists two small children, a boy and a girl, described as boarders, living with her and her daughters.[2] At some point, she reportedly became mute and suffered serious heath problems until her death. At the time she died, Mrs. Palsgraf was sixty-one, and living in Richmond Hill, Queens, with her daughter Elizabeth. On October 27, 1945, she was taken to a Queens hospital suffering from heart failure and died within an hour. The death certificate includes as contributory causes of death diabetes and chronic nephritis. Her body was cremated a few days later.[3] Elizabeth Palsgraf appears never to have married; she died in 1971. Lillian Palsgraf Farmer died in 1985.

Over the years, members of the Palsgraf family have encountered attorneys who were pleasantly surprised to meet a member of the family. However, in what they characterize as the "Curse of *Palsgraf*," family members continued to suffer misadventures in the legal system.[4] In 1965, grandson William Palsgraf fell off an allegedly defective ladder, breaking his wrist and arm, but failed to obtain any compensation. His wife, Barbara, lost her left thumb after catching it in a collapsing ping pong table at a local school, but received only a small settlement. Finally, their son, William III, tripped over a broken curb, broke his ankle, and never received any compensation. However, the family's history with the LIRR includes one positive event. While driving in Douglaston, Queens, William Palsgraf's oil delivery truck slid down an icy street and was saved from going over an embankment when its wheels caught on LIRR track ties. An additional family story is related by Professor Kaufman. He reports that in 1991, J. Scott Garvey, a great-grandson of Mrs. Palsgraf, married Lisa Newell, the first cousin four times removed of Benjamin Cardozo.[5]

Matthew W. Wood's long-running quest to get a judgment for Gladalyn Richter ended in failure. After the Appellate Division ordered a third trial,[6] Wood won a $35,000 default judgment, but within days, the defendant driver declared bankruptcy; Wood then unsuccessfully attempted to have the judgment excluded from discharge on the grounds that by hitting the girl with his car the driver had committed a willful and malicious act.[7] After *Palsgraf*, Wood won a $8,185.83 verdict for Peter J. Duffy, a Brooklyn carpenter seriously injured while working at an Edison facility,[8] and $4,825.80 for Martin J. O'Leary who slipped and fell in a men's room in a building owned by the Standard Oil Company.[9] He lost in a defective-sidewalk case against New York City, but made a successful appeal to the Appellate Division which ordered a new trial.[10] Wood also had two more cases involving injuries suffered by women under unusual circumstances. In 1935, he brought actions against F.W. Woolworth on behalf of both Kathryn G. Treacy, a bookkeeper and cashier who had been severely burned when water-wave combs in her hair burst into flames, and the estate of her daughter who was fatally burned when she attempted to assist her. Like *Palsgraf*, they were factually difficult cases, with the added element of contributory negligence. The mother's action concluded in 1938, when a jury found Woolworth not liable for her injuries.[11] The case of the deceased daughter continued on until 1941, when Wood's motion to amend the original bill of particulars was denied.[12] Wood's post-*Palsgraf* legal career also included several more appearances before the Court of Appeals, including successes in the *O'Leary* slip-and-fall action,[13] and a defeat in a landlord-tenant case on behalf of the Boyd H. Wood Corporation.[14]

The attorney finally married for the first time in 1929. His wife, the French-born Guillemette Riou, had come to America to marry an army officer she had met during World War I, but broke the engagement when her fiance's parents, members of Boston society, disapproved of the match. Opting to stay in the United States, she took a position in a New York bank and met Wood when he came in to check his accounts. Over the years, their names appeared periodically in the *New York Times* society pages as attendees at French-American charitable events. Wood apparently out-lived every other attorney and judge involved with *Palsgraf*; he continued practicing law at his Woolworth Building office until his death in June 1972 at the age of ninety-six. He appears to have done well financially in his law practice and business activities. His funeral was held at the fashionable Frank E. Campbell Funeral Home in Manhattan, and he left a testamentary estate valued at $600,000.[15]

Around the time of the *Palsgraf* appeals, or shortly thereafter, William McNamara left Brooklyn for the suburbs, buying a home in Baldwin, N.Y., that was within walking distance of the LIRR station. Regarded as a "nice guy" by colleagues, he enjoyed a long career with the LIRR's legal department, handling the same type of negligence cases as did his predecessors — trespassers killed or injured,[16] grade-crossing accidents,[17] and one more injured woman passenger.[18] In four more appearances before the Court of Appeals, he won three times and lost once.[19] McNamara's last reported case occurred in 1957;[20] he retired in 1959. McNamara's superior, Joseph F. Keany, continued to serve as the railroad's general solicitor until his death in January 1935. Present among the hundreds at his funeral mass were Brooklyn Bishop Thomas E. Molloy, a United States circuit judge, and nine state supreme court justices. Thomas J. Brennan, who defended the LIRR in so many personal injuries cases during the 1920s and early 1930s retired in April 1940 because of ill health, and died in December at age seventy-one. His brother, Philip A. "Doc" Brennan accepted Boss McCooey's

offer of a supreme court nomination in 1932. He was elected easily, finishing second in a five-man race in which the two Republican candidates trailed badly.
Brennan served on the bench until his retirement in 1942. After his death at
seventy-one in 1944, 600 people, including Justices Lazansky and Hagarty,
attended his funeral services, where a solemn requiem high mass was celebrated by Bishop Molloy.

The LIRR itself continued to have problems. In July 1928, a train on the
Rockaway line went through an open drawbridge, plunging one car into the
water, and injuring twenty-eight people. The next month, its East New York station was again briefly in the news when safecrackers stole over $1,000 from the
ticket office. Ironically, construction related to the elimination of the dangerous
grade-crossings that had caused so many accidents in the 1920s led to the railroad's then-worst disaster, a collision between two trains at Rockville Centre, in
February 1950, that killed twenty-nine people and sent another seventy-seven
to the hospital,[21] dramatically shattering the railroad's record of not having had
a passenger fatality since 1926.[22] This accident was followed in November by an
even worse collision in Richmond Hill, Queens, which killed seventy-seven and
injured 153.[23] One of the dead was an attorney who had gained a $150,000 set-
tlement for the family of a victim of the earlier Rockville Centre crash. After
World War II, the LIRR went into a steady economic decline. Suffering from
chronic financial problems, it finally declared bankruptcy in 1965 and was
taken over by the state. Today, the LIRR is part of the regional Metropolitan
Transportation Authority; it carried 79.9 million riders in 2004.[24]

Justice Burt J. Humphrey's later career included several newsworthy trials,
including one only a few weeks after *Palsgraf* involving a car's plunge off a pier,
and a high-profile criminal case where five Long Beach policemen were acquitted of rum-running charges. His most notable decision, granting an injunction
barring union dockworkers and teamsters from refusing to handle freight delivered by non-union workers, led to a one-day wildcat strike in January 1935 and
briefly threatened to shut down the Brooklyn piers.[25] The next month,
Humphrey was again the subject of news articles when he presided at the first
marriage of eccentric heiress Doris Duke, and again in May, when his house was
burglarized. He retired as a New York Supreme Court justice in 1936, and then
headed an inquiry into ambulance chasing in Brooklyn and Queens that produced many headlines and led to multiple disbarments. After suffering health
problems, Humphrey died of a heart attack at his home in December 1940.

In 1932, Benjamin Cardozo was appointed to the United States Supreme
Court by President Herbert Hoover. It was not an entirely happy move. Although
Cardozo wrote some notable opinions while on the Court, its docket did not
include the kind of common law issues that he had handled with so much success on the New York Court of Appeals. It was also a far less collegial atmosphere than the one he had enjoyed in Albany, and included being subjected to
the overt anti-Semitism of Justice James McReynolds. Judge Andrews retired
from the Court of Appeals at the end of 1928. After leaving the bench, he acted

as an official referee, most notably in a case involving claims by Russian nationals against the Equitable Life Assurance Society.[26] He was also active in the campaign to repeal Prohibition in New York State, believing that it had produced "crime, fraud, corruption and growing disrespect for law."[27] Judges Pound (1932–34), Crane (1934–39), and Lehman (1939–45), in turn succeeded to the position of Chief Judge of the Court of Appeals. All wrote opinions that were considered notable at the time, but the most memorable quote came from Judge Crane in a decision striking down a City of Yonkers ordinance barring the wearing of other than ordinary street attire by persons over sixteen; he wrote: "The Constitution still leaves the opportunity for people to be foolish if they so desire."[28] During the 1930s, Crane joined the exodus to the suburbs, moving from Brooklyn to the Nassau County community of Garden City. After his retirement, he went into law practice in New York City with his son.

There was enough late-life misfortune among the Court of Appeals judges that a selective reading of the facts would support the concept of a judicial "Curse of *Palsgraf*." Cuthbert W. Pound retired at the end of 1934, intending to return to Lockport and practice law. Less than two months later, he collapsed at a Tioga County Bar Association dinner held in his honor, and never regained consciousness. In August 1936, seventy-seven-year-old William S. Andrews fell out of bed the night before his wife's funeral, broke his neck, and was found dead on the floor in the morning. Benjamin Cardozo did not come from a long-lived family — his father, mother, elder brother, and twin sister all died in their fifties.[29] In July 1938, he died at the age of sixty-eight after suffering a heart attack and a stroke. In December 1939, after being ill for several months, John F. O'Brien announced his retirement at the end of the year. However, he died before the end of the month, an event that deprived his widow, Hilda Lockwood O'Brien, of significant retirement benefits. Her action to obtain these benefits went all the way to the Court of Appeals, which unanimously affirmed the Appellate Division ruling against her.[30] Frederick E. Crane's only son, attorney Frederick R. Crane, died of a heart attack after playing badminton in 1941; Crane himself died six years later at seventy-eight. Henry T. Kellogg resigned from the court in 1934 because of ill-health; he died in 1942 at age seventy-three. Like Judge O'Brien, Irving Lehman did not live long enough to retire. In July 1945, he tripped over his pet boxer and broke his ankle in two places; he died of heart attack in September at age sixty-nine.

In contrast, the Appellate Division *Palsgraf* dissenters enjoyed long and active retirements. After serving as presiding justice for fifteen years, Edward Lazansky resumed the practice of law and served on various committees, including one formed in 1945 by Mayor Fiorello La Guardia to investigate racial discrimination in baseball. He was the recipient of several awards, including the title "Brooklyn's Number One Citizen," presented by the Men's League of Brooklyn. He died at age eighty-two on September 13, 1955, a few weeks too soon to see the Dodgers beat the Yankees in the World Series. J. Addison Young finally received his Columbia law degree in 1934 after the Law School tracked down living members of his class and presented them with their diplomas. After his retirement in 1936, he served as an official referee; in this capacity, he added one more newsworthy case to his resume, when, in 1943, he awarded former heavy-weight champion Jack Dempsey custody of his two children. Young continued to hear cases until shortly before his death at eighty-seven in 1953.

The author of the Appellate Division's majority opinion, Albert H.F. Seeger, also had an active retirement, resuming his Newburgh law practice and serving as an official referee. After advancing age forced him to give up trotting horse racing, he continued with horseback riding until a few years before his death from pneumonia in at age eighty-six in 1945. William Hagarty finally took his own advice about lawyers and matrimony at age sixty-five in 1942, marrying his assistant Mary E. McGrath, in a ceremony performed by the Bishop of Brooklyn. He retired in 1947, and died in 1950 at age seventy-two. The only Appellate Division justice who did not live long enough to retire was William B. Carswell. In September 1953, shortly after announcing that he would leave the bench at age seventy, he died during a vacation trip to Quebec.

Dr. Graeme M. Hammond celebrated his eightieth birthday by running four miles at the New York Athletic Club. Afterwards, he hosted a cocktail party at his home where he enjoyed a drink and a cigar. He continued practicing medicine until declining health forced him to curtail his activities; he died at age eighty-six in 1944. Mrs. Palsgraf's physician, Dr. Karl A. Parshall, also enjoyed a long career; he practiced medicine for sixty years, serving as a doctor for the local draft board during World War II. He was eighty-nine when he died in New Jersey in 1967.

Many of the problems that concerned members of the New York bench and bar in the first decades of the twentieth century still persist. Ambulance chasing scandals have vanished in an era of late-night television commercials for personal injuries attorneys, but stories of various forms of lawyer misconduct are still a staple of news articles. In June 2005, it was reported that Long Island had the most dishonest lawyers in the state, accounting for half the reimbursements made by the Lawyers Fund for Client Protection.[31] Imposing a college education prerequisite failed to keep ethnic minorities out of law school,[32] and today's commentary on the social or ethnic composition of the bar involves increasing its diversity. However, the ever-growing number of attorneys still draws comment. According to the Census Bureau, the New York Primary Metropolitan Statistical Area had 42,860 attorneys in November 2003.[33] As for law schools, there are now eleven in the Greater New York area, with a 2004 enrollment of just over 12,000.[34] The number of judges has also continued to increase. Volume 5 of *New York Miscellaneous Reports 3d* lists nineteen Appellate Division justices in the Second Department. The Second Judicial District now includes only Brooklyn and Staten Island, but in that area alone there are sixty-one supreme court justices.[35] Athough Court of Appeals judges are now appointed by the governor, the result of a constitutional amendment approved by voters in 1977,[36] supreme court justices are still elected, and there are periodic reports of judicial misconduct that would seem familiar to the

reformers who targeted Justice Albert Cardozo and his Tammany Hall colleagues. In 2004, a judicial corruption scandal was reported in Brooklyn involving allegations of bribe-taking and the sale of judicial nominations by machine
politicians.

As for Benjamin Cardozo's *Palsgraf* opinion, despite its fame and popularity
with academics and law students, its history in the courts has been problematic.
It was initially praised by many law review articles. As one commentator then
observed, "the logic of the majority . . . seems irrefutable."[37] Another maintained, "under no theory was there any violation of a duty owed to the plaintiff,"[38] while a third expressed the belief that "[t]his decision should go a long
way in avoiding the confusion into which courts have wandered in similar situations."[39] These views have not been uniformly shared by many who subsequently considered the issue. Although the case has certainly stimulated endless
debate, many scholars have questioned its practical influence, noting that its
highly unusual facts limit its actual utility.[40] One commentator has stated,
"The case does not matter. It is a sport: its freakish facts ensure that it will not
be repeated, and no matter how general its language, the case will have (as has
in fact been the case) no precedential importance."[41] Despite its unusual facts,
the opinion's celebrity has enabled it to avoid the slow slide into citation oblivion that is the fate of most appellate decisions.[42] The same strange facts that
limit its value as precedent have helped to provide the fame that has caused it
to be cited with increasing frequency from decade to decade.[43]

CONCLUSION

Palsgraf owes its legendary status to its improbable fact pattern, the endlessly debatable nature of the legal issue it presents, the status of its author, and the natural human interest in the tale of a poor woman who lost her judgment by one vote. On closer inspection, *Palsgraf* also turns out to be the story of an attorney who could take a difficult case a long way, a legal department determined to defend its unloved client to the end, a trial judge who made a close call in favor of the plaintiff, and an intermediate appellate court expeditiously deciding appeals using the standard legal doctrines of the day. As for the accident that set everything in motion, it may have been improbable, but it was certainly not an event that defied the laws of physics.

What then is the result of a fuller understanding of the story of *Palsgraf*? With conventional urban legends or so-called "mysteries" like the Bermuda Triangle or the Curse of King Tut's Tomb, the truth is often regarded as far less interesting than fiction, and too much knowledge simply spoils things. However with *Palsgraf*, additional knowledge about the real people and events does not lessen its appeal. There may be no "mystery" or "riddle," but more information only enhances the unlikely tale of everyday activities of ordinary people at a Brooklyn railroad station suddenly being interrupted by a powerful explosion, and then how a seemingly routine negligence lawsuit was transformed into the most famous torts case in American legal history.

ENDNOTES

INTRODUCTION

[1] 162 N.E. 99 (N.Y. 1928).

[2] Thomas A. Cowan, *The Riddle of the Palsgraf Case*, 23 MINN. L. REV. 46, 46 (1939).

[3] One cartoon, by Leonard Bregman, a 1954 Harvard Law School graduate, and titled "And Lilian Began to Cry," was reprinted in a major torts casebook. *See* WARREN A. SEAVEY ET AL., CASES AND MATERIALS ON THE LAW OF TORTS 236 (1957). For other cartoons, see David Gray Carlson, *Tales of the Unforeseen*, 27 HASTINGS L.J. 776, 776-77 (1975) (a satiric view of the case drawn by a second-year student at Hastings Law School containing such dialogue as "Hit the deck! There's negligence in the air!," and "[o]ut of our way Mrs. Palsgraf, we are looking for appreciable risks of danger"); CHARLES S. DESMOND, SHARP QUILLETS OF THE LAW 212 (1949) (depicting a man being pushed aboard a LIRR train); 14 N.Y.U. INTRAMURAL L. REV. 265 (1959) (depicting an injured Mrs. Palsgraf watching a man driving stakes into the ground around a scale). The film, *Palsgraf: Based on a Story By Benjamin Cardozo* (1983), was filmed at the East New York station where the accident took place.

[4] *See* Jorie Roberts, *Palsgraf Kin Tell Human Side of Famous Case*, HARV. L. REC., Apr. 14, 1978, at 1.

[5] *See* R. Perry Sentell, *The Perils of Palsgraf: At Large and in Georgia*, GEORGIA ST. B.J., Nov. 1991, at 82.

[6] *See* BLACK'S LAW DICTIONARY 1135 (7th ed. 1999).

[7] *See* ANDREW L. KAUFMAN, CARDOZO 286 (1998).

[8] *See* Janeen Kerper, *Creative Problem Solving vs. the Case Method: A Marvelous Adventure in Which Winnie-the-Pooh Meets Mrs. Palsgraf*, 34 CAL. W. L. REV. 351, 369 (1998).

[9] *See* Arthur Machen, Book Review, EXPERIENCE, Fall 1998, at 39 (reviewing KAUFMAN *supra* note 7). For other factual embellishments or new errors, see, e.g., SEAVEY ET AL., *supra* note 3, at 236 (cartoon depicting the event occurring at what appears to be a New York City subway station); James D. Gordon III, *Cardozo's Baseball Card*, 44 STAN. L. REV. 899, 905 (stating that "the rear wheel of the car hit the bundle"); David Margolick, *Classic Cardozo Ruling in a Negligence Case of the 20's is Still Reverberating in an 80's Appeal*, N.Y. TIMES, June 16, 1989, at B4 (stating that Mrs. Palsgraf was hospitalized). For an example of factual alteration as an exercise in literary license, see Edward S. Adams et al., *At the End of* Palsgraf, *There is Chaos: An Assessment of Proximate Cause*

in Light of Chaos Theory, 59 U. PITT. L. REV. 507, 507 (1998) (transforming the falling "scales" into roof tiles).

10 WILLIAM L. PROSSER, HANDBOOK OF THE LAW OF TORTS 342 n.62 (1941).

11 JOHN T. NOONAN, PERSONS AND MASKS OF THE LAW: CARDOZO, HOLMES, JEFFERSON, AND WYTHE AS MAKERS OF MASKS 120 (1976).

12 *Id.* at 150 (citing WILLIAM L. PROSSER, HANDBOOK OF THE LAW OF TORTS 254 (4th ed. 1971)).

13 For definitions of "urban legend," see, e.g., NEW OXFORD AMERICAN DICTIONARY 1861 (2001) ("A humorous or horrific story or piece of information circulated as though true."); THE AMERICAN HERITAGE DICTIONARY OF THE ENGLISH LANGUAGE 1892 (4th ed. 2000) ("An apocryphal story involving incidents of the recent past, often including elements of humor or horror that spreads quickly and is popularly supposed to be true."); THE CHAMBERS DICTIONARY 1834 (1998) ("A story or anecdote of modern life, often untrue or apocryphal.").

14 Richard A. Epstein, *Two Fallacies in the Law of Joint Torts*, 73 GEO. L.J. 1377, 1377 (1985).

15 VICTOR E. SCHWARTZ ET AL., PROSSER, WADE AND SCHWARTZ'S TORTS 311 (10th ed. 2000).

16 ANDREW J. MCCLURG, THE LAW SCHOOL TRAP 118 (2001).

17 *See, e.g.,* RICHARD A. POSNER, CARDOZO: A STUDY IN REPUTATION 43 (1990).

18 *See, e.g.,* DAN B. DOBBS, THE LAW OF TORTS 455 (2000) (stating that scales were located at the other end of the platform); Edward S. Adams et al., *At the End of Palsgraf, There is Chaos: An Assessment of Proximate Cause in Light of Chaos Theory*, 59 U. Pitt. L. Rev. 507, 543 (1998) (stating that the package was "dropped . . . onto the railroad tracks"); Duane J. Desiderio, *Sweet Home on the Range: A Model for As-Applied Challenges to the "Harm" Regulation*, 3 ENVT'L LAW. 725, 763 n.225 (1997) (stating that the fireworks "exploded on the tracks"); Mark G. Grady, *Efficient Negligence*, 87 GEO. L.J. 397, 413 (1998) (stating that the package "fell to the tracks"); Kelly J. Kirkland, *Of Horses, Helpers, and Hayricks: A Brief Re-Examination of Some Basic Principles of the Law of Negligence*, 39 S. TEX. L. REV. 87, 91 (1997) (stating that the fireworks "hit the tracks" and "knocked over scales at the other end of the platform"); John E. Sullivan, III, *Future Creditors and Fraudulent Transfers: When a Claimant Doesn't Have a Claim, When a Transfer Isn't a Transfer, When Fraud Doesn't Stay Fraudulent, and Other Important Limits to Fraudulent Transfers Law for the Asset Protection Planner*, 22 DEL. J. CORP. L. 955, 986 n.110 (1997) (stating that the package struck the tracks and exploded on impact, and that Mrs. Palsgraf was at one end of the platform while the passenger with the fireworks was at the other).

19 NOONAN, *supra* note 11, at 141.

CHAPTER 1

[1] Since the 1990s, numerous projects have been undertaken to revive the area. *See generally* WALTER THABIT, HOW EAST NEW YORK BECAME A GHETTO (2003). For a brief description of the history of the East New York neighborhood, see Ellen Marie Snyder-Grenier, *East New York, in* THE ENCYCLOPEDIA OF NEW YORK CITY 357 (Kenneth T. Jackson ed., 1995).

[2] The total length of the platform cannot be ascertained from contemporary photographs, but a 1920s Brooklyn street atlas shows its length as approximately 600 feet. *See* I.E. BELCHER HYDE MAP CO., DESK ATLAS, BOROUGH OF BROOKLYN, CITY OF NEW YORK 206 (1929). The best photo was taken from the elevated station to the east of the station and offers an good overhead view of much of the LIRR station. The Prosser casebook photo was taken at platform level by a photographer facing east since in the distance are the elevated train tracks that cross the LIRR right-of-way. It initially gives the impression that the eastbound platform was at ground level, but that is a result of the camera angle and the poor quality of the picture. Photos of similar LIRR stations, taken from the same angle also generally make it difficult to discern that the closer platform is above track level. *See* Bob Anderson, Long Island Rail Road History Homepage: Current Stations: Atlantic Ave./Far Rockaway Stations, http://www.lirrhistory.com/farcksta.html (last visited May 26, 2005). Both photos are date from the 1920s, but the exact year they were taken is not available.

[3] *See* VICTOR E. SCHWARTZ, KATHRYN KELLY & DAVID F. PARTLETT, PROSSER, WADE AND SCHWARTZ'S TORTS 303 (10th ed. 2000).

[4] Today, Rockaway can be reached by road from Queens by Cross Bay Boulevard, or from Brooklyn by the Marine Parkway Gil Hodges Memorial Bridge.

[5] *See The Weather*, N.Y. TIMES, Aug. 24, 1924, at 1; *The Weather*, N.Y. TIMES, Aug. 25, 1924, at 17. The high temperature on August 24, 1924, was only 80 degrees Fahrenheit. This is actually below normal for New York City. National Climatic Data Center, U.S. Department of Commerce, Local Climatological Data: New York, N.Y. Central Park 7 (2001) (indicating an average daily high of over 80 degrees for virtually every year since 1951).

[6] Trains to East New York originated in the Brooklyn Flatbush Avenue Terminal. All steam trains from this station were discontinued in 1905; the last wooden coaches were phased out by 1927. Two types of electric cars were in use at the time, most often the MP-54, and the older, smaller MP-41.

[7] Although the trial testimony, briefs, and opinions use such terms as "guard" or "platform man," these employees were popularly known as conductors. The railroad did not employ platform guards. Unlike the New York City subways of the day, it also did not use what were known as "cowpunchers," employees posted on the platforms to push passengers into crowded trains.

[8] *See, e.g., 13 Hurt By Fireworks Exploding Aboard Train*, WASH. POST, Aug. 25, 1924, at 1.

9 Such reports are preserved in the records of a few trials involving the railroad. They consist of an initial report sent immediately from the train involved, and a longer report consisting of over sixty entries that was filled out later.

10 Calls made by the author to various New York City Police Department sources, including the Bomb Squad, which investigated the incident at the station, indicated that no reports survive from the 1920s. Similarly, a call to Edward J. Murphy, then general attorney of the LIRR, indicated that accident reports and the case file were no longer available.

11 The only two accounts omitting the description "Italians" were those appearing in the *New York World* and the *Brooklyn Daily Eagle. See Bomb Blasts Hurl Throng into Panic*, N.Y. WORLD, Aug. 25, 1924, at 15; *Fireworks Blast Which Injured 13 Probed by Police*, BROOKLYN DAILY EAGLE, Aug. 25, 1924, at 18.

12 *Fireworks Blast Injures Many*, N.Y. SUN, Aug. 25, 1924, at 5.

13 *Fireworks Blast Hurts 14*, N.Y. EVENING POST, Aug. 25, 1924, at 3.

14 *Bomb Blast Injures 13 in Station Crowd*, N.Y. TIMES, Aug. 25, 1924, at 1.

15 *Fireworks Blast Rocks Picnickers*, N.Y. DAILY NEWS, Aug. 25, 1924, at 4; *13 Injured as 'Bombs' Explode in L.I. Station*, N.Y. HERALD-TRIB., Aug. 25, 1924, at 1. The men with the fireworks were in possible violation of several sections of the municipal code of ordinances that barred the transportation of fireworks worth over $10 wholesale unless they were securely packaged in marked wooden or metal packages. NEW YORK CITY, N.Y., NEW CODE OF ORDINANCES ch. 10, art. 6, § 92(6) (1926). The use or discharge of fireworks of the type carried by the men was also banned. *Id.* § 93(2) (prohibiting "firecrackers longer than five inches or larger than three-fourths of an inch in diameter" and "bombs and shells"). Had the men carried the fireworks on a train to New Jersey, rather than Long Island, they would have been in violation of a federal statute banning "fireworks, or other similar explosives . . . [from] that part of a vessel, car, or vehicle which is being used for the transportation of passengers." Act of Mar. 4, 1921, ch. 172, 41 Stat. 1444 (repealed 1948).

16 N.Y. WORLD, *supra* note 11, at 15; *Bomb Blast*, N.Y TIMES, *supra* note 14, at 1; N.Y. EVENING POST, *supra* note 13, at 3; N.Y. SUN, *supra* note 12, at 5; N.Y. DAILY NEWS, *supra* note 15, at 4; BROOKLYN DAILY EAGLE, *supra* note 11, at 18.

17 N.Y. HERALD-TRIB., *supra* note 15, at 1.

18 BROOKLYN DAILY EAGLE, *supra* note 11, at 18.

19 *Bomb Blast*, N.Y. TIMES, *supra* note 14, at 1.

20 *Id.*; *Passengers Injured When Fireworks Go Off in L.I. Station*, LONG ISLAND DAILY PRESS, Aug. 24, 1924, at 1.

21 *Bomb Blast*, N.Y. TIMES, *supra* note 14, at 1.

22 *See* N.Y. WORLD, *supra* note 11, at 15; N.Y. SUN, *supra* note 12, at 5; BROOKLYN DAILY EAGLE, *supra* note 11, at 18; N.Y. HERALD-TRIB., *supra* note 15, at 1; *13 Injured When Fireworks Drop*, BROOKLYN DAILY TIMES, August 25, 1924, at 11.

23 N.Y. SUN, *supra* note 12, at 5.

24 N.Y. WORLD, *supra* note 11, at 15.

25 BROOKLYN DAILY EAGLE, *supra* note 11, at 18.

26 As provided by the *Times*, the others injured were: Joseph Coyle, forty-two; Mary Dermody, forty-one (abrasions and contusions to the left shoulder); Leila Eschman, twenty-four (burns on right wrist); Mamie Greenfader, forty-nine (slight abrasions on the left ankle); Mollie Greenfader, nineteen (abrasions on left shoulder); Richard Seeman, forty-four (cuts and burns on face and hands); Herbert Litt, thirty-five (lacerations); Rose Matkowsky, sixteen (burned hair); Emma Moss, fifty (shock); Rose Roseman, sixteen (burns on right wrist); William Schneider, thirty-one (abrasions to the right arm); Eva Shaw, sixteen (burned hair).

27 Dean Prosser once speculated on organized crime's possible connection to the explosion. *See* William L. Prosser, *Palsgraf Revisited*, 52 MICH. L. REV. 1, 2 n.7 (1953) ("Any incurable romantic who visualizes the Mafia and an infernal machine is perhaps not entirely ruled out."). More recently, there has been a humorous suggestion that the explosion may have been related to a bomb plot against the Prince of Wales, who was then visiting the United States. *See* Daniel Ackman, *Perspective: 'Palsgraf' Through the Eyes of Sherlock Holmes*, N.Y.L.J., Nov. 30, 2000, at 2.

28 *Sergeant Gegan Attacked*, N.Y. TIMES, July 23, 1921, at 18. *See also Sues Foe of Reds for Third Degree*, N.Y. TIMES, Mar. 3, 1920, at 17.

CHAPTER 2

1 The standard German spelling of the name is "Pfaltzgraf," meaning Count Palatine. THE NEW CASSELL'S GERMAN DICTIONARY 355, 613 (1971). Her name was again misspelled in a news story about the Appellate Division decision. *See Fireworks Blast Laid to Railroad*, N.Y. TIMES, Dec. 11, 1927, at 29 (spelling name "Palagraf").

2 N.Y. City Department of Health, Certificate of Birth, Jacobine and Rosa Spilger, No. 391698/391699 [herinafter Birth Certificate]. Herman Spilger is listed in the Manhattan city directories published in the 1880s. He is described as a smith/spikemaker located at East 17th St. (in 1885) and later at East 15th St. (in 1889). *See* TROW'S NEW YORK CITY DIRECTORY FOR THE YEAR ENDING MAY 1, 1885, at 1167 (Trow City Directory Co. ed., 1885); TROW'S NEW YORK CITY DIRECTORY FOR THE YEAR ENDING MAY 1, 1889, at 1891 (Trow City Directory Co. ed., 1889).

3 This entire neighborhood no longer exists. After World War II, it was razed to make way for the Stuyvesant Town housing project. The 1880 census provides a profile of the type of people who lived at the East 17th St. address. Their occupations included retail beer dealer, peddler, driver, carriage painter, washerwoman, hairdresser, gas house fireman, butcher, carpenter, and seamstress.

4 Birth Certificate, *supra* note 2.

5 R. Perry Sentell, *The Perils of Palsgraf: At Large and in Georgia*, GEORGIA ST. B.J., Nov. 1991, at 82.

6 *See, e.g.*, N.Y. City Department of Health, Certificate of Death, Lena Palsgraf, No. 8362 (issued Oct. 29, 1945) (copy on file with the author) [hereinafter Death Certificate]. Mrs. Palsgraf's death certificate is signed by Elizabeth Palsgraf, the funeral director, and a physician.

7 Professor Sentell's article, *see supra* note 5, states that Palsgraf relatives reported that the couple had fourteen children, but only William, Elizabeth, and Lillian lived. Whether that number includes miscarriages and/or stillbirths was not indicated.

8 *Id.*

9 *See* THE COST OF LIVING IN NEW YORK CITY 72 chart 1 (1926) (indicating that a family of three living in Brooklyn required a minimum weekly income of $25.90).

10 Record at 19, Palsgraf v. Long Island R.R. Co., 162 N.E. 99 (N.Y. 1928).

11 Telephone interview with Edward J. Murphy. The activities of claims agents were noted during the New York State Bar Association's consideration of contingent fees. Charles G. Signor, an attorney from Albion, described how they pressured poor accident victims to sign statements. *See Discussion of Contingent Fees*, *in* PROCEEDINGS OF THE NEW YORK STATE BAR ASSOCIATION 171 (1927).

12 LONG ISLAND RAILROAD, FORTY-THIRD ANNUAL REPORT: THE LONG ISLAND RAILROAD CO. FOR THE YEAR ENDED 31ST DEC. 1924, at 1 (1925) [hereinafter ANNUAL REPORT].

13 *Id.* at 2-3.

14 *Controls the Long Island Road*, N.Y. TIMES, Mar. 8, 1901, at 2.

15 THE LONG ISLAND RAILROAD: 100TH ANNIVERSARY 14 (1934).

16 FRANK J. SHERMAN, BUILDING UP GREATER QUEENS BOROUGH 58-59 (1929).

17 *Id.* at 2-3.

18 LONG ISLAND R.R. INFO. BULL., June 3, 1925, at 9.

19 Letter to the Editor from L. Amezaga, N.Y. TIMES, Oct. 28, 1927, at 22.

20 The pony, reportedly worth $4,000, was struck by a train at Westbury, Long Island, after its hoof had become stuck underneath a rail.

21 *Warns of 'Plot' By the Long Island*, N.Y. TIMES, May 6, 1924, at 23.

22 *Force to Stand, Commuters Rebel*, N.Y. TIMES, Sept. 15, 1927, at 31.

23 *Long Island R.R. to Spend $84,000,000*, N.Y. TIMES, July 17, 1923, at 21.

24 *Long Island R.R. Plans Big Changes*, N.Y. TIMES, Apr. 4, 1924, at 21.

25 LONG ISLAND AND ITS RAILROAD: EXTRACTS FROM AN ADDRESS BY JOSEPH F. KEANY BEFORE THE LONG ISLAND PRESS ASSOCIATION AT LONG BEACH, L.I. 5 (JUNE 21, 1916) [herinafter KEANY ADDRESS].

26 *News of the Railroads*, N.Y. TIMES, Sept. 19, 1901, at 5.

27 ANNUAL REPORT, *supra* note 12, at 2-3.

28 JOHN T. NOONAN, PERSONS AND MASKS OF THE LAW: CARDOZO, HOLMES, JEFFERSON, AND WYTHE AS MAKERS OF MASKS 128 (1976) (citing MOODY'S MANUAL OF RAILROADS AND CORPORATION SECURITIES 1620, 1622 (Moody Manual Co. ed., 1924)).

29 *See Long Island R.R. To Pay 4% Dividend; Pennsylvania R.R. To Receive $1,364,000 – Disbursement First Since 1896*, N.Y. TIMES, Apr. 10, 1928, at 40.

30 *Long Island Road Pleads Poverty*, N.Y. TIMES, Feb. 12, 1927, at 25.

31 *Higher Rail Fares in Effect Monday*, N.Y. TIMES, Nov. 24, 1920, at 19.

32 *Hylan Takes a Hand in Commuters' War*, N.Y. TIMES, Apr. 17, 1924, at 21. Hylan had worked as a motorman while attending law school, and reportedly hated railroad companies because he had once been fired.

33 *L.I. Road to Spend $63,100,000 on Lines*, N.Y. TIMES, Feb. 4, 1927, at 21. By 1924, grade-crossing accidents had become a state-wide epidemic, prompting Governor Alfred E. Smith to issue a special message to the legislature calling for a constitutional amendment that would permit the lending of state credit to railroads and municipalities to help finance their share of a $400,000,000 grade crossing elimination program.

34 *Will Spend $1,000,000 on Grade Crossings*, N.Y. TIMES, Sept. 1, 1911, at 4.

35 *See Slow Work on Grade Crossings*, N.Y. TIMES, July 1, 1923, at XX8 (letter to the editor from George Flatow, Secretary of the LIRR Committee on Public Relations).

36 *Train Kills Doctor, His Fiance Dying*, N.Y. TIMES, July 22, 1907, at 1.

37 Pell was a fifty-one-year-old New York real estate dealer who once participated in an Arctic expedition searching for gold deposits in Baffin Land. Laimbeer, thirty-nine, was an 1896 Harvard College graduate and a well-known clubman.

38 *Death Dared By 159 Crossing Railroad*, N.Y. TIMES, Sept. 26, 1915, at 12.

39 *Reckless Drivers Continue to Break Crossing Gates Daily*, LONG ISLAND R.R. INFO. BULL., Aug. 25, 1925, at 41.

40 N.Y. TIMES, May 10, 1926, at 23.

41 N.Y. TIMES, Feb. 7, 1923, at 1.

42 N.Y. TIMES, Oct. 12, 1924, at 28.

43 N.Y. TIMES, Nov. 1, 1924, at 30.

44 N.Y. TIMES, Dec. 25, 1924, at 1.

45 N.Y. Times, Aug. 8, 1926, at E1.

46 N.Y. Times, Mar. 28, 1927, at 11.

47 Keany Address, *supra* note 25, at 7.

48 *Car Hurled Against Engine*, N.Y. Times, July 31, 1924, at 1. Overall, there were four deaths and eighty-eight reported injuries connected to LIRR train service operations in 1924. Noonan, *supra* note 25, at 130 (citing Bureau of Statistics, Interstate Commerce Commission, No. 93, Accident Bulletin 111 (1925)).

49 *Heavy Bail for Men Blamed in Wreck*, N.Y. Times, Aug. 1, 1924, at 13.

50 *See* Interstate Commerce Commission, Report of the Director of the Bureau of Safety in re Investigation of an Accident Which Occurred on the Long Island Railroad at Long Island City, N.Y. on July 30, 1924, at 8 (Sept. 20, 1924).

51 *Rail Wreck Halts 55,000 in Rush Hour*, N.Y. Times, Sept. 14, 1926, at 1.

52 *Grand Jury Condemns Long Island Road for Calverton Wreck in Which Six Died*, N.Y. Times, Oct. 21, 1926, at 1. Earlier, the ICC report noted that there was "laxness in the maintenance of switches as well as in the supervision and inspection of the same." Interstate Commerce Commission, Report of the Director of the Bureau of Safety in re Investigation of an Accident Which Occurred on the Long Island Railroad at Calverton, N.Y., on August 13, 1926, at 6 (Sept. 25, 1926).

53 *Held for Fireman's Death*, N.Y. Times, May 8, 1923, at 23; *5 Held in Crossing Deaths*, N.Y. Times, Mar. 1, 1924, at 9.

CHAPTER 3

1 *Population of Boroughs of New York City (as Defined by Consolidation of 1898), 1790–1890*, *in* Encyclopedia of New York City 923 (Kenneth T. Jackson ed., 1995).

2 *Population of New York City by Borough, 1900–1990*, *in id.* at 921.

3 Andrew L. Kaufman, *The First Judge Cardozo: Albert, Father of Benjamin*, 1994–1995 J.L. & Religion 271, 299 (citing the 1870 census).

4 *Education of a Lawyer Comes to a Test*, N.Y. Times, Feb. 27, 1927, at XX4.

5 *Law School Attendance, 1910–1911*, 2 Am. L. Sch. L. Rev. 522, 522 (1911).

6 *Registration in Law Schools – Fall of 1924*, 2 Am. L. Sch. L. Rev. 417, 421 (1924).

7 *Registration in Law Schools – Fall of 1928*, 6 Am. L. Sch. L. Rev. 356, 361 (1928).

8 Michael J. Powell, From Patrician to Professional Elite: The Transformation of the New York City Bar Association 34-35 (1988) (discussing Alfred Z. Reed, Training for the Public Profession of Law (1921)).

9 *Id.* at 24.

10 *Admission to the Bar*, N.Y. TIMES, Jan. 1, 1914, at 14.

11 John H. Wigmore, *Should the Standard of Admission to the Bar Be Based on Two Years or More of College-Grade Education? It Should*, 4 AM. L. SCH. L. REV. 30, 30 (1915).

12 *Excellence Vital in Law, Says Dean*, N.Y. TIMES, Jan. 8, 1922, at 26.

13 *Insists Applicants for Bar Have A.B.*, N.Y. TIMES, Jan. 1, 1927, at 28.

14 I. Morris Wormser, *The Problem of Evening Law Schools*, 4 AM. L. SCH. REV. 544, 547 (1920).

15 *Want College Men in Bar*, N.Y. TIMES, Dec. 31, 1926, at 12.

16 *Id.*

17 POWELL, *supra* note 8, at 35.

18 *Assails Critics of Bar Candidates*, N.Y. TIMES, Jan. 13, 1927, at 21.

19 *Demand Lawyers of Higher Quality*, N.Y. TIMES, Mar. 5, 1927.

20 Julius Henry Cohen, *Training for the Law*, N.Y. TIMES, May 21, 1922, at 105.

21 POWELL, *supra* note 8, at 35.

22 *Philip A. "Doc" Brennan; Candidate for Supreme Court Justice*, BROOKLYN DAILY EAGLE, Aug. 15, 1916 (unpaginated news clipping on file at the Brooklyn Public Library).

23 *Edward J. Reilly Differs From Taft*, BROOKLYN DAILY EAGLE, Mar. 25, 1929, at 4. Before becoming a lawyer, Reilly was an insurance company clerk. His own courtroom sartorial style featured a cutaway coat, striped trousers, and spats. He is best known for his role as chief defense counsel for Bruno Richard Hauptmann who was convicted of the kidnap-murder of the Lindbergh baby in 1935.

24 *Asks Crusade to Rid Courts of Shady Accident Cases*, N.Y. TIMES, Mar. 27, 1927, at XX16 (letter to the editor from "Legal Practitioner").

25 *Censor for Mulberry St.*, N.Y. TIMES, Dec. 11, 1907, at 18.

26 *See In re* Clark, 77 N.E. 1 (N.Y. 1904).

27 1917 N.Y. Laws ch. 783.

28 *Jurist Says Courts Wink at Chasing*, N.Y. TIMES, July 14, 1928, at 30.

29 *See Lawyers Act to Stop Ambulance Chasing*, N.Y. TIMES, Dec. 24, 1927, at 27.

30 Wood's original given name appears to have been Mathias. This name appears in the reports for both the 1892 New York State census and the 1900 United States census.

31 A 1902 newspaper article described the area as "experiencing mushroom growth." *Down Bay Ridge Way*, BROOKLYN DAILY EAGLE, Apr. 19, 1902, at 11. Real estate news entries in the *Daily Eagle* between 1896 and 1902 list several purchases by Boyd H.

Wood, and libers at the Kings County Clerk's office list some twenty different sales of property in Bay Ridge by his company between 1906 and 1920.

32 *Former Citizen Dies in Brooklyn*, MIDDLEBURGH NEWS, Mar. 9, 1922, at 1.

33 Will of Boyd H. Wood, Book 152, at 427 (on file at the King's County Clerk's Records Room).

34 Ironically, his one identifiable written contribution was a review of an 823-page book on railroad accidents. *See* M.W.W., Book Note, 14 YALE L.J. 60 (1904) (reviewing ANDREW NELLIS, STREET RAILROAD ACCIDENT LAW (1904)).

35 *Root Warns Against Abuse of Public Trust*, N.Y. TIMES, June 28, 1904, at 5. Wood once wrote that he'd been told that he was the first Yale one-year student to receive a degree *magna cum laude*. *See* Letter to Tommy from Matthew W. Wood (Nov. 8, 1904) (copy on file with the author).

36 Elihu Root, *Some Duties of American Lawyers to American Law*, 14 YALE L.J. 63, 68 (1904).

37 Letter to Tommy from Matthew W. Wood (Nov. 14, 1904) (copy on file with the author).

38 In a letter to the editor published on October 31, 1925, he objected to the characterization of the Penn team as an "upstart" and complained that a previous letter had been edited beyond recognition.

39 Wood's rating is worth noting since Judge Noonan questions the propriety of the content of his listing in *Hubbell's Legal Directory* and the possible financial arrangements behind Mrs. Palsgraf's lawsuit. *See* JOHN T. NOONAN, PERSONS AND MASKS OF THE LAW: CARDOZO, HOLMES, JEFFERSON, AND WYTHE AS MAKERS OF MASKS 124-25 (1976).

40 Advertisement, N.Y. TIMES, Feb. 23, 1912, at 16.

41 *See* Penn-Yale Corp. v. Commissioner of Internal Revenue, 7 B.T.A. 1228, 1228-29 (1927).

42 Record at 386, People v. Chapman, 121 N.E. 381 (N.Y. 1918) (summation of William R. Murphy).

43 MARTINDALE'S AMERICAN LAW DIRECTORY 1187 (1920).

44 HUBBELL'S LEGAL DIRECTORY 352 (Joseph A. Lynch ed., 1924).

45 MARTINDALE'S AMERICAN LAW DIRECTORY 1418 (1928).

46 *See In re* Dollard, 133 N.Y.S. 1107 (Surr. Ct. Kings County 1911).

47 *See* McLaughlin v. Mendelson, 144 N.Y.S. 1073 (App. Div. 1913).

48 *See* Hock v. Hock, 149 N.Y.S. 1027 (Sup. Ct. Kings County 1914).

49 *See In re* Walsh, 164 N.Y.S. 553 (App. Div. 1917).

50 *See* Holmes v. Langdon, 171 N.Y.S. 30 (App. T. N.Y. County 1918).

51 *See* Clyde v. Wood, 179 N.Y.S. 252 (App. Div. 1919), *aff'd*, 135 N.E. 949 (N.Y. 1922).

52 *See* Wensley v. City of New York, 159 N.Y.S. 510, 514 (App. Div. 1916).

53 Day v. Brooklyn City R.R. Co, 191 N.Y.S. 484, 489 (App. Div. 1921) (Kelly, J., dissenting), *aff'd*, 148 N.E. 481 (N.Y. 1923).

54 *Id.*

55 *See* Day v. Brooklyn City R.R. Co., 148 N.E. 481 (N.Y. 1923).

56 *See* Hild v. McClintic-Marshall Co., 152 N.E. 444 (N.Y. 1926).

57 Richter v. Hallaren, 218 N.Y.S. 880, 880 (App. Div. 1926).

58 *See Ask Court To Tie Up All New City Work; Brooklyn Citizens Demand the Fourth Avenue Subway Before Anything Else*, N.Y. TIMES, July 16, 1908, at 14.

59 *See* Levy v. McClellan, 89 N.E. 569 (N.Y. 1909).

60 For profiles of White, see Helen S. Farrell, *Charles Bouck White: The Sculptor*, SCHOHARIE COUNTY HIST. REV., Spring-Summer 1984, at 2; Patricia Edwards Clyne, *A Maverick Among Us*, HUDSON VALLEY, Oct. 1996, at 25.

61 Jacob H. Dorn, *In Spiritual Communion: Eugene V. Debs and the Socialist Christians*, J. OF THE GILDED AGE AND PROGRESSIVE ERA 2.3 (2003), *available at* http://www.historycooperative.org/journals/jga/2.3/dorn.html.

62 *See Middleburg Wants Novel Suppressed: Villagers Say the Rev. Bouck White Libeled Them in "The Mixing"*, N.Y. TIMES, Jan. 23, 1914, at 5.

63 *See* CHARLES BOUCK WHITE, THE MIXING: WHAT THE HILLPORT NEIGHBORS DID 114-15 (1913).

64 Letter from Matthew W. Wood to the Editor (Jan. 14, 1914), *reprinted in The Mixing Still Goes On*, MIDDLEBURGH NEWS, Jan. 22, 1914, at 1.

65 *Jail Bouck White! Is Middleburg Cry*, BROOKLYN DAILY EAGLE, Jan. 22, 1914, at 1.

66 *Id.*

67 Letter from Charles S. Whitman to Matthew W. Wood, June 8, 1914, *microfilmed on* Roll 68, M.N. #11519 (New York City Municipal Archives).

68 White went to the workhouse again during World War I for burning the American flag. After the war, he married a young French woman who subsequently fled his upstate New York home with tales of White's peculiar behavior, resulting in his being tarred and feathered by local residents. White later withdrew from public life, built an odd castle-like home in the Helderberg Mountains near Albany and started a ceramics business, selling pottery known as "Bouckware." In 1951, he died in men's residence in Albany.

69 *Choirboy Tells of Double Murder*, N.Y. TIMES, Feb. 8, 1918, at 8.

70 *No Chapman Leniency*, BROOKLYN DAILY EAGLE, Mar. 9, 1918, at 6 (letter to the editor from M.G.E.).

71 *Chapman's Lawyer Pleads for Mercy*, BROOKLYN DAILY EAGLE, Mar. 14, 1918, at 12 (letter to the editor from Matthew W. Wood).

72 *More Appeals to Save Chapman*, BROOKLYN DAILY EAGLE, Apr. 1, 1918, at 10.

73 *To Save Chapman's Life; Make Sentence 20 Years is Report*, BROOKLYN DAILY EAGLE, Nov. 29, 1918, at 1.

74 *Paul Chapman's Age Figures in Appeal*, BROOKLYN DAILY EAGLE, Oct. 10, 1918, at 16.

75 *Id.*

76 People v. Chapman, 121 N.E. 381, 387 (N.Y. 1918).

77 *Id.* Because Wood and Murphy did not bring on the appeal for argument within the time allotted after the taking of the appeal, they were denied compensation for their services and for disbursements. The court rejected their argument that the clerk of the trial court did not print the record within the required time. They were allowed only appeal-related personal and incidental expenses. *See* People v. Chapman, 122 N.E. 240 (N.Y. 1919).

78 *Paul Chapman Gets Life Imprisonment as Governor Acts*, BROOKLYN DAILY EAGLE, Nov. 30, 1918, at 1. Even after the commutation of his death sentence, interest in Chapman continued. Articles in the *New York Times* described his role in a Sing Sing Prison show and his efforts on behalf of the prison football team.

Wood reportedly defended an accused murderer before the Chapman case, but there is only one other reported criminal case where he was the defendant's attorney. *See* People v. Royall, 281 N.Y.S. 875 (N.Y. Ct. Sp. Sess. 1935) (involving Wood as co-counsel in an unsuccessful appeal of conviction of Brooklyn hotel proprietor for knowingly allowing prostitution to take place on his premises).

79 *Will Fight to Stay in Love Nest, Says Jilted Widow of 30*, BROOKLYN DAILY EAGLE, Nov. 30, 1926, at 3.

80 *Id.*

81 Wood's niece, Elizabeth W. Smith, recalled him having a romantic involvement sometime before 1922, but the name of the woman was Jenny Purvis, who lived in their Bay Ridge neighborhood.

82 *See Woman Drops Suit for Title to Home of Alleged Lover*, BROOKLYN DAILY EAGLE, Apr. 18, 1927, at 1.

83 THE NEW YORK IMPROVEMENT AND TUNNEL EXTENSION OF THE PENNSYLVANIA RAILROAD 3 (1910). In what the late Senator Daniel Patrick Moynihan regarded as "an act of vandalism," the station was torn down in 1965, and was replaced by a building complex that includes Madison Square Garden.

84 Pharoah v. Benson, 126 N.Y.S. 1035 (Sup. Ct. Equity T. Suffolk County 1910) (holding that the sale of tribal lands to a non-Indian was valid).

85 United States v. Long Island R.R. Co., 4 F.2d 750 (E.D.N.Y. 1925).

86 *See, e.g.* People ex rel. Long Island R.R. Co. v. State Bd. of Tax Commissioners, 183 N.Y.S. 733 (App. Div. 1920).

87 *See, e.g.,* People ex rel. Long Island R.R. Co. v. Pub. Serv. Comm'n, 168 N.Y.S. 832 (App. Div. 1918).

88 *Dick Suit Answered by Long Island R.R.; Joseph F. Keany Holds Control by the Pennsylvania Has Benefited the Property,* N.Y. TIMES, May 30, 1915, at XX9.

89 Speech to the Association of Editors, June 21, 1916 (unpublished manuscript included with the Keany Papers at the St. John's University Archives).

90 For a profile of Carruthers, see *Louis Carruthers, Lawyer Dies; U.S. Lawn Tennis Head, '31-32,* N.Y. TIMES, Nov. 30, 1960, at 37.

91 *See In re* Park Lane South in City of New York, 200 N.Y.S. 555 (App. Div. 1923).

92 *See In re* Eighty-Fourth St. in Borough of Queens, 178 N.Y.S. 517 (App. Div. 1919).

93 Ramme v. Long Island R.R., 123 N.E. 747 (N.Y. 1919).

94 For a profile of Gardner, see *A.A. Gardner Dies; Railroad Counsel,* N.Y. TIMES, Mar. 28, 1947, at 23.

95 *See* Terwilliger v. Long Island R.R. Co., 209 N.Y. 522 (N.Y. 1913); *see also* Hoyt v. Long Island R.R. Co., 120 N.E. 865 (N.Y. 1918) (bicyclist killed at grade crossing); DeBaud v. Long Island R.R. Co., 148 N.Y.S. 581 (App. Div. 1914) (pedestrian killed at grade crossing).

96 People ex rel. Long Island R.R. Co. v. State Bd. of Tax Commissioners, 131 N.E. 896 (N.Y. 1921) (tax assessment dispute); Long Island R.R. Co. v. Hylan, 148 N.E. 189 (N.Y. 1925) (dispute over grade crossing elimination costs).

97 Other than Carruthers and Gardner, the members of the LIRR legal department were compiled by consulting the 1927 *Bender's Lawyers' Directory* to locate attorneys who shared Joseph F. Keany's office address of 341 Pennsylvania Station. One of these, Dominic Bodkin Griffin, was described in his obituary as "an outstanding trial lawyer." The earliest reported case where Griffin represented the railroad occurred in 1907. Although his 1927 address is given as 341 Pennsylvania Station, the last reported case where he appears as a counsel for the LIRR is in 1919. After that date, he appears in the law reports as an attorney only in decisions unrelated to the railroad. Another, Edward Newburn, was admitted to the bar in 1906. The first reported case where he appeared as the attorney for the LIRR was in 1920.

98 *See* Long Island R.R. Co. v. Sherwood, 98 N.E. 169 (N.Y. 1912).

99 *See* People v. Long Island R.R. Co., 186 N.Y.S. 589 (App. Div. 1921).

100 *Henry Uterhart, Lawyer 50 Years*, N.Y. TIMES, Apr. 13, 1946, at 17. Uterhart also represented plaintiffs in negligence actions against the LIRR. *See generally* Record, Horvath v. Long Island R.R. Co., 183 N.Y.S. 950 (App. Div. 1920); Record, Kinsley v. Long Island R.R. Co. 216 N.Y.S. 867 (App. Div. 1926).

101 The jury awarded the Commission damages of $32,200, but on appeal Griffing and Keany were able to have the judgment reduced to $200. *See* People v. Long Island R.R. Co., 149 N.Y.S. 765 (App. Div. 1912), *aff'd*, 101 N.E. 1015 (N.Y. 1913).

102 Littleton also represented the railroad in the $40,000 suit over the death of the Pell chauffeur, Charles Gambino. For a profile of Littleton, see *M.W. Littleton Sr., Lawyer, Dies at 62*, N.Y. TIMES, Dec. 20, 1934, at 1. For descriptions of his activities during the Pell trial, *see Blew His Whistle To Warn Pell Auto*, N.Y. TIMES, June 19, 1915, at 7; *Four Watched Pell Speeding to Death*, N.Y. TIMES, June 22, 1915, at 11.

103 Thaw fatally shot White in front of many witnesses at Madison Square Garden on June 25, 1906, because the architect had once had an affair with his wife, former show-girl Evelyn Nesbit. Littleton convinced the jury that Thaw was insane at the time of the shooting.

104 *See* People ex rel. Shane v. Gittens, 137 N.Y.S. 670 (Sup. Ct. N.Y. County 1912).

105 In both grade-crossing cases, the plaintiffs won verdicts that were reversed by the Appellate Division. *See* Bonert v. Long Island R.R. Co., 130 N.Y.S. 271 (App. Div. 1911) (reversing judgment for plaintiff); Hoyt v. Long Island R.R. Co., 162 N.Y.S. 792 (App. Div. 1917) (reversing $8,000 verdict for plaintiff). A suit by an injured trespasser, a teenager who lost both legs when a freight train backed over him, was dismissed. *See* Freeman v. Long Island R.R. Co., 167 N.Y.S. 1100 (App. Div. 1917).

106 Miles defended the railroad against suits arising from the death of woman who had been hit by a train, a motorist injured in a grade-crossing accident, and two child passengers injured in another grade-crossing crash. In the first two cases, the railroad was found liable, but the Appellate Division reversed. *See* Darnell v. Long Island R.R. Co., 225 N.Y.S. 812 (App. Div. 1927) (reversing $4,602.73 judgment for plaintiff); Stark v. Long Island R.R. Co., 166 N.Y.S. 1115 (App. Div. 1917) (reversing $1,604.93 judgment for plaintiff). In the last case, the action against the LIRR was dismissed. *See* Psota v. Long Island R.R. Co., 220 N.Y.S. 912 (App. Div. 1927).

107 Sinclair claimed the sellers had misrepresented the quality of the horse. The $100,000 verdict was upheld on appeal. *See* Sinclair v. Johnson, 194 N.Y.S. 980 (App. Div. 1922).

108 Record at 56, Whiting v. Long Island R.R. Co., 193 N.Y.S. 958 (App. Div. 1922).

109 *See* D'Aurio v. Long Island R.R. Co., 219 N.Y.S. 796 (App. Div. 1926).

110 *See* Goodrich v. Long Island R.R. Co., 219 N.Y.S. 823 (App. Div. 1926).

111 *See* Brick v. Long Island R.R. Co., 215 N.Y.S. 820 (App. Div. 1926), *rev'd*, 157 N.E. 93 (N.Y. 1927).

112 *See* Kelly v. Long Island R.R. Co., 222 N.Y.S., 832 (App. Div. 1927).

113 *See* Maiorano v. Long Island R.R. Co., 215 N.Y.S. 883 (App. Div. 1926), *rev'd*, 155 N.E. 681 (N.Y. 1927). Other cases where the record indicates that Philip A. Brennan acted as the LIRR's trial attorney include: *Metzler v. Long Island Railroad Co.*, 159 N.Y.S. 1129 (App. Div. 1916); *Zatulove v. Long Island Railroad Co.*, 167 N.Y.S. 1135 (App. Div. 1917); Ullman v. Long Island Railroad Co., 172 N.Y.S. 923 (App. Div. 1918); *Hammond v. Long Island Railroad Co.*, 167 N.Y.S. 908 (App. Div. 1918); *Southard v. Long Island Railroad Co.*, 170 N.Y.S. 1114 (App. Div. 1918); *Meyers v. Long Island Railroad Co.*, 191 N.Y.S. 773 (App. Div. 1922); *Meyers v. Hines*, 191 N.Y.S. 773 (App. Div. 1922); *Whiting v. Long Island Railroad Co.*, 193 N.Y.S. 958 (App. Div. 1922); *Kinsley v. Long Island Railroad Co.*, 216 N.Y.S. 857 (App. Div. 1926). The last reported case where he represented the LIRR is *Ahlgren v. Long Island Railroad Co.*, 255 N.Y.S. 927 (App. Div. 1932). Other cases where Thomas J. Brennan represented the LIRR at trial were: *Flood v. Hines*, 190 N.Y.S. 925 (App. Div. 1921); *O'Donnell v. Long Island Railroad Co.*, 204 N.Y.S. 933 (App. Div. 1924); *Michel v. Long Island Railroad Co.*, 205 N.Y.S. 938 (App. Div. 1924); *Lierness v. Long Island Railroad Co.*, 216 N.Y.S. 656 (App. Div. 1926); *Harrigan v. Long Island Railroad Co.*, 219 N.Y.S. 829 (App. Div. 1926). Later reported cases where he represented the railroad include: *Bowers v. Long Island Railroad Co.*, 232 N.Y.S. 701 (App. Div.), *aff'd*, 168 N.E. 414 (N.Y. 1929); *McCarthy v. Long Island Railroad Co.*, 244 N.Y.S. 919 (App. Div. 1930); *Thomas Roulston Co. v. Long Island Railroad Co.*, 243 N.Y.S. 834 (App. Div.), *aff'd*, 175 N.E. 307 (N.Y. 1930); *Hansen v. Long Island Railroad Co.*, 175 N.E. 307 (N.Y. 1930); *Orr v. Long Island Railroad Co.*, 245 N.Y.S. 831 (App. Div. 1930) and 254 N.Y.S. 971 (App. Div. 1931); *Nicoll v. Long Island Railroad Co.*, 250 N.Y.S. 356 (App. Div. 1931); *Cullen v. Long Island Railroad Co.*, 259 N.Y.S. 957 (App. Div. 1932); *Underhill v. Long Island Railroad Co.*, 277 N.Y.S. 985 (App. Div. 1935).

114 *See* Wiren v. Long Island R.R. Co., 226 N.Y.S. 103 (App. Div. 1923).

CHAPTER 4

1 1909 N.Y. Laws ch. 88, § 274(2) ("An attorney or counselor shall not . . . [b]y himself, or in the name of any other person, either before or after action brought, promise or give, or procure to be promised or given, a valuable consideration to any person, as an inducement to placing, or in consideration of having placed, in his hands, or in the hands of another person, a demand of any kind, for the purpose of bringing an action thereon, or of representing the claimant in the pursuit of any civil remedy for the recovery thereof."). This section was derived from § 74 of the old Code of Civil Procedure. For the few cases before 1928 where attorneys were found in violation of § 272(2), see *In re* an Attorney, 154 N.Y.S. 703 (App. Div. 1915); *In re* Newman, 158 N.Y. S. 375 (App. Div. 1916); *In re* Tunnicliff, 195 N.Y.S. 449 (App. Div. 1922). *See also* McCoy v. Gas Engine & Power Co., 137 N.Y.S. 591 (App. Div. 1912), *aff'd*, 102 N.E. 1106 (N.Y. 1913) (holding an agreement by an attorney "to pay all expenses of every kind whatsoever" was invalid under § 274(2)).

2 *In re* Gilman's Administratrix, 167 N.E. 437, 438 (N.Y. 1929). Cardozo also quoted *Hawkin's Pleas of the Crown*, c. 27(6), § 26, at 460 ("It seems to be agreed that anyone may lawfully give money to a poor man to enable him to carry on his suit.").

3 *Juror's Bulletin Assails Chicanery*, N.Y. TIMES, May 8, 1927, at 27.

4 *Tuttle Denounces Delay in the Courts*, N.Y. TIMES, Aug. 25, 1927, at 1.

5 *Untermyer Wants Curb on Legal Fees*, N.Y. TIMES, Aug. 27, 1927, at 19.

6 *Discussion of Contingent Fees*, *in* PROCEEDINGS OF THE NEW YORK STATE BAR ASSO-CIATION 157 (1927).

7 *Tuttle Wants Curb on Contingent Fee*, N.Y. TIMES, Sept. 29, 1927, at 19.

8 *See Slash in Fees Urged to Combat 'Chasing'*, N.Y. TIMES, Oct. 4, 1928, at 31.

9 *See Scores Remedies for 'Chasing' Evil*, N.Y. TIMES, Feb. 3, 1929, at 22.

10 *See Kill Bills to Stop Ambulance Chasing*, N.Y. TIMES, Mar. 6, 1929, at 32.

11 Record at 1, Palsgraf v. Long Island R.R. Co., 162 N.E. 99 (N.Y. 1928).

12 *Id.* at 5.

13 *Id.*

14 *Id.* at 7.

15 *Id.*

16 *Id.*

17 *Id.* at 8.

18 *See Widow's Record Verdict*, N.Y. TIMES, Dec. 3, 1902, at 1 (awarded for the death of a dry goods store superintendent earning $20,000 a year).

19 *Heirs of Tunnel Victims Get $500,000 in Damages*, N.Y. TIMES, Apr. 21, 1903, at 2 (settlement for the death of the secretary of the United States Paper Bag Co.).

20 Record at 2, Terwilliger v. Long Island R.R. Co., 136 N.Y.S. 733 (App. Div. 1912).

21 Terwilliger v. Long Island R.R. Co., 136 N.Y.S. 733 (App. Div. 1912), *aff'd*, 102 N.E. 1114 (N.Y. 1913).

22 BRIAN J. CUDAHY, THE MALBONE STREET WRECK 114 (1999).

23 *Id.*

24 MINORITY REPORT OF THE COMMITTEE TO INQUIRE INTO DELAYS AND CONGESTION IN THE COURTS OF THE SECOND JUDICIAL DISTRICT 4 (Leg. Doc. No. 62, 1928).

25 *Id.* at 8. In contrast, only 5% were contract actions.

26 *Id.* at 6.

27 *Low Fees Make Courts Paradise for Chasers Here*, BROOKLYN DAILY EAGLE, Sept. 11, 1927, at 24A. For detailed information on court congestion at the time, see generally REPORT TO THE LEGISLATURE OF THE COMMITTEE TO INQUIRE INTO DELAYS AND CONGESTION IN THE COURTS OF THE SECOND JUDICIAL DISTRICT (Leg. Doc. No. 61, 1928) [hereinafter MAJORITY REPORT]; *see also Congestion in Courts Increases Each Year*, N.Y. TIMES, June

6, 1926, at XX20; *Sweeping Changes Urged for Courts to End Congestion*, N.Y. TIMES, June 22, 1927, at 1.

[28] *Longer Court Day Urged By Cropsey*, N.Y. TIMES, July 25, 1927, at 23.

[29] *Justice Lazansky Breaks Record for Disposing of Cases*, BROOKLYN DAILY EAGLE, May 29, 1925.

[30] *See Five Justices to Try 600 Cases in a Week*, N.Y. TIMES, Sept. 27, 1925, at 22.

[31] *See Will Cut Calendar of Supreme Court*, N.Y. TIMES, Jan. 8, 1927, at 35.

[32] *Courts Speed Calendars*, N.Y. TIMES, Feb. 9, 1927, at 4.

[33] MAJORITY REPORT, *supra* note 27, at 8.

[34] Crater later became a supreme court justice and is best remembered for vanishing without a trace in August 1930. The disappearance has never been solved.

[35] *Judges Seek Relief for Crowded Courts*, N.Y. TIMES, Mar. 9, 1927, at 10.

[36] MAJORITY REPORT, *supra* note 27, at 19.

[37] *Id.* at 16.

[38] *Supreme Court Trial Term*, N.Y.L.J., May 24, 1927, at 947.

CHAPTER 5

[1] *Veteran Jurist is 70 Today*, L.I. DAILY PRESS, Apr. 23, 1936, at 2.

[2] *Id.*

[3] *Lazy Bench Issue Soft-Pedaled by Judgeship Rivals*, BROOKLYN DAILY EAGLE, Oct. 25, 1927, at 1.

[4] *Found the Court A-Milking, Lawyer Made His Argument While His Honor Finished the Job*, N.Y. TIMES, Aug. 8, 1908, at 3.

[5] 4 HENRY I. HAZLETON, THE BOROUGHS OF BROOKLYN AND QUEENS; COUNTIES OF NASSAU AND SUFFOLK LONG ISLAND NEW YORK 249 (1925).

[6] *Burt Jay Humphrey Dies; Boro Jurist Many Years*, BROOKLYN DAILY EAGLE, Dec. 11, 1940, at 3.

[7] Humphrey's Washington cases included: *Port v. Parfit*, 30 P. 328 (Wash. 1892) (mortgage foreclosure); *Sayward v. Nunan*, 32 P. 1022 (Wash. 1893) (chattel mortgage); *Blumenthal v. Pacific Meat Co.*, 41 P. 47 (Wash. 1895) (breach of sales contract); *Fairfield v. Binnian*, 42 P. 632 (Wash. 1895) (chattel mortgage).

8 Every court challenge was unsuccessful. After the Court of Appeals upheld segregated schools, special legislation, pushed through the legislature by Governor Theodore Roosevelt, finally ended the practice in incorporated municipalities.

9 For a profile of Cassidy, see *Joseph Cassidy of Queens Dies*, N.Y. TIMES, Nov. 22, 1920, at 14.

10 N.Y. CONST. of 1846 art. VI, § 12.

11 *Why Are New York's Judges Elected?*, N.Y. TIMES, Feb. 17, 1915, at 10 (letter to the editor from J. Hampden Dougherty).

12 In the 1920s, it was said that the going rate for appointment as a magistrate was $10,000, and for a place on the general sessions or supreme court, the cost was $25,000 to $50,000. HERBERT MITGANG, THE MAN WHO RODE THE TIGER: THE LIFE AND TIMES OF JUDGE SAMUEL SEABURY 161 (1963).

13 *Ingraham Assails Bossism in Courts*, N.Y. TIMES, May 28, 1915, at 5.

14 *Id.*

15 *Cropsey is "Cruel" Declares Brennan*, BROOKLYN DAILY EAGLE, Oct. 22, 1916, at 5. Cropsey had the reputation of being a curmudgeon, and it was said that many members of the legal community attended his funeral less to pay their respects than to assure themselves that he was really dead.

16 *'Jekyll and Hyde' Retort of Dr. Brennan to Cropsey*, BROOKLYN DAILY EAGLE, Oct. 5, 1916, at 2.

17 *Cropsey an Ingrate, Brennan Charges*, BROOKLYN DAILY EAGLE, Oct. 10, 1916, at 7.

18 *"Cropsey is Hammer Thrower" – Brennan*, BROOKLYN DAILY EAGLE, Oct. 19, 1916, at 20.

19 *The City Vote*, N.Y. TIMES, Nov. 9, 1916, at 4. Whitman's margin of victory was over 21,000 votes. *State Vote for Governor*, N.Y. TIMES, Nov. 9, 1916, at 4.

20 *Vote the Ticket*, DAILY STAR (Long Island City), Oct. 31, 1903, at 8.

21 *For County Judge*, DAILY STAR (Long Island City), Nov. 4, 1903, at 1.

22 *See Judge Finds Lost Boy*, WASH. POST, Apr. 20, 1909, at 6.

23 *Politics and Crime in Queens*, N.Y. TIMES, June 18, at 1914, at 10.

24 *Judge Humphrey Helped Mrs. Eno*, N.Y. TIMES, June 30, 1914, at 10 (letter to the editor from Florence Eno).

25 *The City Vote*, N.Y. TIMES, Nov. 5, 1925, at 6.

26 *See Sentenced to Die in Chair*, N.Y. TIMES, July 3, 1923, at 8.

27 *See* People v. Nunziato, 135 N.E. 827 (N.Y. 1922).

28 *See* People v. Mastrota, 143 N.E. 766 (N.Y. 1924).

29 *Incendiery Gets 39 Years*, N.Y. TIMES, Feb. 8, 1921, at 5.

30 *Bandits in Queens Risk Life Terms*, N.Y. TIMES, Mar. 8, 1921, at 9.

31 *Fake Dry Agents Got $2000 Weekly*, N.Y. TIMES, Jan. 23, 1923, at 23.

32 *See generally* Record, Terry v. Long Island R.R. Co., 153 N.Y.S. 1147 (App. Div. 1915) (affirming judgment of $608.27).

33 *See generally* Record, Martini v. Long Island R.R. Co., 141 N.Y.S. 1131 (App. Div. 1913) (affirming judgment of $663.96).

34 *See generally* Record, Mahnken Bldg. Material Co. v. Long Island R.R. Co., 148 N.Y.S. 1128 (App. Div. 1914) (affirming judgment of $961.75).

35 For reports on the debate over women as jurors, see *Talley Opposes Women As Jurors*, N.Y. TIMES, Jan. 26, 1920, at 15; *Women as Jurors Called a Failure*, N.Y. TIMES, Apr. 29, 1923, at XX2.

36 Gary T. Schwartz, *Tort Law and the Economy in Nineteenth Century America: A Reinterpretation*, 90 YALE L.J. 1717, 1743 (1981).

37 *Id.* at 1769.

38 The 70% figure is based on reported negligence cases where a verdict can determined with reasonable certainty.

39 *See, e.g.*, *Woman Loses $100,000 Suit*, N.Y. TIMES, Dec. 4, 1924, at 26.

40 Robert H. Elder, *Trial by Jury: Is It Passing?*, 6 AM. L. SCH. REV. 290, 294 (1928).

41 Regarded as too small and outmoded, the courthouse was razed during the 1960s.

42 For example, in the *Whiting* case, the railroad submitted a map and two photos of the station, the conductor's list of cars on the train in question, photos of each of these cars, and a photo of a LIRR baggage car.

43 RICHARD A. POSNER, CARDOZO: A STUDY IN REPUTATION 48 (1990).

44 Record at 52, Palsgraf v. Long Island R.R. Co., 162 N.E. 99 (N.Y. 1928) [hereinafter *Palsgraf* Record].

45 *Id.* at 11.

46 JOHN T. NOONAN, PERSONS AND MASKS OF THE LAW: CARDOZO, HOLMES, JEFFERSON, AND WYTHE AS MAKERS OF THE MASKS 123 (1976).

47 Other trials in reported cases held between 1916 and 1927 where the record shows that the railroad did not put in a case include: *Wolchieck v. Long Island Railroad*, 160 N.Y.S. 1151 (App. Div. 1916) (employee killed in railyard); *Hamilton v. Long Island Railroad Co.*, 165 N.Y.S. 1089 (App. Div. 1917) (passenger injured when pushed off crowded platform); *Stark v. Long Island Railroad Co.*, 166 N.Y.S. 1115 (App. Div. 1917) (pedestrian killed at grade-crossing); *Kovarik v. Long Island Railroad Co.*, 178 N.Y.S. 705 (App. Div. 1919) (would-be passenger tripped over cattle guard at station); *O'Donnell v. Long Island Railroad Co.*, 204 N.Y.S. 933 (App. Div. 1924) (employee maimed in workplace accident); *Maiorano v. Long Island Railroad*, 215 N.Y.S. 883 (App. Div. 1926) (grade-crossing fatality); *Brick v. Long Island Railroad Co.*, 215 N.Y.S. 820 (App. Div. 1926), rev'd, 157 N.E. 93 (N.Y. 1927) (drowned tugboat crewman); *Kelly v. Long Island Railroad Co.*, 222 N.Y.S. 832 (App. Div. 1927) (passenger killed when she fell from moving train); *Kuhn v. Long Island Railroad*, 226 N.Y.S. 846 (App. Div. 1928) (boy injured on Penn Station escalator).

[48] Telephone interview with Edward J. Murphy, retired LIRR general attorney.

[49] McNamara's lone objection came when medical expert Dr. Graeme M. Hammond appeared to connect Mrs. Palsgraf's alleged insomnia with the accident. The reference to insomnia was stricken out. *See Palsgraf* Record at 50.

[50] Mrs. Palsgraf said that since the accident she had moved to a new residence with a slightly higher rent. However, this does not indicate any great improvement in living standards. Her new address, 102-33 Jamaica Avenue, was on a main street covered by an elevated train trestle.

[51] *Palsgraf* Record at 24.

[52] *Id.* at 25, 28. He also related that he unsuccessfully offered to identify the man with the package.

[53] Unfortunately, the only other fact about the Gerhardts that can be currently ascertained is that they appear to have moved frequently. At the trial, Herbert Gerhardt indicated that he had moved since the date of the accident. His new address in 1927, as provided in the record, was 81 New Jersey Avenue in the East New York section of Brooklyn. However, a check of the 1930 census records did not list him or his wife at that address.

[54] *Id.* at 25-26.

[55] *Id.* at 45.

[56] *Id.* at 26.

[57] *Id.* at 36.

[58] *Id.* at 25, 27.

[59] *Id.* at 40.

[60] *Id.* at 45.

[61] *Id.* at 23.

[62] *Id.* at 24.

[63] *Id.* at 25.

[64] *Id.* at 37.

65 *Id.*

66 *Id.* at 46.

67 *Id.* at 43.

68 *Id.* at 27.

69 *Id.* at 21.

70 *Id.* at 19.

71 *Id.* at 47.

72 *Id.* at 40.

73 *Id.* at 37.

74 *Id.* at 48. McNamara made this motion when Wood's medical expert, Dr. Graeme M. Hammond, was late getting to court.

75 *Id.* at 34.

76 *Id.* at 33.

77 For a thorough account of William A. Hammond's contributions to American medicine, see BONNIE ELLEN BLUSTEIN, PRESERVE YOUR LOVE FOR SCIENCE: THE LIFE OF WILLIAM A. HAMMOND, AMERICAN NEUROLOGIST (1991).

78 *See* WILLIAM A. HAMMOND & GRAEME M. HAMMOND, A TREATISE ON THE DISEASES OF THE NERVOUS SYSTEM (9th ed. with corrections and additions 1898).

79 *See* Graeme M. Hammond, *On the Proper Method of Executing the Sentence of Death by Hanging*, 22 MED. REC. 426 (1882).

80 *See* Graeme M. Hammond, *The Bicycle in the Treatment of Nervous Diseases*, J. NERVOUS & MENTAL DISORDERS (Jan. 1892).

81 *Blames Bridge*, WASH. POST, July 1, 1906, at E4.

82 *See X-Ray to Stamp Out Crime*, WASH. POST, Mar. 24, 1908, at 6.

83 *See* Graeme M. Hammond, *Spirit Idea Utterly Absurd*, N.Y. TIMES, Dec. 13, 1908, at SM9.

84 *See Science Says Psychic Force Makes Champs*, CHI. TRIB., Sept. 9, 1928, at G8.

85 *Setting Free the Tiger in Woman*, ATLANTA CONST., Jan. 6, 1918, at 13, 14.

86 *Dr. Hammond, Athlete at 80, to Run Four Miles*, N.Y. HERALD-TRIB., Jan. 31, 1938, at 1, 9.

87 S.J. Woolf, *Hammond Tells What Makes an Athlete at 80*, N.Y. TIMES, Mar. 13, 1938, at 138.

88 BLUSTEIN, *supra* note 77, at 15.

89 *Thaw Testimony May Close To-day*, N.Y. TIMES, Mar. 19, 1907, at 1. Thaw escaped conviction when the jury failed to agree, and was acquitted on the grounds of insanity in a second trial. He later declared bankruptcy, and Hammond was not paid his $1,000 fee. Unlike some other alienists, he did not sue, saying, "I never take that course with a patient, and I shall not break my rule in this case." *Thaw's Wife Fears He'll Cut Her Off*, N.Y. TIMES, Aug. 11, 1908, at 2.

90 *Palsgraf* Record at 50.

91 *Id.*

92 *Id.* at 51.

93 Telephone interview with Dr. Rachel Yehuda, Professor of Psychiatry, Mount Sinai School of Medicine, New York (Feb. 2005).

94 *Palsgraf* Record at 51.

95 For a discussion of the development of medical thinking on psychological trauma, see Ralph Harrington, *The Railway Accident: Trains, Trauma and Technological Crises in Nineteenth Century Britain*, *in* TRAUMATIC PASTS: HISTORY, PSYCHIATRY, AND TRAUMA IN THE MODERN AGE 44 (Mark S. Micale & Paul Lerner eds., 2001).

96 *Id.* (citing JOHN E. ERICHSEN, ON RAILWAY AND OTHER INJURIES OF THE NERVOUS SYSTEM 112-13 (1866)).

97 For a discussion of Charcot, see Mark Micale, *John-Martin Charcot and les nevoses traumatiques: From Medicine to Culture in French Trauma Theory of the Late Nineteenth Century*, *in* TRAUMATIC PASTS, *supra* note 95, at 115.

98 Clark Bell, *Railway Spine*, 12 MEDICO-LEGAL J. 133 (1894–95), *cited in* Eric Caplan, *Trains and Trauma in the American Gilded Age, in* TRAUMATIC PASTS, *supra* note 95, at 71.

99 HAMMOND & HAMMOND, *supra* note 78, at 737.

100 *Id.* at 52.

101 *See, e.g.*, NOONAN, *supra* note 46, at 127.

102 Francis X. Dercum, *The Back in Railway Spine*, 102 AM. J. MED. SCI. 264 (1891), *cited in* Caplan, *supra* note 98, at 71.

103 *Palsgraf* Record at 55.

104 *Id.*

105 *Id.* at 56. Judge Noonan regards Humphrey's charge as "balanced." NOONAN, *supra* note 46, at 130.

106 Holding that another part of the charge constituted reversible error, the Appellate Division ordered a new trial. *See* Kelly v. Long Island R.R. Co., 222 N.Y.S. 832 (App. Div. 1927).

[107] *See* Leibowitz v. Long Island R.R. Co., 157 N.Y.S. 1132 (App. Div. 1916) (reversing trial court and ordering a new trial) (verdict amount provided by the Record at 11).

[108] Here, there was testimony that the woman would never be able to eat solid food again. *See $25,000 for Broken Jaw*, N.Y. TIMES, May 28, 1916. This award was upheld by the Appellate Division. *See* Zatulove v. Long Island R.R. Co., 167 N.Y.S. 1135 (App. Div. 1917).

[109] *See* Ullmann v. Long Island R.R. Co., 130 N.E. 888 (N.Y. 1920), *aff'g* 172 N.Y.S. 923 (App. Div. 1918) (reversing trial court and dismissing complaint) (verdict amount provided by the Record at 11).

[110] *See* O'Donnell v. Long Island R.R. Co., 204 N.Y.S. 933 (App. Div. 1924) (verdict amount provided by the Record at 17).

[111] Like Mrs. Palsgraf, the plaintiff was diagnosed as suffering from hysteria with no certain prognosis for when she would recover. *See Woman Wins Injury Suit*, N.Y. TIMES, Jan. 9, 1925, at 6.

[112] Meyers v. Hines, 191 N.Y.S. 773, 774 (App. Div. 1922).

[113] Brown v. Long Island R.R. Co., 147 N.Y.S. 730 (App. Div. 1914) (per curium opinion affirming trial court and reprinting its opinion). *See also* Hunt v. Long Island R.R. Co., 115 N.Y.S. 478 (App. Div. 1909); Meanley v. Long Island R.R. Co., 141 N.Y.S. 1131 (App. Div. 1913); Harrigan v. Long Island R.R. Co., 219 N.Y.S. 829 (App. Div. 1926).

[114] *Brown*, 147 N.Y.S. at 732.

[115] *Palsgraf* Record at 58.

CHAPTER 6

[1] 2 REVISED RECORD OF THE CONSTITUTIONAL CONVENTION OF THE STATE OF NEW YORK 897 (William H. Steele reviser, 1900).

[2] N.Y. CONST. of 1894 § 9.

[3] *Table Showing the Number of Decisions and Opinions of the Appellate Divisions for the Years 1920–1922*, REPORT OF THE COMMISSION ON THE ADMINISTRATION OF JUSTICE IN NEW YORK STATE (Leg. Doc. No. 50, 1934).

[4] *Justice Lazansky Explains Duties of Appellate Court*, BROOKLYN DAILY EAGLE (press clipping from 1927 or 1928 on file at the Brooklyn Public Library).

[5] *La Guardia Calls M'Cooey Grasping*, N.Y. TIMES, Oct. 19, 1929, at 4.

[6] *Curry and M'Cooey Caused City Crisis Seabury Charges*, N.Y. TIMES, Dec. 10, 1932, at 1.

[7] *M'Cooey's Estate Put At $719,288*, N.Y. TIMES, Jan. 9, 1937, at 28.

8 *See* HERBERT MITGANG, THE MAN WHO RODE THE TIGER: THE LIFE AND TIMES OF JUDGE SAMUEL SEABURY 234-36 (1963).

9 *Asks Extra Session to Bar Bench Deal*, N.Y. TIMES, Oct. 28, 1931, at 4.

10 *Judicial Spoils*, N.Y. TIMES, Oct. 24, 1931, at 16.

11 *Will Seek Reforms in Picking Judges*, N.Y. TIMES, Nov. 30, 1931, at 25. The voters proved less upset by the bipartisan judicial deal than the *New York Times* editorial writers and good government reformers. Even McCooey's son, who fared less well at the polls than others on the ticket, outpolled the leading No Deal Judiciary Party candidate by a margin of 5 to 1. *See Bench Deal Protest Unheeded at Polls*, N.Y. TIMES, Nov. 4, 1931, at 1.

12 *E. Lazansky Dies; A Former Justice*, N.Y. TIMES, Sept. 13, 1955, at 31.

13 *Hylan's Victory is a Tammany Record*, N.Y. TIMES, Nov. 8, 1917, at 2.

14 *In re* Grilli, 179 N.Y.S. 795 (Sup. Ct. Sp. T. Kings County 1920).

15 *See* Ottinger v. Vorhies, 211 N.Y.S. 861 (Sup. Ct. Sp. T. Kings County), *aff'd*, 210 N.Y.S. 193 (App. Div.), *aff'd*, 148 N.E. 784 (N.Y. 1925).

16 *See* Minns v. Crossman, 193 N.Y.S. 714 (Sup. Ct. Kings County 1922).

17 *Blushing Spooners Untangle and Court Trial Resumes*, BROOKLYN DAILY EAGLE (1925 press clipping on file at the Brooklyn Public Library).

18 *Lawyer is Denounced by Justice Lazansky*, N.Y. TIMES, Dec. 17, 1922, at 3. Axtell, known for his battles for seamen's rights, was disbarred for soliciting cases, but was reinstated in 1933. He also represented the estate of Thomas V. Brick, the crewman who drowned after falling off a LIRR tugboat.

19 *See In re* Murphy, 151 N.Y.S. 267 (App. Div. 1914). In 1912, Carswell had won by a comfortable margin of 2,525 votes.

20 *Carswell for O'Neill of Course*, BROOKLYN DAILY EAGLE, Oct. 20, 1916. The support of McCooey and Carswell did O'Neill little good in the general election; he lost by a wide margin to Republican Harry Lewis, becoming another Democratic victim of the landslide victory of Republican gubernatorial candidate Charles S. Whitman.

21 *See* Parkes v. N.Y. Tel. Co., 198 N.Y.S. 698 (Sup. Ct. Queens County), *aff'd*, 201 N.Y.S. 930 (App. Div. 1923).

22 *Would Organize as Peasants; No Classes Here*, BROOKLYN DAILY EAGLE, Apr. 28, 1926 (press clipping on file at the Brooklyn Public Library).

23 *See* McConnell v. Morse Iron Works & Dry Dock Co., 80 N.E. 190 (N.Y. 1907).

24 *See* Mengis v. Fitzgerald, 95 N.Y.S. 436 (App. Div. 1905). A second trial resulted in a hung jury. The case was later reportedly settled for $300,000.

25 *See City Vote*, N.Y. TIMES, Nov. 10, 1921, at 4.

26 Smith won New York City by over 478,000 votes. Carswell with 324,511 votes, and Hagarty with 312,100, easily outpolled the Republican candidates, supreme court Justice Frank S. Gannon, and former Kings County Judge William R. Bayes. *The City Vote*, N.Y. TIMES, Nov. 9, 1922, at 4.

27 *Dolphin Sends New Apology to Court*, N.Y. TIMES, Dec. 11, 1923, at 15.

28 *Justice Hagarty Admits He'll Miss Bench*, BROOKLYN DAILY EAGLE, Dec. 21, 1947 (press clipping on file at the Brooklyn Public Library). The level of interest in the case was so high that a *New York Daily News* reporter strapped a small camera to his ankle and photographed Snyder as she sat in the electric chair; his photo appeared on the front page of the paper under the one-word headline, "DEAD!"

29 *See* Standard Trust Co. v. N.Y. Cent. & Hudson River R.R. Co., 70 N.E. 925 (N.Y. 1904), *aff'g* 84 N.Y.S. 1147 (App. Div. 1903) (Perrin); Dimon v. N.Y. Cent. & Hudson River R.R. Co., 66 N.E. 1 (N.Y. 1903), *aff'g* 77 N.Y.S. 1125 (App. Div. 1902).

30 *See* People v. Pierson, 68 N.E. 243 (N.Y. 1903); *see also Faith Curist's Belief*, N.Y. TIMES, Nov. 21, 1902, at 1.

31 For a profile of Ward, see *W.L Ward Dies at 76 After an Operation*, N.Y. TIMES, July 17, 1933, at 1.

32 *Supreme Court Vote Close*, N.Y. TIMES, Nov. 7, 1915, at 23.

33 *Judge Platt Wins Justiceship*, N.Y. TIMES, Nov. 10, 1915, at 22.

34 *Republicans Split in Judiciary Fight*, N.Y. TIMES, Aug. 22, 1922, at 3.

35 *J. Addison Young, a Retired Justice*, N.Y. TIMES, Sept. 25, 1953, at 21. A LexisNexis search located 206 reported decisions by Young.

36 *Mount Vernon Bars Hearst Newspapers*, N.Y. TIMES, May 15, 1918, at 7.

37 Star Co. v. Brush, 172 N.Y.S. 661, 662 (Sup. Ct. Westchester County), *rev'd*, 172 N.Y.S. 851 (App. Div. 1918).

38 *Hearst Paper Ban Upheld by Court*, N.Y. TIMES, July 19, 1918, at 13.

39 *Star Co.*, 172 N.Y.S. at 851-52.

40 *See* Hammond v. Long Island R.R. Co., 173 N.Y.S. 908 (App. Div. 1918).

41 One folder in the Seeger papers at the State Library in Albany contains nothing but horse-related receipts.

42 *Two Judges in Horse Race*, N.Y. TIMES, Dec. 17, 1912, at 4.

43 *See* People v. Pollock, 4 N.Y.S. 297 (Sup. Ct. Gen. T. 1889).

44 *Little Stories of Fact and Fancy*, N.Y. TIMES, Sept. 21, 1913, at SM8.

45 *See* Hintze v. New York Cent. R.R. Co., 125 N.Y.S. 644 (App. Div. 1910); Brooks v. Erie R.R. Co., 163 N.Y.S. 1111 (App. Div. 1917).

[46] *See In re* Thaw, 143 N.Y.S. 854 (App. Div. 1913).

[47] The governor then ordered the attorney general to investigate, an intervention that was later enjoined by Justice Henry T. Kellogg. *See* Ward Baking Co. v. Western Union Telegraph Co., 200 N.Y.S. 865 (App. Div. 1923). Ward was later indicted, but was quickly acquitted.

[48] *See* Stein v. Brown, 211 N.Y.S. 822 (Sup. Ct. Westchester County 1925).

[49] *Conflicting Evidence Halts Alimony Plea*, N.Y. TIMES, July 24, 1922, at 16.

[50] Browning v. Browning, 220 N.Y.S. 651, 655 (Sup. Ct. Putnam County 1927).

CHAPTER 7

[1] Record at 12, Palsgraf v. Long Island R.R. Co., 162 N.E. 99 (N.Y. 1928) [hereinafter *Palsgraf* Record].

[2] Cases between 1912 and 1927 where the opinion and/or the record indicate that the plaintiff was a passenger include: *Blaisdell v. Long Island Railroad Co.*, 136 N.Y.S. 768 (App. Div. 1912) (assault in waiting room); *Hamilton v. Long Island Railroad Co.*, 165 N.Y.S. 1089 (App. Div. 1917) (pushed off crowded platform); *Kovarik v. Long Island Railroad Co.*, 178 N.Y.S. 705 (App. Div. 1919) (would-be passenger tripped over cattle guard at station); *Meyers v. Hines*, 191 N.Y.S. 773 (App. Div. 1922) (attempt to board moving train); *Whiting v. Long Island Railroad Co.*, 193 N.Y.S. 958 (App. Div. 1922) (fall from moving train); *Wiren v. Long Island Railroad Co.*, 226 N.Y.S. 103 (App. Div. 1923) (fall while getting off train); *Kelly v. Long Island Railroad Co.*, 222 N.Y.S. 832 (App. Div. 1927) (fatal fall from moving train). A case that involved the railroad's liability for the conduct of another passenger was *Davis v. Long Island R.R. Co.*, 143 N.Y.S. 1112 (1st Dep't App. T. 1913), holding the railroad not liable where one passenger dropped a board on the foot of another.

[3] *See* JOHN T. NOONAN, PERSONS AND MASKS OF THE LAW: CARDOZO, HOLMES, JEFFERSON, AND WYTHE AS MAKERS OF MASKS 126 (1976).

[4] *See* Pell v. Long Island R.R. Co., 139 N.Y.S. 1132 (App. Div. 1916). The court held that the jury's finding that the train whistle did not blow was against the greater weight of the evidence and that certain charges were either confusing or erroneous.

[5] *See* Wiren v. Long Island R.R. Co., 226 N.Y.S. 103 (App. Div. 1923).

[6] *See* Brick v. Long Island R.R. Co., 215 N.Y.S. 820 (App. Div. 1926), *rev'd*, 157 N.E. 93 (N.Y. 1927).

[7] *See* D'Aurio v. Long Island R.R. Co., 219 N.Y.S. 796 (App. Div. 1926).

[8] *See* Kelly v. Long Island R.R. Co., 222 N.Y.S. 832 (App. Div. 1927).

[9] *See In re* Walsh, 164 N.Y.S. 553 (App. Div. 1917) (attorney disbarred for converting $200 of client's funds and then failing to make restitution).

10 *See* McLaughlin v. Mendelson, 144 N.Y.S. 1073 (App. Div. 1913).

11 *See* Clyde v. Wood, 179 N.Y.S. 252 (App. Div. 1919).

12 *See* Huott v. Wood, 167 N.Y.S. 754 (App. Div. 1917).

13 Brief of Plaintiff-Respondent at 2. Palsgraf v. Long Island R.R. Co., 225 N.Y.S. 412 (App. Div. 1927) [hereinafter Plaintiff-Respondent's Brief].

14 *Id.* at 3.

15 *Id.*

16 *Id.*

17 *Id.* at 5.

18 *Id.* at 4.

19 *Id.* at 7.

20 Scott v. Shepard, 2 Wm. Black. 892, 96 Eng. Rep. 525 (K.B. 1773).

21 Vandenburgh v. Truax, 4 Den. 464 (N.Y. 1847).

22 Guille v. Swan, 19 Johns. 381 (N.Y. Sup. Ct. 1822).

23 Plaintiff-Respondent's Brief at 10 (quoting Saugerties Bank v. Delaware & Hudson Co., 141 N.E. 904, 907 (N.Y. 1923) (Andrews, J., dissenting)).

24 Plaintiff-Respondent's Brief at 14. In his brief, Wood stated: "The platform man and the train guard certainly knew how this accident occurred. They were not produced and did not testify." *Id.*

25 Brief for Defendant-Appellant at 5, Palsgraf v. Long Island R.R. Co., 225 N.Y.S. 412, 413 (App. Div. 1927).

26 113 N.E. 529, 529 (N.Y. 1916) (boy killed by nitroglycerine caps stolen from an unlocked company storage chest).

27 125 N.E. 93, 93 (N.Y. 1919) (boy shocked and burned when he touched an electric trolley wire with an eight-foot-long wire).

28 Brief for Defendant-Appellant at 8, Palsgraf v. Long Island R.R. Co., 225 N.Y.S. 412, 413 (App. Div. 1927) (emphasis in original).

29 *Id.*

30 *Id.*

31 Five additional Seeger opinions appear in *Appellate Division Reports* between 1921 and 1926. These are cases from special term, where Seeger's opinion was reprinted along with the Appellate Division decision.

[32] Palsgraf v. Long Island R.R. Co., 225 N.Y.S. 412, 413 (App. Div. 1927), *rev'd*, 162 N.E. 99 (N.Y. 1928).

[33] *Id.*

[34] *Id.* at 414.

[35] DAVID W. ROBERTSON ET AL., CASES AND MATERIALS ON TORTS 192 (1989).

[36] *Palsgraf*, 225 N.Y.S. at 414 (Lazansky, P.J., dissenting).

[37] *Id.* at 415.

CHAPTER 8

[1] By 1915, even with extra judges, the court was two years behind on its calendar. A proposal to reestablish a second division was included in the proposed 1915 Constitution that was rejected by the voters; only a marked decrease in cases caused by World War I brought an end to the calendar problem.

[2] Although it is no longer utilized, the provision allowing the appointment of temporary judges is still part of the New York State Constitution. *See* N.Y. CONST. art. 6, § 2(b) (McKinney Supp. 2005).

[3] 94 N.E. 431 (N.Y. 1911).

[4] 1910 N.Y. Laws ch. 674.

[5] HERBERT MITGANG, THE MAN WHO RODE THE TIGER: THE LIFE AND TIMES OF JUDGE SAMUEL SEABURY 108 (1963). Privately, Seabury characterized the court's chief judge, Willard Bartlett as "a seasoned ultraconservative who slavishly retarded social growth." *Id.* at 109.

[6] *Roosevelt Answers Cry of Revolution*, N.Y. TIMES, Feb. 27, 1912, at 1.

[7] ANDREW L. KAUFMAN, CARDOZO 138 (1998).

[8] Irving Lehman, *Judge Cardozo in the Court of Appeals*, 52 HARV. L. REV. 364, 369 (1939).

[9] 111 N.E. 1050 (N.Y. 1916).

[10] 118 N.E. 214 (N.Y. 1917).

[11] 129 N.E. 889 (N.Y. 1921).

[12] 159 N.E. 173 (N.Y. 1927).

[13] KAUFMAN, *supra* note 7, at 40.

[14] *Id.* at 20.

[15] *Id.* at 309.

16 McCunn and Barnard were convicted and removed from office. McCunn died only a few days after his removal; Barnard returned to private life and died in 1879.

17 The 1880 census report shows the family living at 803 Madison Avenue with six Irish domestics, including three servants, a cook, a waitress, and a maid.

18 *Ex-Judge Cardozo's Will*, N.Y. TIMES, Nov. 17, 1885, at 8.

19 KAUFMAN, *supra* note 7, at 21-22

20 *Id.* at 22.

21 Among Cardozo's siblings, only his twin sister, Emily, married.

22 KAUFMAN, *supra* note 7, at 69.

23 MITGANG, *supra* note 5, at 109.

24 KAUFMAN, *supra* note 7, at 24.

25 *See* Carpenter v. City of New York, 101 N.Y.S. 402 (App. Div. 1906).

26 *See* Devine v. Alphons Custodis Chimney Constr. Co., 91 N.E. 791 (N.Y. 1910).

27 *See* Perley v. Shubert, 106 N.Y.S. 593 (App. Div. 1907).

28 *See* Perley v. Shubert, 128 N.Y.S. 925 (App. Div.), *aff'd*, 93 N.E. 1129 (N.Y. 1910).

29 *See* Ziegfeld v. Norworth, 133 N.Y.S. 208 (App. Div.), *aff'd*, 96 N.E. 1135 (1911).

30 *See* Masterson v. Commercial Advertiser Ass'n, 144 N.Y.S. 1129 (App. Div. 1913).

31 KAUFMAN, *supra* note 7, at 119.

32 *Justice Candidates All of High Grade*, N.Y. TIMES, Oct. 31, 1913, at 5.

33 *Fusion Appeals for Its Judges*, N.Y. TIMES, Nov. 2, 1913, at 12.

34 KAUFMAN, *supra* note 7, at 125.

35 *Id.* Cardozo did especially well in the 32nd and 34th assembly districts.

36 *See* Felberbaum v. Union Ry. (Sup. Ct. N.Y. County), N.Y. L.J., Feb. 4, 1914, at 2230; KAUFMAN, *supra* note 7, at 127.

37 KAUFMAN, *supra* note 7, at 127-28. The annual salary of supreme court justices in the First Department was several thousand dollars higher than those on the Court of Appeals.

38 *Judges Heed Bars Request*, N.Y. TIMES, Jan. 21, 1917, at B4.

39 *Id.* at 164.

40 N.Y. TIMES, *supra* note 38, at B4.

41 Cardozo reportedly sometimes regretted his lack of trial experience, believing that only in this way would an appellate judge learn how to "appraise the possible effects of errors committed during a trial; that only a judge who knows the atmosphere of a trial is fitted to determine whether error committed in its heat is prejudicial." Lehman, *supra* note 8, at 383.

42 *See* Dean v. Dean, 149 N.E. 844 (N.Y. 1925).

43 *See* Finlay v. Finlay, 148 N.E. 624 (N.Y. 1925).

44 *See* Hoadley v. Hoadley, 155 N.E. 728 (N.Y. 1927).

45 *See* Mirizio v. Mirizio, 161 N.E. 461 (N.Y. 1928).

46 *See* People v. Chiagles, 142 N.E. 583 (N.Y. 1923).

47 *See* People v. Bertlini, 113 N.E. 541 (N.Y. 1916).

48 *See* People v. Gerks, 153 N.E. 36 (N.Y. 1924).

49 *See* People v. Werblow, 148 N.E. 786 (N.Y. 1925).

50 *See* People v. Schmidt, 110 N.E. 945 (N.Y. 1916); People v. Emieleta, 144 N.E. 487 (N.Y. 1924) (Chinese laundryman beaten to death during a robbery); People v. Moran, 158 N.E. 35 (N.Y. 1927) (fatal shooting of two police officers). In *Moran*, Cardozo reversed the conviction and ordered a second trial. A second conviction was affirmed in a per curium opinion in which Cardozo concurred. *See* 163 N.E. 553 (N.Y. 1928).

51 For a critical look at Cardozo's opinion in *Schmidt*, see Christopher Hawthorne, Comment, *"Deific Decree": The Short, Happy Life of a Pseudo-Doctrine*, 33 LOYOLA L.A. L. REV. 1755 (2000).

52 125 N.E. 93 (N.Y. 1919) (verdict amount provided in the Record at 135).

53 *See* Baker v. Lehigh Valley R.R. Co., 161 N.E. 445 (N.Y. 1928).

54 *See* Hynes v. N.Y. Cent. R.R. Co., 131 N.E. 898 (N.Y. 1921). Here, Cardozo supplied the name of the victim, and described him as a "lad of sixteen." *Id.* at 898.

55 *See* Hinz v. Eighth Ave. Ry. Co., 152 N.E. 475 (N.Y. 1926).

56 133 N.E. 437 (N.Y. 1921). Unlike *Palsgraf*, Cardozo supplied the names of the victims and provided accurate details about the accident, although he gives the impression by the use of the term "body" that the man who was thrown from the trolley was killed. Ironically, the trial record reveals that the would-be rescuer was far more seriously injured. Herbert Wagner dislocated a shoulder and was knocked unconscious by his fall, but he completely recovered and was drafted during World War I. Arthur Wagner suffered permanent disabling injuries to his legs and feet.

57 *Id.* at 437, *rev'g* 180 N.Y.S. 957 (App. Div. 1919).

58 *Judge Pound, Made Appeals Chief, Sworn in at Lockport* (undated press clipping on file at the Lockport Public Library).

59 *Cerebral Hemorrhage Fatal to Judge Pound*, BUFF. COURIER EXPRESS, Feb. 4, 1935, at 1.

60 In Memoriam: Minutes of the Court of Appeals in Reference to Honorable Cuthbert W. Pound, A Former Chief Judge of the Court of Appeals, 266 N.Y. vii (1935).

61 KARL L. LLEWELLYN, THE COMMON LAW TRADITION: DECIDING APPEALS 106 (1960).

62 BUFF. COURIER EXPRESS, *supra* note 59, at 1.

63 Ives v. S. Buffalo Ry., 94 N.E. 431 (N.Y. 1911).

64 Ives v. S. Buffalo Ry., 124 N.Y.S. 920, 924 (Sup. Ct. Erie County), *aff'd*, 125 N.Y.S. 1125 (App. Div. 1910), *rev'd*, 94 N.E. 431 (N.Y. 1911).

65 *See* 1913 N.Y. Laws ch. 816.

66 Burritt v. Burritt, 102 N.Y.S. 475, 476 (Sup. Ct. Erie County 1907).

67 *See, e.g.*, Goodrich v. Village of Otego, 110 N.E. 162 (N.Y. 1915) (married woman's property rights); Matter of Thorne, 148 N.E. 630 (N.Y. 1925) (child custody); Seyford v. S. Pac. Co., 111 N.E. 248 (N.Y. 1916) (injured employee); McGuire v. N.Y. Rys. Co., 128 N.E. 905 (N.Y. 1920) (dissenting) (contributory negligence).

68 *See* Carr v. Pennsylvania R.R. Co., 121 N.E. 473 (N.Y. 1918); Chamberlain v. Lehigh Valley R.R. Co., 144 N.E. 512 (N.Y. 1924).

69 *See* Goldstein v. Pullman Co., 116 N.E. 376 (N.Y. 1917).

70 Frederick W.H. Crane played in twenty-one games during the 1875 season, and batted .210. THE BASEBALL ENCYCLOPEDIA 54 (Joseph L. Reichler ed., 7th ed. 1988).

71 *Illustrations on the Judiciary*, BROOKLYN DAILY EAGLE, Nov. 3, 1901, at 8.

72 *Who's Who in Brooklyn: Justice Frederick Crane*, BROOKLYN DAILY EAGLE (1911 press clipping on file at the Brooklyn Public Library).

73 *Court Scores Divorce Evil*, N.Y. TIMES, June 3, 1915, at 5.

74 *See* People v. Fitzgerald, 155 N.E. 584 (N.Y. 1927).

75 *See* Sydney v. McFadden Newspaper Publ'g Corp., 151 N.E. 209 (N.Y. 1926).

76 *See* Horton v. N.Y. Cent. R.R. Co., 142 N.E. 345 (N.Y. 1923) (verdict amount provided in the Record at 15).

77 *See* McDade v. Int'l Ry. Co., 138 N.E. 488 (N.Y. 1923).

78 *See* Unger v. Belt Line Ry. Corp., 136 N.E. 303 (N.Y. 1922) (verdict amount provided in the Appellant's brief at 1).

79 *See* Fitch v. N.Y. Cent. R.R. Co., 135 N.E. 598 (N.Y. 1922) (verdict amount provided in the Record at 34).

80 *See* Castle v. Director Gen. of Railroads, 134 N.E. 334 (N.Y. 1922) (verdict amount provided in the Record at 21).

81 *See* Psota v. Long Island R.R. Co., 159 N.E. 180 (N.Y. 1927) (verdict amounts provided in the Record at 3).

82 *Irving Lehman*, N.Y. TIMES, Oct. 19, 1908, at 2.

83 MITGANG, *supra* note 5, at 161.

84 *Murphy Advanced Steadily to Power*, N.Y. TIMES, Apr. 26, 1924, at 2.

85 *C.F. Murphy Estate Valued at $2,170,761*, N.Y. TIMES, Nov. 28, 1925, at 1.

86 *Parsons Questions Straus*, N.Y. TIMES, Oct. 20, 1908, at 1.

87 *City Vote Revised*, N.Y. TIMES, Nov. 5, 1908, at 3.

88 *Id.*

89 *Dicks Lose Railroad Suit*, N.Y. TIMES, Mar. 21, 1917, at 5.

90 1922 N.Y. Laws ch. 590.

91 *See* People v. Weller, 143 N.E. 205 (N.Y. 1924).

92 *See* Interborough Rapid Transit Co. v. Lavin, 159 N.E. 408 (N.Y. 1928).

93 *See* People v. Buzzi, 144 N.E. 653 (N.Y. 1924).

94 *See* People v. Soper, 153 N.E. 433 (N.Y. 1926).

95 *See* People v. Pantano, 146 N.E. 646 (N.Y. 1925).

96 *See* People v. Snyder, 159 N.E. 863 (N.Y. 1927).

97 *See* Canudo v. N.Y. Int'l Ry. Co., 159 N.E. 879 (N.Y. 1928).

98 *Current Topics*, 60 ALBANY L.J. 209, 212 (1899).

99 *See* Nat'l Cash Register Co. v. South Bay Club House Ass'n, 118 N.Y.S. 1044 (Sup. Ct. Onondaga County 1909).

100 *See* George v. Pierce, 148 N.Y.S. 230 (Sup. Ct. Onondaga County 1914).

101 *See* 1908 N.Y. Laws ch. 429.

102 *See* Lindsley v. Nat'l Carbonic Gas Co., 220 U.S. 61 (1911).

103 *Court Deals Blow to Barnes's Case*, N.Y. TIMES, May 11, 1915, at 10.

104 *See* People v. Westchester County Nat'l Bank of Peekskill, 132 N.E. 241 (N.Y. 1921).

105 *To Oppose Andrews for Appeals Judge*, N.Y. TIMES, Sept. 16, 1921, at 3.

106 *Nominate Andrews; Urge Tariff to Aid Foodstuff Exports*, N.Y. TIMES, Sept. 24, 1921, at 1, 2.

107 *Judge Andrews*, N.Y. TIMES, Oct. 25, 1921, at 13.

108 *Andrews Elected by 65,152 Majority*, N.Y. TIMES, Dec. 16, 1921, at 6.

109 Halsey v. New York Soc'y for Suppression of Vice, 136 N.E. 219, 220 (N.Y. 1922).

110 *Id.* at 223 (Crane, J., dissenting).

111 Moses v. Bd. of Educ. of the City of Syracuse, 156 N.E. 631, 632 (N.Y. 1927).

112 *See* Exchange Bakery & Restaurant v. Rifkin, 157 N.E. 130 (N.Y. 1927).

113 *See* Globe Malleable Iron & Steel Co. v. N.Y. Cent. & Harlem River R.R. Co., 124 N.E. 109 (N.Y. 1919).

114 *See* Campbell v. Richmond Light & R.R. Co., 127 N.E. 271 (N.Y. 1920).

115 *See* DiCaprio v. N.Y. Cent. R.R. Co., 131 N.E. 746 (N.Y. 1921).

116 Editorial, TROY TIMES, *reprinted in* ELIZABETHTOWN POST & GAZETTE, July 2, 1903, at 2.

117 *See* Klauder v. Gabriels, 147 N.Y.S. 862 (App. Div. 1914).

118 *See* Goodrich v. Erie R.R. Co., 170 N.Y.S. 394 (App. Div. 1918); Troy v. Rutland R.R. Co., 173 N.Y.S. 895 (App. Div. 1919); Cassidy v. Fonda, Johnstown & Gloversville R.R. Co., 193 N.Y.S. 275 (App. Div. 1922); Behrens v. N.Y. Cent. R.R. Co., 218 N.Y.S. 274 (App. Div. 1926).

119 *See* D'Angelo v. N.Y. Cent. R.R. Co., 205 N.Y.S. 435 (App. Div. 1924).

120 *See* Ward v. Erie R.R. Co., 172 N.Y.S. 691 (App. Div. 1918).

121 *See* Hodas v. Davis, 196 N.Y.S. 801 (App. Div. 1922).

122 *See* Kentfield v. N.Y. Cent. R.R. Co., 199 N.Y.S. 860 (App. Div. 1923).

123 *See* Maiorano v. Long Island R.R. Co., 155 N.E. 681 (N.Y. 1927). On the appeal, the LIRR was represented by Doc Brennan and the Keanys.

124 A Westlaw search located 145 reported Court of Appeals cases with O'Brien listed as one of the attorneys. His one Supreme Court case was dismissed for lack of jurisdiction. *See* City of New York v. McEntree, 263 U.S. 688 (1924).

125 *See* Eckert v. City of New York, 207 N.Y.S. 168 (App. Div. 1924); Carroll v. City of New York, 155 N.E. 886 (N.Y. 1926).

126 *See* Kellman v. City of New York, 200 N.Y.S. 295 (App. T. 1st Dep't 1923); Fessenden v. City of New York, 143 N.E. 734 (N.Y. 1923); Van den Bergh v. City of New York, 203 N.Y.S. 127 (App. Div. 1924); Martin v. City of New York, 154 N.E. 593 (N.Y. 1926).

127 *See* Foley v. City of New York, 194 N.Y.S. 98 (App. T. 1st Dep't 1922).

128 *See* Sweeney v. City of New York, 130 N.E. 884 (N.Y. 1920).

129 *See* Metzroth v. City of New York, 150 N.E. 519 (N.Y. 1926).

130 *See* Horton v. City of New York, 210 N.Y.S. 433 (App. Div. 1925).

131 *See* Cohen v. City of New York, 213 N.Y.S. 710 (App. Div. 1926).

132 *Judge J.F. O'Brien Dies at Home Here*, N.Y. TIMES, Dec. 26, 1939, at 23.

133 *Smith Ire is 'Bunk,' Republicans Say*, N.Y. TIMES, June 15, 1927, at 29.

134 *Butler for O'Brien for Appeals Bench*, N.Y. TIMES, Sept. 14, 1927, at 3.

CHAPTER 9

1 Grounds for appeals to the Court of Appeals were governed by § 588 of the Civil Practice Act, ch. 925, 1920 N.Y. Laws 486 (current version at N.Y. C.P.L.R. § 5601 (McKinney 1995)).

2 Brick v. Long Island R.R. Co., 157 N.E. 93, 93 (N.Y. 1927). Other cases where the LIRR prevailed include: *Ullman v. Long Island Railroad Co.*, 130 N.E. 888 (N.Y. 1920) (woman's foot injured by allegedly defective board at grade-crossing); *D'Aurio v. Long Island Railroad Co.*, 148 N.E. 333 (N.Y. 1925) (trackwalker struck and killed by train); *Psota v. Long Island Railroad Co.*, 159 N.E. 180 (N.Y. 1927) (two children injured in grade-crossing accident).

3 Plaintiff-Respondent's Brief at 5-6, *Palsgraf*, 162 N.E. 99.

4 As he had in his Appellate Division brief, Wood cited *Saugerties Bank v. Delaware & Hudson Co.*, 141 N.E. 904, 905 (N.Y. 1923), where Chief Judge Frank H. Hiscock, citing *Milwaukee & St. Paul Railway v. Kellogg*, 94 U.S. 469, 475 (1876), wrote, "ordinarily it is to be determined as a question of fact whether there has been such a connection between cause and effect as to make the former proximate." In his Court of Appeals brief, he added a citation to Judge Frederick Collin's opinion in *Boyce v. Greeley Square Hotel Company*, 126 N.E. 647, 650 (N.Y. 1920), that states: "It is a rule in actions for negligence that it must be generally left to the jury to determine under the evidence the natural, proximate and fairly to be apprehended consequences of the negligence. It is likewise a rule that in actions for acts tortious in character it must be generally left to the jury to determine under the evidence the direct consequences of the acts."

5 The evidence for this discussion is a type-written memo given to Professor Robert E. Keeton by Warren A. Seavey in 1956 or 1957, bearing the hand-written date of "around 1926–27?." *See* Robert E. Keeton, *A Palsgraf Anecdote*, 56 TEX. L. REV. 513, 514 (1978).

6 ANDREW L. KAUFMAN, CARDOZO 654 n.14 (1998).

7 American Law Institute, Torts Conference Minutes, I, 39-43 (Oct. 23, 1927), *reprinted in* KAUFMAN, *supra* note 6, at 291.

8 *See* KAUFMAN, *supra* note 6, at 292.

9 *Id.* at 446.

10 What is clearly a reference to *Palsgraf* subsequently appeared in the *Restatement of the Law of Torts*. An illustration for § 281(b) (the liability for "conduct [that] is negligent with respect to such interest or any other similar interest of the other which is protected against unintentional invasion") stated:

> A, a passenger of the X and Y Railway Company is attempting to board a train while encumbered with a number of obviously fragile parcels. B, a trainman of the company, in assisting A, does so in a manner as to make it probable that A will drop one or more of the parcels. A drops a parcel which contains fireworks, although nothing in its appearance indicates this. The fireworks explode, injuring A's eyes. The railway company is not liable to A.

2 RESTATEMENT OF THE LAW OF TORTS § 281, at 737-38 (1934) (illus. under (g)).

11 52 MICH. L. REV. 1 (1953).

12 *See id.* at 4-5. A more embellished version of this tale has Cardozo telling those at the ALI meeting that his court currently has before it a case that raises the issue of whether negligence, to be actionable, must be in relation to the plaintiff. Convinced by his arguments, they then purportedly adopt that position. On his return to Albany, Cardozo then supposedly sways the other judges during the conference on *Palsgraf* by telling them that the Restaters are going to define negligence as relational. *See* Guido Calabresi & Jeffrey O. Cooper, *New Directions in Tort Law*, 30 VALPARAISO UNIV. L. REV. 859, 867 (1996). This story, which the authors indicated might be apocryphal, appeared before the publication of Professor Kaufman's Cardozo biography. In addition to the points made by Professor Kaufman, the credibility of this version also suffers severely from the fact that it purports to relate remarks made during a confidential Court of Appeals conference.

13 KAUFMAN, *supra* note 6, at 294.

14 *Id.* at 295.

15 *See Fireworks Blast Laid to Railroad*, N.Y. TIMES, Dec. 10, 1927, at 29. The Appellate Division opinion appears to have been noted only in the *Boston University Law Review* and the *Yale Law Journal*. *See* Robert A. Welsh, Comment, *Negligence – Cause and Condition – Natural and Probable – Consequence –* Palsgraf v. Long Island R. Co., *225 N.Y. Supp. 412 (1928)*, B.U. L. REV. 159 (1928) (finding the precedent of the *Squib Case* unconvincing since the actions there were sudden and compulsive, not careless); *Torts – Negligence – Duty of Carrier to Passenger on Station Platform*, Note, 37 YALE L.J. 1002 (1928) (concluding that "under no theory was there any violation of the duty owed the plaintiff").

16 N.Y.L.J., Dec. 10, 1927, at 1218.

17 Benjamin N. Cardozo, *The Bench and Bar*, 34 N.Y. ST. B.J. 444, 447 (1962) (speech to the Broome County Bar Association given on March 9, 1929).

18 Palsgraf v. Long Island R.R. Co., 162 N.E. 99, 101 (N.Y. 1928).

19 *Id*. at 101.

20 *Id*. at 99.

21 *Id*. at 100.

22 *Id*.

23 2 Wm. Black. 892, 96 Eng. Rep. 525 (K.B. 1773).

24 105 N.E. 795 (N.Y. 1914).

25 82 U.S. (15 Wall.) 534 (1872).

26 125 N.E. 93 (N.Y. 1919).

27 Palsgraf v. Long Island R.R. Co., 162 N.E. 99, 99 (N.Y. 1928) (citing SIR FREDERICK POLLOCK, THE LAW OF TORTS 455 (11th ed. 1920)). For a more extensive discussion of the authorities used by Cardozo, see JOHN T. NOONAN, PERSONS AND MASKS OF THE LAW: CARDOZO, HOLMES, JEFFERSON, AND WYTHE AS MAKERS OF MASKS 135-39 (1976).

28 William Powers, Jr., *Reputology*, 12 CARDOZO L. REV. 1941, 1946 (1991) (reviewing RICHARD A. POSNER, CARDOZO: A STUDY IN REPUTATION (1990)).

29 POSNER, *supra* note 28, at 38.

30 This is not unusual for Cardozo's negligence opinions. A survey of non-workplace negligence cases revealed that in only a few was the plaintiff mentioned by name. In some, however, a few details, most often age, were provided.

31 *Palsgraf*, 162 N.E. at 99.

32 *Id*.

33 Record at 36, Palsgraf v. Long Island R.R. Co., 162 N.E. 99 (N.Y. 1928) [hereinafter *Palsgraf* Record].

34 *Palsgraf*, 162 N.E. at 100.

35 *Palsgraf* Record, *supra* note 33, at 27, 36.

36 *Palsgraf*, 162 N.E. at 100.

37 *Palsgraf* Record, *supra* note 33, at 42.

38 *Id*. at 46-47.

39 *Palsgraf*, 162 N.E. at 99-100.

40 *Id*. at 99.

[41] Affidavit of Helen Palsgraf at 4, Palsgraf v. Long Island R.R. Co., 164 N.E. 564 (N.Y. 1928) (per curiam) [hereinafter *Palsgraf* Affidavit].

[42] POSNER, *supra* note 28, at 43.

[43] KAUFMAN, *supra* note 6, at 446.

[44] Benjamin N. Cardozo, *Law and Literature*, *in* SELECTED WRITINGS 339, 341 (1947).

[45] KAUFMAN, *supra* note 6, at 299.

[46] *Id.* at 445. For another favorable view, see William Powers, Jr., *Reputology*, 12 CARDOZO L. REV. 1941, 1946 (1991) ("But the generality of a statement of facts is always open to dispute, and in any event, abstractness is not disingenuousness.").

[47] James A. Henderson, Jr., MacPherson v. Buick Motor Company: *Simplifying the Facts While Reshaping the Law*, *in* TORTS STORIES 41 (2003).

[48] *Id.* at 53.

[49] 166 N.E. 173 (N.Y. 1929).

[50] Kenneth W. Simons, Murphy v. Steeplechase Amusement Co.: *While the Timerous Stay at Home, the Adventurous Ride the Flopper*, *in* TORTS STORIES, *supra* note 47, at 182.

[51] *Id.* at 204.

[52] Powers, *supra* note 28, at 1946.

[53] POSNER, *supra* note 28, at 38.

[54] Judith M. Schelly, *Interpretation in Law: The Dworkin-Fish Debate (Or Soccer Amongst the Gahuku-Gama)*, 73 CAL. L. REV. 158, 174 n.72 (1985).

[55] *Id.* at 171.

[56] Palsgraf v. Long Island R.R. Co., 162 N.E. 99, 101 (N.Y. 1928) (Andrews, J., dissenting).

[57] POSNER, *supra* note 28, at 45.

[58] *Palsgraf*, 162 N.E. at 102 (Andrews, J., dissenting).

[59] *Id.* at 105 (Andrews, J., dissenting).

[60] *See* POSNER, *supra* note 28, at 45.

[61] *Palsgraf*, 162 N.E. at 103.

[62] *Id.* at 104.

[63] Keeton, *supra* note 5, at 516.

[64] *Palsgraf*, 162 N.E. at 104.

[65] *Id.*

[66] *Id.*

[67] *Id.* at 105.

[68] *Id.*

[69] *Id.*

[70] *Id.* at 7.

[71] *Id.* at 10.

[72] *Id.* at 11.

[73] *Palsgraf* Affidavit, *supra* note 41, at 17.

[74] *Id.*

[75] *See* Lewine v. Nat'l City Bank of New York, 162 N.E. 284 (N.Y.), *reargument granted*, 164 N.Y. 564 (N.Y. 1928). For an example of another Cardozo decision where reargument was denied, see Berkey v. Third Ave. Ry. Co, 155 N.E. 58 (N.Y. 1926), *reargument denied*, 155 N.E. 914 (N.Y. 1927).

[76] Learned Hand, Tribute to the Memory of the late Benjamin Cardozo of the Supreme Court of the United States 2-3, *quoted in* KAUFMAN, *supra* note 6, at 165.

[77] KAUFMAN, *supra* note 6, at 165 (quoting former Cardozo clerk Ambrose Doskow).

[78] Palsgraf v. Long Island R.R. Co., 164 N.E. 564, 564 (N.Y. 1928) (per curium).

CHAPTER 10

[1] Defendant-Appellant's Memorandum in Opposition to Plaintiff-Respondent's Motion for Reargument at 3, Palsgraf v. Long Island R.R. Co., 164 N.E. 564 (N.Y. 1928) (per curium).

[2] *Id.*

[3] Affidavit of Helen Palsgraf at 7, Palsgraf v. Long Island R.R. Co., 164 N.E. 564 (N.Y. 1928) (per curium) [hereinafter *Palsgraf* Affidavit].

[4] *See* RICHARD A. POSNER, CARDOZO: A STUDY IN REPUTATION 43 n.19 (1990).

[5] The standard gauge for American railroad tracks is four feet, eight and one-half inches. San Diego Railway Museum, SDRM Rail Gauge Derivation, http://www.sdrm.org/faqs/gauge/index.html (last modified Jan. 18, 2002).

[6] At the trial, Mrs. Palsgraf estimated the width of the platform as twelve to fifteen feet. Record at 17, Palsgraf v. Long Island R.R. Co., 162 N.E. 99 (N.Y. 1928) [hereinafter *Palsgraf* Record].

7 *Id.*

8 Telephone Interview with Ron Ziel. For photographs showing the space between the side of a car and the typical LIRR platform, see RON ZIEL, THE LONG ISLAND RAIL ROAD IN EARLY PHOTOGRAPHS 62 (1990); Vincent F. Seyfried, *Kew Gardens, in* THE ENCYCLOPEDIA OF NEW YORK CITY 635 (Kenneth T. Jackson ed., 1995).

9 *Palsgraf* Record, *supra* note 6, at 27, 36, 45.

10 VICTOR E. SCHWARTZ ET AL., PROSSER, WADE AND SCHWARTZ'S TORTS 305 (10th ed. 2000).

11 Alice Marie Beard, *One Hell: December Thoughts on Law School*, http://www.members.aol.com/alicebeard/thoughts/december.html (last modified Dec. 3, 1999).

12 In a video shown to the author by Detective Dennis M. Small of the Nassau County Police Department Arson and Bomb Squad, the entire back half of an automobile was blown off by the detonation of one hundred "blockbuster" firecrackers that had been placed in the vehicle's trunk. For a news report of a similar demonstration, see Denise M. Bonilla, *Cops: Fourth Can Be Explosive, Officials Blow Up a Car To Demonstrate Dangers of Fireworks*, NEWSDAY (New York, N.Y.), June 28, 2001, at A30 (describing an explosion of M80's, M100's and assorted other fireworks that gutted the interior of a Pontiac Firebird TransAm).

13 J.C. Cackett, *Pyrotechnics, in* CHEMICAL WARFARE, PYROTECHNICS, AND THE FIREWORKS INDUSTRY 82 (T.F. Watkins et al. eds., 1968).

14 Telephone Interviews with Charles P. Weeth, Weeth & Associates (a fireworks consulting firm) (June 4, 2002, July 8, 2002, July 31, 2002) [hereinafter Weeth Interviews]. In the 1920s, chlorate compounds were cheaper and more available than the more stable perchlorates used in modern fireworks. *Id.*; *see also* RONALD LANCASTER, FIREWORKS: PRINCIPLES AND PRACTICE 61 (2d ed. 1992).

15 *See* VICTOR E. SCHWARTZ ET AL., PROSSER, WADE AND SCHWARTZ'S TORTS 311 (10th ed. 2000).

16 *Id.* at 137.

17 Telephone Interview with Philip Butler, Fireworks by Grucci (July 23, 2001). The *Palsgraf* fireworks may not necessarily have been of commercial manufacture since good quality homemade pyrotechnics were common during the 1920s. Weeth Interviews, *supra* note 14.

18 LANCASTER, *supra* note 14, at 186.

19 *Id.*

20 *Id.* In contrast, ordinary black powder contains charcoal, sulfur, and saltpeter.

21 *Id.*

22 *Id.*

23 Weeth Interviews, *supra* note 14.

24 *Id.*

25 PAUL W. COOPER, EXPLOSIVES ENGINEERING 407 (1996).

26 Weeth Interviews, *supra* note 14. A blast wave is produced "when the atmosphere surrounding the explosion is forcibly pushed back . . . by the gases from a conventional chemical explosive." GILBERT F. KINNEY & KENNETH J. GRAHAM, EXPLOSIVE SHOCKS IN AIR 88 (1985).

27 Telephone Interviews with Dale S. Preece, Sandia National Laboratories (2002–05) [hereinafter Preece Interviews].

28 *See* KINNEY & GRAHAM, *supra* note 317, at 6 (stating that "distance offers sure protection against damage from explosions"). A well-known example of distance and intervening objects affecting the strength of an explosion was the 1944 bomb plot against Adolf Hitler. Had Hitler been standing closer to the site of the blast, and if the satchel containing the bomb not been pushed against a table leg, the conspirators might have succeeded in killing him.

29 COOPER, *supra* note 25, at 420.

30 Weeth Interviews, *supra* note 14.

31 *Palsgraf* Record, *supra* note 6, at 18.

32 William L. Prosser, *Palsgraf Revisited*, 52 MICH. L. REV. 1, 3 n.9 (1953).

33 Weeth Interviews, *supra* note 14.

34 *See* KINNEY & GRAHAM, *supra* note 26, at 81.

35 Weeth Interviews, *supra* note 14.

36 *Palsgraf* Record, *supra* note 6, at 27.

37 SCHWARTZ ET AL., *supra* note 10, at 305.

38 E-mail from Bob Butler, Curator of the Coin-Operated Machine Museum, Newport News, VA (Apr. 22, 2002) (copy on file with the author).

39 E-mail from Jeff Storck, Coin-Operated Scales Collector (May 11, 2002) (copy on file with the author).

40 *Id.*

41 *Id.*

42 When, at the request of the author, fireworks consultant Charles Weeth queried persons experienced with fireworks on this question, the consensus was that it was not just possible, but probable that the powerful salutes could have knocked over the scale. Weeth Interviews, *supra* note 14. An analysis of the fireworks explosion based on the

TNT equivalent estimate of 0.4–0.6 for the salutes and 0.2–0.4 for the color breaks, and assuming for simplicity's sake that the explosives contained black powder (instead of their unknown exact chemical composition), produced the following estimate of peak incident pressure (psi) at a range of ten feet:

Type of Firework	Assumed TNT Equiv. Factor	PSI*
Salute	0.6	25.17
Salute	0.4	18.77
Color	0.4	18.77
Color	0.2	11.67

* These numbers also do not take into account variables caused by intervening objects or the angle of the blast wave.

Effects of different psi levels:

Peak Incident Overpressure	Results
0.5 – 1 psi	Shattered windows
1.8 – 2.9 psi	Failure of concrete block wall
29 – 72 psi	Lung damage to humans
101 – 217 psi	Lethality to humans

Dale S. Preece, Sandia National Laboratories, Analysis of Fireworks Accident (June 29, 2005) (copy on file with the author).

43 *See* Prosser, *supra* note 32, at 3 n.8.

44 Jorie Roberts, *Palsgraf Kin Tell Human Side of Famous Case*, HARV. L. REC., Apr. 14, 1978, at 1, 9. Her name was then Lillian Palsgraf Farmer.

45 *See* POSNER, *supra* note 4, at 33.

46 SCHWARTZ ET AL., *supra* note 10, at 305.

47 MP-54 passenger cars weighed 107,100 pounds. VINCENT F. SEYFRIED, THE LONG ISLAND RAIL ROAD: A COMPREHENSIVE HISTORY 263 (1975).

48 *See* Preece Interviews, *supra* note 27.

49 *Palsgraf* Record, *supra* note 6, at 58.

50 *Id.*

51 Palsgraf v. Long Island R.R. Co., 162 N.E. 93, 100 (N.Y. 1928) (emphasis added).

52 *In re* Kinsman Transit Co., 338 F.2d 708, 721 n.5 (2d Cir. 1964). This is not everyone's view. One commentator found Cardozo's statements about the doubtful evidence of negligence to be "a puzzling remark given the facts of the case." DAVID W. ROBERTSON ET AL., CASES AND MATERIALS ON TORTS 191 (1989); *see also* Mark G. Grady, *Efficient Negligence*, 87 GEO. L.J. 397, 413 (1998) (stating that "the defendant's guards clearly committed a breach of duty" because they should have "either stopped the passenger from boarding or helped him more carefully").

53 The identification of Italians with fireworks was not mere stereotyping. Italians were long famous for their fireworks displays and are often given credit for pioneering such events in Europe. However, on the day of the accident, there was no particular reason to expect Italian-looking men to be carrying fireworks. The closest major Italian holiday to August 24 is the Feast of San Gennaro, which takes place in September.

54 Points for Appellant at 5, *Palsgraf*, 162 N.E. 99.

55 *Id.*

56 *Palsgraf*, 162 N.E. at 100. This statement is virtually the only part of either brief that is reflected in the opinion.

57 *Id.* at 101 (Andrews, J., dissenting).

58 *Id.*

59 *See* Solomon v. Manhattan Ry. Co., 9 N.E. 430 (N.Y. 1886); *see also* Hunter v. Cooperstown & Susquehanna Valley R.R. Co., 26 N.E. 958 (N.Y. 1891).

60 Distler v. Long Island R.R. Co., 45 N.E. 937, 938 (N.Y. 1897). For a post-*Palsgraf* case holding this position, see Feil v. Long Island R.R. Co., 81 N.Y.S.2d 803 (Sup. Ct. 1948). For other New York cases involving attempts by passengers to board moving trains, see, e.g., Reinberg v. New York Life Ins. Co., 139 N.E. 728 (N.Y. 1923); Pakulski v. New York Central & Harlem R.R. Co., 114 N.E. 1075 (N.Y. 1916); Meyers v. Hines, 191 N.Y.S. 773 (App. Div. 1916) (involving a moving LIRR train); Jones v. New York Cent. R.R., 177 N.Y.S.2d 492 (App. Div. 1958).

61 THOMAS G. SHEARMAN & AMASA A. REDFIELD, A TREATISE ON THE LAW OF NEGLIGENCE 1436 (6th ed. 1913). This was the rule in a majority of states, particularly when the one making the attempt was a young man in good physical condition. M.L. Cross, Annotation, *Attempt To Board Moving Car or Train as Contributory Negligence or Assumption of Risk*, 31 A.L.R.2d 931, 935 (1953).

62 *See* Eppendorf v. Brooklyn City & Newtown R.R. Co., 69 N.Y. 195, 197 (1877) ("But there may be exceptional cases, when the car is moving rapidly, or when the person is infirm and clumsy, or is incumbered with children, packages or other hindrances, or when there are other unfavorable conditions, when it would be reckless to do so, and a court might, upon undisputed evidence, hold as matter of law that there was negligence in doing so.").

63 In the Matter of the Long Island R.R. Co., Case No. 2016 (N.Y. Pub. Serv. Comm'n June 15, 1917).

64 *See* LONG ISLAND RAILROAD COMPANY, RULES OF THE LONG ISLAND RAILROAD CO. FOR THE GOVERNMENT OF THE OPERATING DEPARTMENT R. 707, at 162 (1926) (listing instances when doors are to be kept closed).

65 For other New York cases involving passengers thrown out of open vestibule doors, see Scott v. New York Cent. R.R. Co., 216 N.Y.S. 163 (App. Div. 1926); Fox v. New York, Ontario & Western Ry. Co., 173 N.E. 879 (N.Y. 1930); Bunt v. N.Y. Cent. R.R. Co., 23 N.E.2d 557 (N.Y. 1939).

66 *See, e.g.*, Scott v. N.Y. Cent. R.R. Co., 216 N.Y.S. 163 (App. Div. 1926) (holding that there was a question of fact where a passenger fell through an open vestibule door); *see also* Mearns v. Cent. R.R. of N.J., 158 N.E. 1089 (N.Y. 1900) (holding the railroad not liable where passenger stepped from moving train as it pulled into station).

67 For a discussion of this issue, see J.E. Keefe, Jr., Annotation, *Open Door as Ground of Liability of Carrier for Injury to Passenger Falling or Alighting from Vehicle*, 7 A.L.R.2d 1427 (1950).

68 The typical negligence case arising from an open car door generally involved trains operating between stations, doors opening before the train came to a complete stop, or trains making sudden jerks or stops. *See generally id.*

69 WILLIAM L. PROSSER & YOUNG B. SMITH, CASES AND MATERIALS ON TORTS 360 (4th ed. 1967).

70 CHARLES O. GREGORY & HENRY KALVEN, JR., CASES AND MATERIALS ON TORTS 339 (2d ed. 1969).

71 Ken Durham, *Coin Operated Scales History & Gameroom Stuff* (1996), http://www.gameroomantiques.com/ HistoryScale.htm.

72 *Id.*

73 *See, e.g.*, Nye v. Louis K. Liggett Co., 113 N.E. 201 (Mass. 1916); Seabridge v. Poli, 119 A. 214 (Conn. 1922); Reed v. L. Hammel Dry Goods Co., 111 So. 237 (Ala. 1927); Dowling v. MacLean Drug Co., 248 Ill. App. 270 (App. Ct. 1928); Denue v. Whelan Drug Stores, 195 N.E. 161 (N.Y. 1934); Mick v. John R. Thompson Co., 77 S.W.2d 470 (Mo. Ct. App. 1934); Thompson v. F.W. Woolworth Co., 192 N.E. 893 (Ind. Ct. App. 1934); Drake v. Corning Bldg. Co., 281 N.Y.S. 680 (App. Div. 1935); Engdal v. Owl Drug Co., 48 P.2d 232 (Wash. 1935); Solomon v. Alps Kandy Shoppe, Inc., 182 A. 844 (N.J. Super. 1936); City of Hazlehurst v. Matthews, 176 So. 384 (Miss. 1937); Walsh v. Maurice Mercantile, 66 P.2d 181 (Cal. Ct. App. 1937); Lombardi v. F.W. Woolworth Co., 22 N.E.2d 28 (Mass. 1939); Baird v. Goldberg, 142 S.W.2d 120 (Ky. Ct. App. 1940); McDonald v. Heinemann, 141 S.W.2d 177 (Mo. Ct. App. 1940); Burckhalter v. F.W. Woolworth Co., 16 A.2d 716 (Pa. 1941); Wurster v. Armstrong, 21 A.2d 650 (Pa. Super. Ct. 1941); Simmons v. Penn Fruit Co., 47 A.2d 231 (Pa. 1946); Hodgson v. Anastasio, 50 So. 2d 511 (La. 1951); Johnson v. Brand Stores, 63 N.W.2d 370 (Minn. 1954); Harbourn v. Katz Drug Co., 318 S.W.2d 226 (Mo. 1958).

74 *See* Bannon v. Peerless Weighing & Vending Mach. Corp., 63 N.E.2d 335 (Mass. 1945).

75 PROSSER & YOUNG, *supra* note 69, at 360.

76 Palsgraf v. Long Island R.R. Co., 162 N.E. 99, 100 (N.Y. 1928).

77 *See* United States v. Carroll Towing Co., 159 F.2d 169, 173 (2d Cir. 1947).

78 RICHARD A. EPSTEIN, TORTS § 10.13 (1999) (citing RESTATEMENT (SECOND) OF TORTS 281 cmt. c (1979)).

79 PROSSER AND KEETON ON THE LAW OF TORTS 287 (W. Page Keeton et al. eds., 1984).

80 Prosser, *supra* note 32, at 27.

81 *See* POSNER, *supra* note 4, at 43.

82 DAN B. DOBBS, THE LAW OF TORTS 182 (2000).

83 JOHN T. NOONAN, PERSONS AND MASKS OF THE LAW: CARDOZO, HOLMES, JEFFERSON, AND WYTHE AS MAKERS OF MASKS 131 (1976).

84 Ernest J. Weinrib, *The Passing of* Palsgraf, 54 VAND. L. REV. 803, 803 (2001).

85 RESTATEMENT (THIRD) OF TORTS: GENERAL PRINCIPLES 6 (Discussion Draft Apr. 5, 1999).

86 *See* NOONAN, *supra* note 83, at 136-38.

87 Bowen v. N.Y. Cent. R.R. Co., 18 N.Y. 408, 411 (1858).

88 Alden v. N.Y. Cent. R.R. Co., 26 N.Y. 102, 104 (1862). In a subsequent decision, the court did rule the railroad could not be liable where the active intervention of a third party caused an accident. *See* Deyo v. N.Y. Cent. R.R. Co., 34 N.Y. 9 (1865) (rails tampered with by unknown persons).

89 35 N.Y. 210, 216 (1866) ("To sustain such a claim . . . would subject to a liability against which no prudence could guard, and to meet which no private fortune would be adequate.").

90 McPadden v. N.Y. Cent. R.R. Co., 44 N.Y. 478 (1871) (railroad not liable when the effects of cold weather caused a rail to break, derailing train).

91 Massouth v. Delaware & Hudson Canal Co., 64 N.Y. 524, 528 (1876).

92 ANDREW L. KAUFMAN, CARDOZO 301 (1998).

93 542 N.Y.S.2d 542 (App. Div.), *aff'd*, 545 N.E.2d 627 (N.Y. 1989). A jury verdict for the plaintiff of $174,976.85 was reversed on the law and dismissed. The claim that the Transit Authority was liable rested on the allegation that the motorman had reopened the doors in response the shouts of the running passenger.

94 NOONAN, *supra* note 83, at 143.

95 Richard H. Weisberg, *Law, Literature and Cardozo's Judicial Poetics*, 1 CARDOZO L. REV. 283, 295, 304 (1979).

96 KAUFMAN, *supra* note 92, at 142 (quoting internal memoranda for Foster v. City of New York, 118 N.E. 1058 (N.Y. 1917), Cardozo Memoranda, Box 1, Folder 554). These memoranda are held by the New York State Archives, and are available only by special permission. When inquiries were made about the possible existence of internal memoranda for *Palsgraf*, the archivist reported that the index to the documents made no mention of the case.

97 *Id.* (quoting internal memoranda for City of New York v. Voris, 143 N.E. 746 (N.Y. 1924), Cardozo Memoranda, Box 2, Folder 1829).

98 *Have Lawyers a Sense of Humor?*, 6 N.Y. L. REV. 148 (1928).

99 Benjamin N. Cardozo, *The Bench and Bar*, 34 N.Y. ST. B.J., 444, 453 (1962) (speech to the Broome County Bar Association given on March 9, 1929).

100 An $8,000 verdict for the plaintiff was set aside at the end of the first trial. After the Appellate Division affirmed this order (*see* Hynes v. N.Y. Cent. R.R. Co., 176 N.Y.S. 795 (App. Div. 1919)), a second trial was held. Here, the case was dismissed, and again the Appellate Division affirmed. *See* Hynes v. N.Y. Cent. R.R. Co., 179 N.Y.S. 927 (App. Div. 1919).

101 *Palsgraf* Affidavit, *supra* note 3, at 19.

102 NOONAN, *supra* note 83, at 144.

103 James D. Gordon III, *Cardozo's Baseball Card*, 44 STAN. L. REV. 899, 908 (1992).

104 Retired LIRR general attorney Edward J. Murphy indicated to the author that during his career the railroad never attempted to collect costs. In addition, the *Harvard Law Record* and *Georgia Bar Journal* articles that contain comments by Palsgraf family members make no mention of any attempt to collect.

105 Record at 214, Goodrich v. Long Island R.R. Co., 219 N.Y.S. 823 (App. Div. 1926).

CHAPTER 11

1 Cardozo once said about blame for the loss of a case: "I fancy the weight of odium is borne by the judge." Benjamin N. Cardozo, *The Bench and Bar*, 34 N.Y. St. B.J. 444, 449 (1962) (speech to the Broome County Bar Association given on March 9, 1929).

2 The children are identified as George Schwarz, three, and Catherine Bryzalsky, two. No occupation is listed for Mrs. Palsgraf. Her daughters are recorded as working as clerks. Their residence appears to be a two-family house at 108-11 88th Ave., Richmond Hill, Queens.

3 In her *Harvard Law Record* interview, Lillian Palsgraf Farmer blamed the fireworks accident for her mother's diabetes. Jorie Roberts, *Palsgraf Kin Tell Human Side of Famous Case*, HARV. L. REC., Apr. 14, 1978, at 1, 9, 15. However, as Judge Posner points out, this is not credible since diabetes cannot be caused by trauma. RICHARD A. POSNER, CARDOZO: A STUDY IN REPUTATION 36 (1990) (citing 3A ROSCOE N. GRAY & LOUISE J. GORDY, TEXTBOOK OF MEDICINE & 74.11 (3d ed. 1986)).

4 For the complete story of the family's legal misadventures, see Mark Fass, *Palsgrafs Say Claim to Fame Has Been Years of Bad Luck*, N.Y. L.J., Dec. 9, 2004, at 1.

5 ANDREW L. KAUFMAN, CARDOZO 303 (1998).

6 Richter v. Hallaren, 224 N.Y.S. 896 (App. Div. 1927).

7 *See* Application of Hallaren, 248 N.Y.S. 925 (App. Div. 1931).

8 *See* Duffy v. Thomas A. Edison, Inc., 268 N.Y.S. 959 (App. Div. 1933).

9 *See* O'Leary v. Standard Oil Co., 271 N.Y.S. 980 (App. Div.), *aff'd*, 193 N.E. 417 (N.Y. 1934) (judgment amount provided by the Record at 1).

10 *See* Beller v. City of New York, 278 N.Y.S. 131 (App. Div. 1935).

11 The cases were factually difficult because the injured woman may been using combs purchased from both Woolworth and other stores, and she was wearing eyeglasses with plastic rims at the time of the accident. Woolworth also claimed contributory negligence since the woman was using a hair dryer while the combs were in place. For the final reported decisions actions that ensued, see Treacy v. F.W. Woolworth Co., 1 N.Y.S.2d 919 (App. Div. 1938) (unsuccessful appeal of verdict for Woolworth in the mother's personal injury action); Treacy v. F.W. Woolworth Co., 28 N.Y.S.2d 736 (App. Div. 1941) (affirming an order denying the defendant's motion for summary judgment in the action by the daughter's estate).

12 Order, Treacy v. F.W. Woolworth (Sup. Ct. Westchester County July 31, 1941).

13 *See* O'Leary v. Standard Oil Co., 193 N.E. 417 (N.Y. 1934).

14 *See* Boyd H. Wood Co. v. Horgan, 52 N.E.2d 932 (N.Y. 1943) (unsuccessful appeal of holding that provision in lease waiving notice requirement of automatic renewal clause was void as against public policy). Wood's other post-*Palsgraf* Court of Appeals Cases include: *Pershall v. Elliott*, 163 N.E. 554 (N.Y. 1928) (unsuccessful defense of Appellate Division affirmation of the trial court in a will case); *Germann v. Reynolds*, 164 N.E. 600 (N.Y. 1928) (unsuccessful opposition to motion to dismiss appeal in a will case); *Burroughs Adding Machine Co. v. Hosack*, 168 N.E. 414 (N.Y. 1929) (unsuccessful appeal in a salary and commissions case); *In re Bartlett's Estate*, 83 N.E.2d 149 (N.Y. 1948) (successful defense of decree in dispute over deceased person's dental bill). In 1969, Wood's nephew, Alan W. Borst, won the family's most significant legal victory — a patent infringement case where Justice William O. Douglas held that a patent on an asphalt paving machine was invalid for obviousness. *See* Anderson's-Black Rock, Inc. v. Pavement Salvage Co., 396 U.S. 57 (1969).

15 Probate Petition, *In re* Will of Wood, No. 3656 (Surr. Ct. N.Y. County, June 15, 1972) (copy on file with the author).

16 *See* Krowtzoff v. Long Island R.R. Co., 274 N.Y.S. 770 (App. Div. 1934); Skypeck v. Long Island R.R. Co., 292 N.Y.S. 169 (App. Div. 1936), *aff'd*, 11 N.E.2d 318 (N.Y. 1937); Donnelly v. Long Island R.R. Co., 299 N.Y.S. 464 (App. Div. 1937).

17 *See* Buckin v. Long Island R.R. Co., 24 N.Y.S.2d 501 (App. Div. 1940), *aff'd*, 36 N.E.2d 88 (N.Y. 1941); Lavine v. Long Island R.R. Co., 83 N.Y.S.2d 251 (App. Div. 1948) (successful defense in case where a woman was hit by a hand truck in a waiting room).

18 *See* Drachenberg v. Long Island R.R. Co., 44 N.Y.S.2d 892 (App. Div. 1943).

19 For later Court of Appeals cases involving McNamara, see Weis v. Long Island R.R. Co., 186 N.E. 861 (N.Y. 1933) (successful appeal of Appellate Division ruling reversing trial term dismissal of plaintiff's complaint where automobile had struck beam on railroad-owned bridge); Skzypek v. Long Island R.R. Co., 11 N.E.2d 318 (N.Y. 1937) (unsuccessful appeal against judgment for plaintiff where pedestrian was electrocuted by third rail); Buckin v. Long Island R.R. Co., 36 N.E.2d 88 (N.Y. 1941) (affirming Appellate Division ruling that occupants of automobile struck by train were guilty of contributory negligence); Tomasetti Construction Co. v. Long Island R.R. Co., 63 N.E.2d 78 (N.Y. 1945) (affirming Appellate Division holding reversing trial court in dispute over a grade crossing construction contract).

20 *See* Long Island R.R. Co. v. Grossman, 160 N.Y.S.2d 237 (App. Div. 1957). Efforts to obtain McNamara's date of death from the LIRR were not successful. One William McNamara, born in 1894, and who had a Railroad Board Social Security number is listed in the online Social Security Death Index. He died in June 1972. However, it is uncertain if this is the railroad attorney considering the commonness of the name and the index's small number of listings for deaths before 1970.

21 *Dewey's Aid Asked for Safety Device To Halt L.I.: Mayor of Rockville Centre Calls for Automatic Control on Passing Red Light*, N.Y. TIMES, Feb. 20, 1949, at 1.

22 At a Public Service Commission hearing held in 1950, the LIRR claimed that from 1926 to 1949 it had completed 2,309,844,120 runs without a fatality. *See Record of No Passenger Fatalities Over 24 Years Cited by L.I. Road: Safety Mark Claimed at P.S.C. Hearing*, N.Y. TIMES, Mar. 8, 1950, at 22.

23 *See 4-Way Investigation Starts into Long Island Rail Wreck: Toll Now 77 Dead, 153 Injured*, N.Y. TIMES, Nov. 24, 1950, at 1; *Train Passengers Tell of Horrors*, N.Y. TIMES, Nov. 23, 1950, at 1.

24 *Fewer Riders on Railroad*, NEWSDAY, Feb. 16, 2005, at A14.

25 *See* New York Lumber Trade Ass'n v. Lacey, 277 N.Y.S. 519 (Sup. Ct. Kings County 1935), *rev'd*, 281 N.Y.S. 647 (App. Div.), *aff'd*, 199 N.E. 688 (N.Y. 1935).

26 *See* Doughtery v. Equitable Life Assurance Soc'y of the U.S., 259 N.Y.S. 146 (Sup. Ct. N.Y. County 1932).

27 *W.S. Andrews Joins Wets*, N.Y. TIMES, July 10, 1930, at 17.

28 People v. O'Gorman, 8 N.E.2d 862, 863 (N.Y. 1937).

29 In contrast, many of Cardozo's first cousins lived into their eighties and nineties.

30 *See* O'Brien v. Tremaine, 33 N.E.2d 536 (N.Y. 1941). By then, the only judge who had served with O'Brien remaining on the court was Chief Judge Irving Lehman.

[31] *Long Island Tops the Docket for Dishonesty Among Lawyers*, N.Y. TIMES, June 16, 2005, at B1.

[32] *See* MICHAEL J. POWELL, FROM PATRICIAN TO PROFESSIONAL ELITE: THE TRANSFORMATION OF THE NEW YORK CITY BAR ASSOCIATION 37 (1988).

[33] U.S. Department of Labor, Occupational Employment and Wages, Nov. 2003, http://www.bls.gov/oes231011.htm.

[34] AMERICAN BAR ASSOCIATION – LAW SCHOOL ADMISSION COUNCIL, OFFICIAL GUIDE TO ABA-APPROVED LAW SCHOOLS 55 (2005).

[35] *See* 5 Misc. 3d v, vii-viii. There are over 100 additional justices in Queens, Nassau, and Suffolk counties that were part of the Second Judicial District in the 1920s. These include retired justices serving as temporary or additional members of the court.

[36] *See* N.Y. CONST. art. 6, § 2(e) (McKinney Supp. 2005).

[37] Harold S. Quigley, *Note, Torts–Negligence–Necessity for Duty to Plaintiff*, 13 MINN. L. REV. 397 (1928).

[38] Note, *Torts – Negligence – Duty of Carrier to Passenger on Station Platform*, 37 YALE L.J. 1002 (1928). *See also* George B. Weisiger, *Negligence – Legal Cause*, 24 ILL. L. REV. 325, 327-28 (1928) ("The decision in the principal case seems sound and if negligence is considered as a term of relation some of the problems in this field will be simplified.").

[39] Note, *Torts – Negligence – Necessity for*, 27 MICH. L. REV. 114 (1928). For other favorable contemporary comments, see John H. Weidner, Note, *Negligence: Liability for Consequences of Negligent Acts to Those Outside the Forseeable Zone of Danger*, 14 CORNELL L.Q. 94 (1928); J.W.B., Note, *The Nature of Actionable Negligence*, 3 ST. JOHN'S L. REV. 117 (1929). For a critical view, see Note, *The Extent to Which Forseeability as to the Persons Injured is Required in Imposing Liability for Negligence*, 29 COLUM. L. REV. 53, 61 (1929) ("The rule proposes that emphasis be laid on the relation between the plaintiff and the defendant. It seems wiser to lay the emphasis on the standard of conduct imposed on the defendant and hold the defendant liable for all the consequences of his dereliction from that standard.").

[40] *See, e.g.*, Thomas A. Cowan, *The Riddle of the* Palsgraf *Case*, 23 MINN. L. REV. 46, 56 n.10 (1939) ("[A] rule of law containing as many elements as that of the *Palsgraf Case* is very likely to be applicable only to a Palsgraf situation.").

[41] Richard A. Epstein, *Two Fallacies in the Law of Joint Torts*, 73 GEO. L.J. 1377, 1377 (1985). Although *Palsgraf* is not the most-cited New York Court of Appeals decision or Cardozo's most-followed case, it has still garnered a significant number of citations. Statistical evidence of this is provided by the LexisNexis *Shepard's* service that provides both the number of "citing decisions" and "following decisions." Comparative results as of late June 2005 were as follows:

Case	"citing decisions"	"following decisions"
Palsgraf v. Long Island R.R. Co. 162 N.E. 99 (N.Y. 1928)	1,433	41
MacPherson v. Buick Motor Co., 111 N.E. 1050 (N.Y. 1916)	1,159	47
Ultramares v. Touche, 174 N.E. 441 (N.Y. 1931)	768	44
People v. Contes, 454 N.E.2d 932 (N.Y. 1980)	6,639	14
People v. Bleakley, 508 N.E.2d 672 (N.Y. 1987)	3,450	73
People v. Baldi, 429 N.E.2d 400 (N.Y. 1981)	2,591	94

[42] In 2000, only eighteen of 874 New York appellate decisions cited by the Court of Appeals dated from the 1920s. William H. Manz, *The Citation Practices of the New York Court of Appeals: A Millennium Update*, 49 BUFF. L. REV. 1273, 1304 tbl.9 (2001).

[43] As Dean Prosser has observed: "It has become fashionable to cite *Palsgraf* in every kind of negligence case, and most of the long array of references to it must be disregarded as insignificant and immaterial." William L. Prosser, Palsgraf *Revisited*, 52 MICH L. REV. 1, 8 (1953). A LexisNexis *Shepard's* comparison of "citing decisions" for *Palsgraf* and *MacPherson* produced the following results:

	1910s	1920s	1930s	1940s	1950s	1960s	1970s	1980s	1990s	2000+
Palsgraf	–	2	63	57	124	150	172	322	380	163
MacPherson	12	56	115	105	213	224	153	165	86	30

SOURCES

Facts about the East New York fireworks accident were drawn from newspaper accounts and the trial transcript. Very helpful information regarding fireworks and explosions were provided by fireworks consultant Charles Weeth, and Dr. Dale S. Preece of the Sandia National Laboratories. Information about the Palsgrafs came from the trial transcript; the article by Jorie Roberts in the *Harvard Law Record*, based on an interview with Lillian Palsgraf Farmer; an article by Professor R. Perry Sentell in the *Georgia Bar Journal*, which included facts provided by family members; and Grace White Lohr, a Palsgraf family member, who also assisted Professor Sentell with his article. Additional facts were obtained from census records, and birth, death, and marriage records on file at the New York City Municipal Archives. Chapters dealing with the *Palsgraf* trial and appeals utilized the trial transcript, all briefs prepared for the Appellate Division and the Court of Appeals, and the affidavit that accompanied the motion for reargument.

With the exception of the sections on Benjamin N. Cardozo, which relied heavily on Professor Andrew L. Kaufman's definitive biography, *Cardozo*, information about judges and attorneys was derived largely from newspaper articles and the case reporters. Additional information about Matthew W. Wood was provided by the alumni offices of the University of Pennsylvania, the Yale Law School Archives, and by his niece, Ms. Elizabeth W. Smith. Further information about Wood's law practice came from news articles and the trial records from his other appellate cases. Additional facts about Justice Albert H.F. Seeger and LIRR legal department head Joseph F. Keany were found in the Seeger Papers in the New York State Archives and the Keany Papers in the St. John's University Archives. Insights into the likely strategy and methods of the 1920s Long Island Railroad Legal Department were provided by Edward J. Murphy, the retired general attorney of the LIRR. Additional information about the department's activities in the years before the *Palsgraf* accident came through examination of the trial records of numerous negligence actions against the railroad where the Appellate Division and/or the Court of Appeals issued an opinion or order.

The section on the life, career, and medical expertise of expert witness Dr. Graeme Hammond was drawn from newspaper articles, medical journals, and his treatise on nervous diseases. Extra details about Mrs. Palsgraf's personal physician were provided by the alumni office of Albany Medical College. The discussion of traumatic hysteria relied on several chapters in *Traumatic Pasts: History, Psychiatry, and Trauma in the Modern Age*. Details on post-traumatic stress disorder came through a telephone interview with Dr. Rachel Yehuda of the Mt. Sinai School of Medicine.

Deriving information from newspapers was greatly facilitated by the availability of the digitized *New York Times* on ProQuest, and the digitized *Brooklyn Daily Eagle* on the Brooklyn Public Library's Web site. Also useful was the collection of digitized upstate New York papers posted at the Web site of the Northern New York Library Network, and the digitized historical Syracuse papers provided by the Onondaga County Library. Also of considerable value were the digitized, searchable census records available online through *Ancestry.com*, and digitized historical legal periodicals provided by HeinOnline.

A complete list of newspapers utilized is listed below.

> *Atlanta Constitution*
> *Brooklyn Daily Eagle*
> *Brooklyn Daily Times*
> *Buffalo Courier-Express*
> *Canton Commercial Advertiser*
> *Chicago Tribune*
> *Daily Star* (Long Island City)
> *Elizabethtown Post & Gazette*
> *Lockport Union Sun & Journal*
> *Long Island Daily Press*
> *Malone Farmer*
> *Malone Palladium*
> *Middleburgh News*
> *Newburgh News*
> *New Rochelle Daily Star*
> *Newsday* (Long Island)
> *New York Daily News*
> *New York Evening Journal*
> *New York Evening Post*
> *New York Herald-Tribune*
> *New York Law Journal*

New York Sun
New York Times
New York World
Plattsburgh Daily Press
Plattsburgh Sentinel
Syracuse Herald
Syracuse Post-Standard
Ticonderoga Sentinel
Wall Street Journal
Washington Post
Watertown Daily Times

In addition to the journal articles and Web sites mentioned in the notes, major sources consulted included:

SECONDARY SOURCES

Bergan, Francis, *The History of the Court of Appeals, 1847-1932* (1985).

Chemical Warfare, Pyrotechnics and the Fireworks Industry (T.F. Watkins et al. eds., 1968).

Cooper, Paul, *Explosives Engineering* (1996).

Cudahy, Brian J., *The Malbone Street Wreck* (1999).

Hammond, William A. & Graeme M. Hammond, *A Treatise on the Diseases of the Nervous System* (9th ed. with corrections 1898).

Kaufman, Andrew L., *Cardozo* (1998).

Kinney, Graham F. & Kenneth J., *Graham, Explosive Shocks in Air* (1985).

Lancaster, Ronald, *Fireworks: Principles and Practice* (2d ed. 1992).

Mitgang, Herbert, *The Man Who Rode the Tiger: The Life and Times of Judge Samuel Seabury* (1963).

Nevins, Allan, *Herbert Lehman and His Era* (1963).

Noonan, John T., *Persons and Masks of the Law: Cardozo, Holmes, Jefferson, and Wythe as Makers of Masks* (1976).

Posner, Richard A., *Cardozo: A Study in Reputation* (1990).

Powell, Michael J., *From Patrician to Professional Elite: The Transformation of the New York City Bar Association* (1988).

Second Department: Celebrating the First 100 Years (1996).

Seyfried, Vincent, *The Long Island Rail Road: A Comprehensive History* (1975).

Thabit, Walter, *How East New York Became a Ghetto* (2003).

There Shall Be a Court of Appeals (1997).

Traumatic Pasts: History Psychiatry, and Trauma in the Modern Age (Mark S. Micale & Paul Lerner eds., 2001).

Ziel, Ron, *The Long Island Rail Road in Early Photographs* (1990).

DOCUMENTS AND REPORTS

Long Island R.R., Forty-Third Annual Report: The Long Island Railroad Co. for the Year Ended 31st Dec. 1924.

Minority Report of the Committee to Inquire Into Delays and Congestion in the Courts of the Second Judicial District (N.Y. Leg. Doc. 62, 1928).

Report of the Director of the Bureau of Safety in re Investigation of an Accident Which Occurred on the Long Island Railroad Calverton, N.Y., on August 13, 1926 (Sept. 25, 1926).

Report of the Director of the Bureau of Safety in re Investigation of an Accident Which Occurred on the Long Island Railroad at Long Island City, N.Y., on July 30, 1924 (Sept. 20, 1924).

Report of the Director of the Bureau of Safety in re Investigation of an Accident Which Occurred on the Long Island Railroad Near Central Islip, N.Y., on April 15, 1918 (Aug. 5, 1918).

Report on the Administration of Justice in New York State (N.Y. Leg. Doc. No. 50, 1934).

Report to the Legislature of the Committee to Inquire Into Delays and Congestion in the Courts of the Second Judicial District (N.Y. Leg. Doc. 61, 1928).

Revised Record of the Constitutional Convention of the State of New York (1900).

APPENDIX A

HELEN PALSGRAF, RESPONDENT

v.

THE LONG ISLAND RAILROAD COMPANY, APPELLANT

Supreme Court of New York, Appellate Division, Second Department

222 A.D. 166, 225 N.Y.S. 412

December 9, 1927

COUNSEL: *William McNamara* [*Joseph F. Keany* with him on the brief], for the appellant.

Matthew W. Wood, for the respondent.

JUDGES: Seeger, J. Hagarty and Carswell, JJ., concur; Lazansky, P.J., with whom Young, J., concurs, dissents and reads for reversal.

SEEGER, J.: The action was brought to recover damages resulting from negligence. The plaintiff was a passenger intending to take a train of the defendant at the defendant's East New York passenger station on the 24th day of August, 1924. While plaintiff was at the station waiting for her train, another train came into the station. After this train had started from the station, two young men came up and undertook to board it while the train was in motion. One of these men had a bundle under his arm. Two of the defendant's employees undertook to help him on the train while it was in motion, one of them the trainman and the other the man on the platform. During their efforts to assist the man onto the moving train these men knocked the bundle out from under the passenger's arm and it fell under the train. The bundle contained explosive fireworks which exploded and caused a large scale, near which the plaintiff was standing, to be thrown against the plaintiff, severely injuring her. There was no evidence to show that the passenger carrying the bundle had any authority or permit under the Code of Ordinances of the City of New York to carry or transport fireworks, or of the value of the fireworks, and it does not appear that the provisions of such Code of Ordinances were violated. (Code of Ordinances of City of N.Y. chap. 10, art. 6, § 92, subd. 6.)

The defendant contends that the accident was not caused by the negligence of the defendant.

The sole question of defendant's negligence submitted to the jury was whether the defendant's employees were "careless and negligent in the way they handled this particular passenger after he came upon the platform and while he was boarding the train." This question of negligence was submitted to the jury by a fair and impartial charge and the verdict was supported by the evidence. The jury might well find that the act of the passenger in undertaking to board a moving train was negligent, and that the acts of the defendant's employees in assisting him while engaged in that negligent act were also negligent. Instead of aiding or assisting the passenger engaged in such an act, they might better have discouraged and warned him not to board the moving train. It is quite probable that without their assistance the passenger might have succeeded in boarding the train and no accident would have happened, or without the assistance of these employees the passenger might have desisted in his efforts to board the train. In any event, the acts of defendant's employees, which the jury found to be negligent, caused the bundle to be thrown under the train and to explode. It is no answer or defense to these negligent acts to say that the defendant's employees were not chargeable with notice that the passenger's bundle contained an explosive. While there seems to be no precedent for this case, every case must stand upon its own facts. In principle the case is similar to the squib case (*Scott v. Shepherd*, 2 Wm. Bl. 892), where a lighted squib was thrown in or near a crowd of people, and it was successively thrown by two or more persons until it landed upon and burned the plaintiff; or the negro boy case (*Vandenburgh v. Truax*, 4 Den. 464), where a boy in escaping a threatened attack of the party pursuing him ran against and knocked out the faucet of a cask of valuable wine, destroying it. The pursuing party was held liable for the loss. Also the balloon case (*Guille v. Swan*, 19 Johns. 381), where the defendant, while in a balloon, descended in a garden under circumstances which tended to invite people to go to his assistance and in doing so the vegetables in plaintiff's garden were trampled upon and destroyed, for which the defendant was held liable.

It must be remembered that the plaintiff was a passenger of the defendant and entitled to have the defendant exercise the highest degree of care required of common carriers.

The judgment and order appealed from should be affirmed, with costs.

LAZANSKY, P.J. (dissenting). The facts may have warranted the jury in finding the defendant's agents were negligent in assisting a passenger in boarding a moving train in view of the fact that a door of the train should have been closed before the train started, which would have prevented the passenger making the attempt. There was also warrant for a finding by the jury that as a result of the negligence of the defendant a package was thrown between the platform and train, exploded, causing injury to plaintiff, who was on the station platform. In my opinion, the negligence of defendant was not a proximate cause of the injuries to plaintiff. Between the negligence of defendant and the injuries, there intervened the negligence of the passenger carrying the package containing an explosive. This was an independent, and not a concurring act of negligence. The explosion was not reasonably probable as a result of defendant's act of negligence. The negligence of defendant was not a likely or natural cause of the explosion, since the latter was such an unusual occurrence. Defendant's negligence was a cause of plaintiff's injury, but too remote.

The judgment should be reversed, with costs to the appellant, and the complaint dismissed, with costs.

APPENDIX B

HELEN PALSGRAF, RESPONDENT

V.

THE LONG ISLAND RAILROAD COMPANY, APPELLANT

Court of Appeals of New York

248 N.Y. 339, 162 N.E. 99

May 29, 1928

COUNSEL: *William McNamara* and *Joseph F. Keany* for appellant. Plaintiff failed to establish that her injuries were caused by negligence of the defendant and it was error for the court to deny the defendant's motion to dismiss the complaint. (*Paul v. Cons. Fireworks Co.*, 212 N.Y. 117; *Hall v. N.Y. Tel. Co.*, 214 N.Y. 49; *Perry v. Rochester Lime Co.*, 219 N.Y. 60; *Pyne v. Cazenozia Canning Co.*, 220 N.Y. 126; *Adams v. Bullock*, 227 N.Y. 208; *McKinney v. N.Y. Cons. R. R. Co.*, 230 N.Y. 194; *Palsey v. Waldorf Astoria, Inc.*, 220 App. Div. 613; *Parrott v. Wells Fargo & Co.*, 15 Wall. 524; *A., T. & S. Fe Ry. Co. v. Calhoun*, 213 U.S. 1; *Prudential Society, Inc., v. Ray*, 207 App. Div. 496; 239 N.Y. 600.)

Matthew W. Wood for respondent. The judgment of affirmance was amply sustained by the law and the facts. (*Saugerties Bank v. Delaware & Hudson Co.*, 236 N.Y. 425; *Milwaukee & St. Paul Ry. Co. v. Kellogg*, 94 U.S. 469; *Lowery v. Western Union Tel. Co.*, 60 N.Y. 198; *Insurance Co. v. Tweed*, 7 Wall. 44; *Trapp v. McClellan*, 68 App. Div. 362; *Ring v. City of Cohoes*, 77 N.Y. 83; *McKenzie v. Waddell Coal Co.*, 89 App. Div. 415; *Slater v. Barnes*, 241 N.Y. 284; *King v. Interborough R.T. Co.*, 233 N.Y. 330.)

JUDGES: Cardozo, Ch. J. Pound, Lehman and Kellogg, JJ., concur with Cardozo, Ch. J.; Andrews, J., dissents in opinion in which Crane and O'Brien, JJ., concur.

CARDOZO, CH. J.: Plaintiff was standing on a platform of defendant's railroad after buying a ticket to go to Rockaway Beach. A train stopped at the station, bound for another place. Two men ran forward to catch it. One of the men reached the platform of the car without mishap, though the train was already moving. The other man, carrying a package, jumped aboard the car, but seemed unsteady as if about to fall. A guard on the car, who had held the door open, reached forward to help him in, and another guard on the platform pushed him from behind. In this act, the package was dislodged, and fell upon the rails. It was a package of small size, about fifteen inches long, and was covered by a newspaper. In fact it contained fireworks, but there was nothing in its appearance to give notice of its contents. The fireworks when they fell exploded. The shock of the explosion threw down some scales at the other end of the platform, many feet away. The scales struck the plaintiff, causing injuries for which she sues.

The conduct of the defendant's guard, if a wrong in its relation to the holder of the package, was not a wrong in its relation to the plaintiff, standing far away. Relatively to her it was not negligence at all. Nothing in the situation gave notice that the falling package had in it the potency of peril to persons thus removed. Negligence is not actionable unless it involves the invasion of a legally protected interest, the violation of a right. "Proof of negligence in the air, so to speak, will not do" (Pollock, Torts [11th ed.], p. 455; *Martin v. Herzog*, 228 N.Y. 164, 170; *cf.* Salmond, Torts [6th ed.], p. 24). "Negligence is the absence of care, according to the circumstances" (Willes, J., in *Vaughan v. Taff Vale Ry. Co.*, 5 H. & N. 679, 688; 1 Beven, Negligence [4th ed.], 7; *Paul v. Consol. Fireworks Co.*, 212 N.Y. 117; *Adams v. Bullock*, 227 N.Y. 208, 211; *Parrott v. Wells-Fargo Co.*, 15 Wall. [U.S.] 524). The plaintiff as she stood upon the platform of the station might claim to be protected against intentional invasion of her bodily security. Such invasion is not charged. She might claim to be protected against unintentional invasion by conduct involving in the thought of reasonable men an unreasonable hazard that such invasion would ensue. These, from the point of view of the law, were the bounds of her immunity, with perhaps some rare exceptions, survivals for the most part of ancient forms of liability, where conduct is held to be at the peril of the actor (*Sullivan v. Dunham*, 161 N.Y. 290). If no hazard was apparent to the eye of ordinary vigilance, an act innocent and harmless, at least to outward seeming, with reference to her, did not take to itself the quality of a tort because it happened to be a wrong, though apparently not one involving the risk of bodily insecurity, with reference to some one else. "In every instance, before negligence can be predicated of a given act, back of the act must be sought and found a duty to the individual complaining, the observance of which would have averted or avoided the injury" (McSherry, C.J., in *W. Va. Central R. Co. v. State*, 96 Md. 652, 666; *cf. Norfolk & Western Ry. Co. v. Wood*, 99 Va. 156, 158, 159; *Hughes v. Boston & Maine R.R. Co.*, 71 N.H. 279, 284; *U.S. Express Co. v. Everest*, 72 Kan. 517; *Emry v. Roanoke Nav. Co.*, 111 N.C. 94, 95; *Vaughan v. Transit Dev. Co.*, 222 N.Y. 79; *Losee v. Clute*, 51 N.Y. 494; *DiCaprio v. N.Y.C.R.R. Co.*, 231 N.Y. 94; 1 Shearman & Redfield on Negligence, § 8, and cases cited; Cooley on Torts [3d ed.], p. 1411; Jaggard on Torts, vol. 2, p. 826; Wharton, Negligence, § 24; Bohlen, Studies in the Law of Torts, p. 601). "The ideas of negligence and duty are strictly correlative" (Bowen, L.J., in *Thomas v. Quartermaine*, 18 Q.B.D. 685, 694). The plaintiff sues in her own right for a wrong personal to her, and not as the vicarious beneficiary of a breach of duty to another.

A different conclusion will involve us, and swiftly too, in a maze of contradictions. A guard stumbles over a package which has been left upon a platform. It seems to be a bundle of newspapers. It turns out to be a can of dynamite. To the eye of ordinary vigilance, the bundle is abandoned waste, which may be kicked or trod on with impunity. Is a passenger at the other end of the platform protected by the law against the unsuspected hazard concealed beneath the waste? If not, is the result to be any different, so far as the distant passenger is concerned, when the guard stumbles over a valise which a truck-man or a porter has left upon the walk? The passenger far away, if the victim of a wrong at all, has a cause of action, not derivative, but original and primary. His claim to be protected against invasion of his bodily security is neither greater nor less because the act resulting in the invasion is a wrong to another far removed. In this case, the rights that are said to have been violated, the interests said to have been invaded, are not even of the same order. The man was not injured in his person nor even put in danger. The purpose of the act, as well as its effect, was to make his person safe. If there was a wrong to him at all, which may very well be doubted, it was a wrong to a property interest only, the safety of his package. Out of this wrong to property, which threatened injury to nothing else, there has passed, we are told, to the plaintiff by deriva-tion or succession a right of action for the invasion of an interest of another order, the right to bodily security. The diversity of interests emphasizes the futil-ity of the effort to build the plaintiff's right upon the basis of a wrong to some one else. The gain is one of emphasis, for a like result would follow if the inter-ests were the same. Even then, the orbit of the danger as disclosed to the eye of reasonable vigilance would be the orbit of the duty. One who jostles one's neighbor in a crowd does not invade the rights of others standing at the outer fringe when the unintended contact casts a bomb upon the ground. The wrong-doer as to them is the man who carries the bomb, not the one who explodes it without suspicion of the danger. Life will have to be made over, and human nature transformed, before prevision so extravagant can be accepted as the norm of conduct, the customary standard to which behavior must conform.

The argument for the plaintiff is built upon the shifting meanings of such words as "wrong" and "wrongful," and shares their instability. What the plain-tiff must show is "a wrong" to herself, *i.e.*, a violation of her own right, and not merely a wrong to some one else, nor conduct "wrongful" because unsocial, but not "a wrong" to any one. We are told that one who drives at reckless speed through a crowded city street is guilty of a negligent act and, therefore, of a wrongful one irrespective of the consequences. Negligent the act is, and wrong-ful in the sense that it is unsocial, but wrongful and unsocial in relation to other travelers, only because the eye of vigilance perceives the risk of damage. If the same act were to be committed on a speedway or a race course, it would lose its wrongful quality. The risk reasonably to be perceived defines the duty to be obeyed, and risk imports relation; it is risk to another or to others within the range of apprehension (Seavey, Negligence, Subjective or Objective, 41 H. L. Rv. 6; *Boronkay v. Robinson & Carpenter*, 247 N.Y. 365). This does not mean, of course, that one who launches a destructive force is always relieved of liability if the force, though known to be destructive, pursues an unexpected path. "It was not necessary that the defendant should have had notice of the particular method in which an accident would occur, if the possibility of an accident was clear to the ordinarily prudent eye" (*Munsey v. Webb*, 231 U.S. 150, 156; *Condran v. Park & Tilford*, 213 N.Y. 341, 345; *Robert v. U.S.E.F. Corp.*, 240 N.Y. 474, 477). Some acts, such as shooting, are so imminently dangerous to any one who may come within reach of the missile, however unexpectedly, as to impose a duty of prevision not far from that of an insurer. Even today, and much oftener in earlier stages of the law, one acts sometimes at one's peril (Jeremiah Smith, Tort and Absolute Liability, 30 H. L. Rv. 328; Street, Foundations of Legal Liability, vol. 1, pp. 77, 78). Under this head, it may be, fall certain cases of what is known as transferred intent, an act willfully dangerous to A resulting by misadventure in injury to B (*Talmage v. Smith*, 101 Mich. 370, 374). These cases aside, wrong is defined in terms of the natural or probable, at least when unintentional (*Parrot v. Wells-Fargo Co.* [*The Nitro-Glycerine Case*], 15 Wall. [U.S.] 524). The range of reasonable apprehension is at times a question for the court, and at times, if varying inferences are possible, a question for the jury. Here, by concession, there was nothing in the situation to suggest to the most cautious mind that the parcel wrapped in newspaper would spread wreckage through the station. If the guard had thrown it down knowingly and willfully, he would not have threatened the plaintiff's safety, so far as appearances could warn him. His conduct would not have involved, even then, an unreasonable probability of invasion of her bodily security. Liability can be no greater where the act is inadvertent.

Negligence, like risk, is thus a term of relation. Negligence in the abstract, apart from things related, is surely not a tort, if indeed it is understandable at all (Bowen, L.J., in *Thomas v. Quartermaine*, 18 Q.B.D. 685, 694). Negligence is not a tort unless it results in the commission of a wrong, and the commission of a wrong imports the violation of a right, in this case, we are told, the right to be protected against interference with one's bodily security. But bodily security is protected, not against all forms of interference or aggression, but only against some. One who seeks redress at law does not make out a cause of action by showing without more that there has been damage to his person. If the harm was not willful, he must show that the act as to him had possibilities of danger so many and apparent as to entitle him to be protected against the doing of it though the harm was unintended. Affront to personality is still the keynote of the wrong. Confirmation of this view will be found in the history and development of the action on the case. Negligence as a basis of civil liability was unknown to mediaeval law (8 Holdsworth, History of English Law, p. 449; Street, Foundations of Legal Liability, vol. 1, pp. 189, 190). For damage to the person, the sole remedy was trespass, and trespass did not lie in the absence of aggression, and that direct and personal (Holdsworth, op. cit. p. 453; Street, op. cit. vol. 3, pp. 258, 260, vol. 1, pp. 71, 74). Liability for other damage, as where a servant without orders from the master does or omits something to the damage of another, is a plant of later growth (Holdsworth, op. cit. 450, 457; Wigmore, Responsibility for Tortious Acts, vol. 3, Essays in Anglo-American Legal History, 520, 523, 526, 533). When it emerged out of the legal soil, it was thought of as a variant of trespass, an offshoot of the parent stock. This appears in the form of action, which was known as trespass on the case (Holdsworth, op. cit. p. 449; *cf. Scott v. Shepard*, 2 Wm. Black. 892; Green, Rationale of Proximate Cause, p. 19). The victim does not sue derivatively, or by right of subrogation, to vindicate an interest invaded in the person of another. Thus to view his cause of action is to ignore the fundamental difference between tort and crime (Holland, Jurisprudence [12th ed.], p. 328). He sues for breach of a duty owing to himself.

The law of causation, remote or proximate, is thus foreign to the case before us.

The question of liability is always anterior to the question of the measure of the consequences that go with liability. If there is no tort to be redressed, there is no occasion to consider what damage might be recovered if there were a finding of a tort. We may assume, without deciding, that negligence, not at large or in the abstract, but in relation to the plaintiff, would entail liability for any and all consequences, however novel or extraordinary (*Bird v. St. Paul F. & M. Ins. Co.*, 224 N.Y. 47, 54; *Ehrgott v. Mayor, etc., of N.Y.*, 96 N.Y. 264; *Smith v. London & S.W. Ry. Co.*, L.R. 6 C.P. 14; 1 Beven, Negligence, 106; Street, op. cit. vol. 1, p. 90; Green, Rationale of Proximate Cause, pp. 88, 118; *cf. Matter of Polemis*, L.R. 1921, 3 K. B. 560; 44 Law Quarterly Review, 142). There is room for argument that a distinction is to be drawn according to the diversity of interests invaded by the act, as where conduct negligent in that it threatens an insignificant invasion of an interest in property results in an unforseeable invasion of an interest of another order, as, *e.g.*, one of bodily security. Perhaps other distinctions may be necessary. We do not go into the question now. The consequences to be followed must first be rooted in a wrong.

The judgment of the Appellate Division and that of the Trial Term should be reversed, and the complaint dismissed, with costs in all courts.

ANDREWS, J. (dissenting): Assisting a passenger to board a train, the defendant's servant negligently knocked a package from his arms. It fell between the platform and the cars. Of its contents the servant knew and could know nothing. A violent explosion followed. The concussion broke some scales standing a considerable distance away. In falling they injured the plaintiff, an intending passenger.

Upon these facts may she recover the damages she has suffered in an action brought against the master? The result we shall reach depends upon our theory as to the nature of negligence. Is it a relative concept — the breach of some duty owing to a particular person or to particular persons? Or where there is an act which unreasonably threatens the safety of others, is the doer liable for all its proximate consequences, even where they result in injury to one who would generally be thought to be outside the radius of danger? This is not a mere dispute as to words. We might not believe that to the average mind the dropping of the bundle would seem to involve the probability of harm to the plaintiff standing many feet away whatever might be the case as to the owner or to one so near as to be likely to be struck by its fall. If, however, we adopt the second hypothesis we have to inquire only as to the relation between cause and effect. We deal in terms of proximate cause, not of negligence.

Negligence may be defined roughly as an act or omission which unreasonably does or may affect the rights of others, or which unreasonably fails to protect oneself from the dangers resulting from such acts. Here I confine myself to the first branch of the definition. Nor do I comment on the word "unreasonable." For present purposes it sufficiently describes that average of conduct that society requires of its members.

There must be both the act or the omission, and the right. It is the act itself, not the intent of the actor, that is important. (*Hover v. Barkhoof*, 44 N.Y. 113; *Mertz v. Connecticut Co.*, 217 N.Y. 475.) In criminal law both the intent and the result are to be considered. Intent again is material in tort actions, where punitive damages are sought, dependent on actual malice — not on merely reckless conduct. But here neither insanity nor infancy lessens responsibility. (*Williams v. Hays*, 143 N.Y. 442.)

As has been said, except in cases of contributory negligence, there must be rights which are or may be affected. Often though injury has occurred, no rights of him who suffers have been touched. A licensee or trespasser upon my land has no claim to affirmative care on my part that the land be made safe. (*Meiers v. Koch Brewery*, 229 N.Y. 10.) Where a railroad is required to fence its tracks against cattle, no man's rights are injured should he wander upon the road because such fence is absent. (*Di Caprio v. N.Y.C.R.R.*, 231 N.Y. 94.) An unborn child may not demand immunity from personal harm. (*Drobner v. Peters*, 232 N.Y. 220.)

But we are told that "there is no negligence unless there is in the particular case a legal duty to take care, and this duty must be one which is owed to the plaintiff himself and not merely to others." (Salmond, Torts [6th ed.], 24.) This, I think too narrow a conception. Where there is the unreasonable act, and some right that may be affected there is negligence whether damage does or does not result. That is immaterial. Should we drive down Broadway at a reckless speed, we are negligent whether we strike an approaching car or miss it by an inch. The act itself is wrongful. It is a wrong not only to those who happen to be within the radius of danger but to all who might have been there — a wrong to the public at large. Such is the language of the street. Such the language of the courts when speaking of contributory negligence. Such again and again their language in speaking of the duty of some defendant and discussing proximate cause in cases where such a discussion is wholly irrelevant on any other theory. (*Perry v. Rochester Line Co.*, 219 N.Y. 60.) As was said by Mr. Justice Holmes many years ago, "the measure of the defendant's duty in determining whether a wrong has been committed is one thing, the measure of liability when a wrong has been committed is another." (*Spade v. Lynn & Boston R.R. Co.*, 172 Mass. 488.) Due care is a duty imposed on each one of us to protect society from unnecessary danger, not to protect A, B or C alone.

It may well be that there is no such thing as negligence in the abstract. "Proof of negligence in the air, so to speak, will not do." In an empty world negligence would not exist. It does involve a relationship between man and his fellows. But not merely a relationship between man and those whom he might reasonably expect his act would injure. Rather, a relationship between him and those whom he does in fact injure. If his act has a tendency to harm some one, it harms him a mile away as surely as it does those on the scene. We now permit children to recover for the negligent killing of the father. It was never prevented on the theory that no duty was owing to them. A husband may be compensated for the loss of his wife's services. To say that the wrongdoer was negligent as to the husband as well as to the wife is merely an attempt to fit facts to theory. An insurance company paying a fire loss recovers its payment of the negligent incendiary. We speak of subrogation — of suing in the right of the insured. Behind the cloud of words is the fact they hide, that the act, wrongful as to the insured, has also injured the company. Even if it be true that the fault of father, wife or insured will prevent recovery, it is because we consider the original negligence not the proximate cause of the injury. (Pollock, Torts [12th ed.], 463.)

In the well-known *Polemis Case* (1921, 3 K.B. 560), Scrutton, L.J., said that the dropping of a plank was negligent for it might injure "workman or cargo or ship." Because of either possibility the owner of the vessel was to be made good for his loss. The act being wrongful the doer was liable for its proximate results. Criticized and explained as this statement may have been, I think it states the law as it should be and as it is. (*Smith v. London & Southwestern Ry. Co.*, [1870-71] 6 C.P. 14; *Anthony v. Slaid*, 52 Mass. 290; *Wood v. Penn. R.R. Co.*, 177 Penn. St. 306; *Trashansky v. Hershkovitz*, 239 N.Y. 452.)

The proposition is this. Every one owes to the world at large the duty of refraining from those acts that may unreasonably threaten the safety of others. Such an act occurs. Not only is he wronged to whom harm might reasonably be expected to result, but he also who is in fact injured, even if he be outside what would generally be thought the danger zone. There needs be duty due the one complaining but this is not a duty to a particular individual because as to him harm might be expected. Harm to some one being the natural result of the act, not only that one alone, but all those in fact injured may complain. We have never, I think, held otherwise. Indeed in the *Di Caprio* case we said that a breach of a general ordinance defining the degree of care to be exercised in one's calling is evidence of negligence as to every one. We did not limit this statement to those who might be expected to be exposed to danger. Unreasonable risk being taken, its consequences are not confined to those who might probably be hurt.

If this be so, we do not have a plaintiff suing by "derivation or succession." Her action is original and primary. Her claim is for a breach of duty to herself — not that she is subrogated to any right of action of the owner of the parcel or of a passenger standing at the scene of the explosion.

The right to recover damages rests on additional considerations. The plaintiff's rights must be injured, and this injury must be caused by the negligence. We build a dam, but are negligent as to its foundations. Breaking, it injures property down stream. We are not liable if all this happened because of some reason other than the insecure foundation. But when injuries do result from our unlawful act we are liable for the consequences. It does not matter that they are unusual, unexpected, unforeseen and unforseeable. But there is one limitation. The damages must be so connected with the negligence that the latter may be said to be the proximate cause of the former.

These two words have never been given an inclusive definition. What is a cause in a legal sense, still more what is a proximate cause, depend in each case upon many considerations, as does the existence of negligence itself. Any philosophical doctrine of causation does not help us. A boy throws a stone into a pond. The ripples spread. The water level rises. The history of that pond is altered to all eternity. It will be altered by other causes also. Yet it will be forever the resultant of all causes combined. Each one will have an influence. How great only omniscience can say. You may speak of a chain, or if you please, a net. An analogy is of little aid. Each cause brings about future events. Without each the future would not be the same. Each is proximate in the sense it is essential. But that is not what we mean by the word. Nor on the other hand do we mean sole cause. There is no such thing.

Should analogy be thought helpful, however, I prefer that of a stream. The spring, starting on its journey, is joined by tributary after tributary. The river, reaching the ocean, comes from a hundred sources. No man may say whence any drop of water is derived. Yet for a time distinction may be possible. Into the clear creek, brown swamp water flows from the left. Later, from the right comes water stained by its clay bed. The three may remain for a space, sharply divided. But at last, inevitably no trace of separation remains. They are so commingled that all distinction is lost.

As we have said, we cannot trace the effect of an act to the end, if end there is. Again, however, we may trace it part of the way. A murder at Serajevo may be the necessary antecedent to an assassination in London twenty years hence. An overturned lantern may burn all Chicago. We may follow the fire from the shed to the last building. We rightly say the fire started by the lantern caused its destruction.

A cause, but not the proximate cause. What we do mean by the word "proximate" is, that because of convenience, of public policy, of a rough sense of justice, the law arbitrarily declines to trace a series of events beyond a certain point. This is not logic. It is practical politics. Take our rule as to fires. Sparks from my burning haystack set on fire my house and my neighbor's. I may recover from a negligent railroad. He may not. Yet the wrongful act as directly harmed the one as the other. We may regret that the line was drawn just where it was, but drawn somewhere it had to be. We said the act of the railroad was not the proximate cause of our neighbor's fire. Cause it surely was. The words we used were simply indicative of our notions of public policy. Other courts think differently. But somewhere they reach the point where they cannot say the stream comes from any one source.

Take the illustration given in an unpublished manuscript by a distinguished and helpful writer on the law of torts. A chauffeur negligently collides with another car which is filled with dynamite, although he could not know it. An explosion follows. A, walking on the sidewalk nearby, is killed. B, sitting in a window of a building opposite, is cut by flying glass. C, likewise sitting in a window a block away, is similarly injured. And a further illustration. A nursemaid, ten blocks away, startled by the noise, involuntarily drops a baby from her arms to the walk. We are told that C may not recover while A may. As to B it is a question for court or jury. We will all agree that the baby might not. Because, we are again told, the chauffeur had no reason to believe his conduct involved any risk of injuring either C or the baby. As to them he was not negligent.

But the chauffeur, being negligent in risking the collision, his belief that the scope of the harm he might do would be limited is immaterial. His act unreasonably jeopardized the safety of any one who might be affected by it. C's injury and that of the baby were directly traceable to the collision. Without that, the injury would not have happened. C had the right to sit in his office, secure from such dangers. The baby was entitled to use the sidewalk with reasonable safety.

The true theory is, it seems to me, that the injury to C, if in truth he is to be denied recovery, and the injury to the baby is that their several injuries were not the proximate result of the negligence. And here not what the chauffeur had reason to believe would be the result of his conduct, but what the prudent would foresee, may have a bearing. May have some bearing, for the problem of proximate cause is not to be solved by any one consideration.

It is all a question of expediency. There are no fixed rules to govern our judgment. There are simply matters of which we may take account. We have in a somewhat different connection spoken of "the stream of events." We have asked whether that stream was deflected — whether it was forced into new and unexpected channels. (*Donnelly v. Piercy Contracting Co.*, 222 N.Y. 210). This is rather rhetoric than law. There is in truth little to guide us other than common sense.

There are some hints that may help us. The proximate cause, involved as it may be with many other causes, must be, at the least, something without which the event would not happen. The court must ask itself whether there was a natural and continuous sequence between cause and effect. Was the one a substantial factor in producing the other? Was there a direct connection between them, without too many intervening causes? Is the effect of cause on result not too attenuated? Is the cause likely, in the usual judgment of mankind, to produce the result? Or by the exercise of prudent foresight could the result be foreseen? Is the result too remote from the cause, and here we consider remoteness in time and space. (*Bird v. St. Paul F. & M. Ins. Co.*, 224 N.Y. 47, where we passed upon the construction of a contract — but something was also said on this subject.) Clearly we must so consider, for the greater the distance either in time or space, the more surely do other causes intervene to affect the result. When a lantern is overturned the firing of a shed is a fairly direct consequence. Many things contribute to the spread of the conflagration — the force of the wind, the direction and width of streets, the character of intervening structures, other factors. We draw an uncertain and wavering line, but draw it we must as best we can.

Once again, it is all a question of fair judgment, always keeping in mind the fact that we endeavor to make a rule in each case that will be practical and in keeping with the general understanding of mankind.

Here another question must be answered. In the case supposed it is said, and said correctly, that the chauffeur is liable for the direct effect of the explosion although he had no reason to suppose it would follow a collision. "The fact that the injury occurred in a different manner than that which might have been expected does not prevent the chauffeur's negligence from being in law the cause of the injury." But the natural results of a negligent act — the results which a prudent man would or should foresee — do have a bearing upon the decision as to proximate cause. We have said so repeatedly. What should be foreseen? No human foresight would suggest that a collision itself might injure one a block away. On the contrary, given an explosion, such a possibility might be reasonably expected. I think the direct connection, the foresight of which the courts speak, assumes prevision of the explosion, for the immediate results of which, at least, the chauffeur is responsible.

It may be said this is unjust. Why? In fairness he should make good every injury flowing from his negligence. Not because of tenderness toward him we say he need not answer for all that follows his wrong. We look back to the catastrophe, the fire kindled by the spark, or the explosion. We trace the consequences — not indefinitely, but to a certain point. And to aid us in fixing that point we ask what might ordinarily be expected to follow the fire or the explosion.

This last suggestion is the factor which must determine the case before us. The act upon which defendant's liability rests is knocking an apparently harmless package onto the platform. The act was negligent. For its proximate consequences the defendant is liable. If its contents were broken, to the owner; if it fell upon and crushed a passenger's foot, then to him. If it exploded and injured one in the immediate vicinity, to him also as to A in the illustration. Mrs. Palsgraf was standing some distance away. How far cannot be told from the record — apparently twenty-five or thirty feet. Perhaps less. Except for the explosion, she would not have been injured. We are told by the appellant in his brief "it cannot be denied that the explosion was the direct cause of the plaintiff's injuries." So it was a substantial factor in producing the result — there was here a natural and continuous sequence — direct connection. The only intervening cause was that instead of blowing her to the ground the concussion smashed the weighing machine which in turn fell upon her. There was no remoteness in time, little in space. And surely, given such an explosion as here it needed no great foresight to predict that the natural result would be to injure one on the platform at no greater distance from its scene than was the plaintiff. Just how no one might be able to predict. Whether by flying fragments, by broken glass, by wreckage of machines or structures no one could say. But injury in some form was most probable.

Under these circumstances I cannot say as a matter of law that the plaintiff's injuries were not the proximate result of the negligence. That is all we have before us. The court refused to so charge. No request was made to submit the matter to the jury as a question of fact, even would that have been proper upon the record before us.

The judgment appealed from should be affirmed, with costs.

Index

References are to pages.

M

Mack, John E., 83
MacPherson v. Buick Motor Company (1916), 72, 97
Mademoiselle de Maupin, 86
Maine Central's Knickerbocker Limited, 80
Madison Square Garden, 136n83
Mafia, 129n27
Maiorano, Frank, 28
Maiorano grade-crossing case, 89–90, 93
Malbone Street
crash, 31, 56
station, 10
victims, 31
Manhattan, 5, 7, 18, 21, 24, 32, 40, 53, 59, 60, 73, 75, 80, 83, 89
Park Avenue tunnel, 10
Manhattan Beach train, 10
Manlius, New York, 84
Manning, Daniel F., 54
manslaughter, 11
Marshall, Moran, Williamson & Vicker, 82
Martindale's American Law Dictionary, 18
Massachusetts Supreme Judicial Court, 109
Masterson, Bat, 75
Mastrora, Albito, 40
Maujer Street, 5
May, Mitchell, 15
Mazet Committee, 37
McAvoy, John V., 37, 38
McCall, Edward E., 75
McClellan, George B., 39, 56, 82
McCooey, John H., Jr., 55
McCooey, John H. "Uncle John," 54-55, 58, 72, 83, 119
McCooey, Margaret, 54
McCunn, John H., 73
McGrath, Mary E., 121
McKinnley, William, 53
McLaughlin, Chester B., 76, 89
McNamara, William, 26, 43, 44, 45, 48, 49, 50, 66, 93, 96, 107, 118
McQuade, James A., 55
McReynolds, James, 120
Medical College, Albany, 6
Memorial Day, 9

Mengis, Morris C., 59
Men's League of Brooklyn, 120
Metropolitan Statistical Area, New York, 121
Metropolitan Transportation Authority, 119
Meyer, David, 20
Middleburgh News, 21
Middleburg National Bank, 16
Middlebury College, 87
Miles, Rowland C., 27
Miller, Nathan L., 61, 86, 91
minimum weekly income, 130n9, 6
"Miss Yonkers," 63
Mitchell, John Purroy, 56, 75
Mixing, The: What the Hillport Neighbors Did, 21
M'Naughten insanity rule, 76
Molloy, Thomas E., 118
Montauk Indian land claim, 24
Montgomery County, 16
Moore, Harrison S., 38, 39
Morgan, J.P., 26, 60
Mormons, 80
Morris, George K., 91
Morris, William J., 26
motion for a new trial, 65
motion for reargument, 101, 110
MP-41, 102, 127n6
MP-54, 102, 127n6
Murphy, Charles F. "Silent Charlie," 37, 57, 72, 82, 85
Murphy, William R., 22
Murphy v. Steeplechase Amusement Co., 97
Mustard, Elmer, 3

N

Nassau County, 39, 41, 50, 56–57, 80, 86, 120
Nassau Electric Railroad Company, 27, 79
Nathan, Gratz, 73
Nathan, Rebecca, 73
National Carbonic Gas Company, 85
National Democratic Finance Committee, 85
National Marble and Tile Works, 1
National Women's Party, 41

weather, day of accident, 127n5, 2
Weed, Katherine, 88
Weed, Smith M., 88
weekly income, minimum, 130n9, 6
Weeks, Bartow S., 75
Welfare Island Penitentiary, 40
Weller, Royal H., 26
Wensley, Edith M., 19
Wensley case, 66
Werner, William E., 72
Westchester County, 59, 60
Western Electric Company, 1
Western Front, 10
Western Maryland Railroad, 59
Westport, Connecticut, 46–47
Wharton School, 16
White, Charles Bouck, 20, 21
  "Bouckware," 135n68
  flag burning, 135n68
White, Emma, 77
White, Stanford, 27, 47, 72
  death of, 27, 138n103
Whiting, John C., 28, 104
Whiting case, 28, 31
Whitman, Charles S., 21, 22, 23, 38, 75, 78, 80, 89
Who's Who in the East, 18
Who's Who in Law, 18
Who's Who in New York, 18
Wickersham, George, 14
Wiggins, Howard, 85
Wigmore, John Henry, 13
Willard, Jess, 83
Willett, William, 37
Williamsburg, 5
Williams College, 59
William Street, 17
Wills, Harry, 59
Wing, Putnam & Burlingham, 17
Wiren, Myra Paige, 28, 65
witnesses, for Mrs. Palsgraf, 69
Women
  attitudes toward, xi
  law school applicants, 13
Wood v. Lucy, Lady Duff-Gordon (1917), 72
Wood, Abram, 16
Wood, Boyd Hudson, 16, 133n31
Wood, Elizabeth, 16

Wood, Matthew W., 16, 17, 18, 19, 20, 21, 22, 23, 24, 29, 30, 32, 35, 41, 42, 43, 45, 47, 48, 50, 66, 67, 68, 69, 92, 95, 96, 98, 99, 100, 101, 106, 107, 109, 117–18
  briefs, 108
  given name, 133n30
  motion for reargument, 110
  romantic involvement, 136n81
Woolworth, F.W., 89, 118
Woolworth Building, 17, 18, 24, 118
Worcester, Williams & Lehman, 81
World Series, 120
World War I, 4, 17, 40, 46, 61, 118
  veterans' bonuses, 85
World War II, 119, 121
Wreck Lead
  crossing, 9
  grade-crossing accident, 27, 31, 65
Wyse, William S., 47

X

Xavier, Frank E., 60

Y

Yale Equity Company, 18
Yale Law Journal, 17
Yale Law School, 17, 95
Yankees, 120
Yonkers Herald, 60
Young, J. Addison, 54, 59, 61, 69, 93, 113, 115, 120
  Appellate Division, 54, 59–61
Young, James Halsey, 59, 60
Young, Lucy, 59
Young Men's Hebrew Association, 82

Z

Ziegfeld, Florenz, 74
zone of foreseeable harm, 112